EYEWITNESS D-DAY

EYEWITNESS D–DAY

Firsthand Accounts from the Landing at Normandy to the Liberation of Paris

D.M. GIANGRECO with **KATHRYN MOORE**
Edited and with a foreword by **NORMAN POLMAR**

Sterling Publishing Co., Inc.
New York

Published by Sterling Publishing Co., Inc.
387 Park Avenue South, New York, NY 10016

©2005 by Sterling Publishing Co., Inc.

Distributed in Canada by Sterling Publishing
c/o Canadian Manda Group, 165 Dufferin Street
Toronto, Ontario, Canada M6K 3H6

Distributed in the United Kingdom by GMC
Distribution Services
Castle Place, 166 High Street, Lewes, East
Sussex, England BN7 1XU

Distributed in Australia by Capricorn Link
(Australia) Pty. Ltd.
P.O. Box 704, Windsor, NSW 2756, Australia

ISBN-13: 978-0-7607-5045-2
ISBN-10: 0-7607-5045-9

10 9 8 7 6 5 4 3

For information about custom editions,
special sales, premium and corporate
purchases, please contact Sterling Special
Sales Department at 800-805-5489 or
specialsales@sterlingpub.com

FRONT AND BACK ENDPAPERS: The Normandy American
Cemetery at Colleville-sur-Mer, France.

PAGE 1: The rusted, misshapen arms of a beach obstacle
offer mute testimony to the Germans' failed effort to stop
the Allied invasion at the Normandy coast.

PAGE 2, INSET: U.S. Army Rangers board landing craft that
will take them to assault transports in Weymouth harbor.

PAGES 2–3: High tide at UTAH beach, where American
soldiers established the western flank of the invasion.
On the horizon stretches the Grandcamp–Pointe du Hoc
area that separated UTAH and OMAHA Beaches.

PAGE 7: The village of Arromanches-les-Bains, site of the
British artificial harbor at GOLD Beach.

PAGE 9: Soldiers of the 1st Infantry Division pose aboard an
LCT before sailing for the Continent. The African-American
soldier in a different style of field jacket is probably from
the 5th Engineer Special Brigade.

I think the best thing is if you can think of all those who made the supreme sacrifice—remember the real meaning of that. They gave away all of their tomorrows for our today.

—Wally Parr, Corporal,
British 6th Airborne Division

Contents

Foreword

There were several decisive battles in the European theaters of World War II, battles that could have changed the course of the war and of history had the outcome been different. A list of those battles should be led by the aerial Battle of Britain (1940), the battles of Stalingrad (winter 1942–1943) and Kursk (1943) on the Eastern Front, and the Allied invasion of Normandy.

The Allied landings on the coast of Normandy in June 1944 finally brought American and British armies to battle with the main German armies—the long-awaited Second Front. From the summer of 1940, when the main German armies had invaded the Soviet Union along the broad Eastern Front, Soviet dictator Josef Stalin had implored Britain and then the United States to open a Second Front against Germany, a ground invasion of Europe. It was there, on the Eastern Front, that the Germans concentrated most of their troops, tanks, guns, and aircraft.

Although Anglo-American forces landed in North Africa in late 1942, and then invaded Sicily and the Italian mainland in 1943, those actions did not bring to battle the main German armies. The Eastern Front remained the main battleground of the European conflict. But the massive airborne and amphibious landings in Normandy in June 1944 did bring major German armies to battle. The Allied troops included battle-hardened veterans and relatively new units; the defending troops included German soldiers who had been at war for almost five years as well as impressed Russians and other "allied" troops who were used to man defensive positions.

Had the German defenders been able to throw the invaders back into the sea, the next few years of the conflict in Europe would have been quite different. Indeed, in some respects the invasion was a "close thing." General Dwight D. Eisenhower, the Allied commander in Europe, realized the possibility of the invaders being thrown back into the sea, and he even had a speech prepared in the event that his assault forces were thrown back into the sea.

But Adolf Hitler had prevented the proper deployment of defensive troops, fearing that the open-beach landings at Normandy were a feint. He believed that the main Allied thrust had to be closer to a large port—probably to Cherbourg—or directly across the English Channel at its narrowest point, to Calais. Thus, Hitler held back divisions for several days, preventing his Army commanders from employing those divisions in the first few, critical days of the landings. Those additional units might have defeated the Allied landings.

General Eisenhower, in his *Crusade in Europe*, wrote: "The Battle of the Beachhead was a period of incessant and heavy fighting and one which, except for the capture of Cherbourg, showed few geographic gains. Yet it was during this period that the stage was set for the later, spectacular liberation of France and Belgium." And, subsequently, for the eventual Allied thrusts into Holland, Germany, and Austria.

Cherbourg was captured by the U.S. VII Corps after twenty days of fighting. But its value as a major port was limited because of German destruction of its facilities. In place of the early capture of a major French port, the Allies brought their own ports with them— the massive MULBERRY artificial harbors erected offshore.

But the sixty-mile (96.6km) beachhead was held, and by the end of June the beachhead was secure between Cherbourg and the mouth of the Orne River. Casualties had been severe on both sides, but the stage was now set for the Allied advance into northwestern Europe.

The Allies who participated in those landings in June 1944 fought one of the most important battles of World War II. In *Eyewitness D-Day* their voices are heard. In dramatic, first-person accounts—recorded by Emmy Award–winning historical documentarians Rob Lihani and Rob Kirk—D-DAY veterans relate the anguish, the terror, the hopes, the frustration, and the feeling of accomplishment they experienced during those tumultuous days. Their words are placed in perspective by two distinguished American historians, D.M. Giangreco and Kathryn Moore. The juxtaposition of the voices of D-DAY participants with a comprehensive account of the Normandy landings makes this book a most important account of D-DAY.

—Norman Polmar
Coauthor of *America at War: World War II, 1941–1945*

Introduction

In the summer of 1940, Britain stood alone against Nazi Germany. Having secured its eastern front by conquering Poland and entering into a non-aggression treaty with Soviet Russia, Germany had turned its armies west in April of that year, seizing Norway and Denmark in lightning assaults. Then the mighty French Army of more than one hundred combat divisions, supported by eleven British and twenty-two Belgian divisions, was soundly defeated in May and June. For the first time since the reign of Napoleon Bonaparte some 130 years before, Britain faced invasion from a seemingly invincible foe.

The two dozen understrength divisions defending the island nation were terribly deficient in tanks and modern weapons of war, but all was not lost. The same Royal Navy that dominated the narrow English Channel in Napoleon's time and defeated the Spanish Armada in 1588—with more than a little help from the weather—barred the way to a quick victory in the west that would have allowed Germany to throw the full weight of its armies against its unsuspecting Soviet ally. The Royal Navy, however, was vulnerable to air attack, and the German *Luftwaffe*, with nearly three thousand planes now based directly across the Channel from Britain, was by far the world's most powerful air force.

Confident in the ability of the *Luftwaffe*, Germany planned to invade the island nation along sea lanes protected by hoards of fighter aircraft after it swept away all resistance by Britain's Royal Air Force. Although both sides suffered terrible losses in the ensuing Battle of Britain, the outnum-

bered British fighter pilots successfully fought off attacks designed to destroy their bases near the coast. Nazi Germany experienced its first defeat and was forced to call off its invasion.

Germany's leader, Adolf Hitler, viewed the reversal as only a minor setback in his dreams of conquest. Britain's airmen had bought their nation some breathing room, but its puny Army certainly couldn't be viewed as a serious threat, and its stubborn countrymen, under their "lunatic" Prime Minister, Winston Churchill, could be dealt with at a more appropriate time. Hitler also believed the meddlesome Americans to be of little concern, even though their "Jew" president, Franklin D. Roosevelt, had skirted his country's own neutrality laws to help the British.

After the fall of France, Roosevelt sent millions of dollars worth of "surplus" munitions across the Atlantic to replenish Britain's depleted stocks. In September, he sent Britain fifty old destroyers to protect its sea lanes in exchange for leases to British bases near the United States. To Hitler, the troublesome Americans were certainly sticking their noses where they didn't belong. Didn't they realize Britain was doomed? Any suggestion that, in less than four years, America and Britain would hurl millions of soldiers across the very same English Channel that had just foiled the German armies in France would have seemed laughable.

BELOW: Ruins of a German casement at Pointe du Hoc. From this spot, and even well inland, German artillery could fire on ships launching men and equipment to both American invasion beaches.

In England they're filled with curiosity and keep asking, "Why doesn't he come?" Be calm. He's coming! He's coming! The hour will come when one of us will break and it will not be National Socialist Germany.... If Russia is smashed, Britain's last hope will be shattered and Germany will be master of Europe.
—German Führer Adolf Hitler, 1940

Chapter One

OVERTURE TO INVASION

Events were winding down quickly. Barges, coastal steamers, and assorted craft—laboriously gathered from the far reaches of Adolf Hitler's newly conquered empire for the invasion of England—had already completed their move away from the English Channel and beyond the range of Royal Air Force fighters. At Le Havre and Boulogne, Calais and Dunkirk, tired French railroad workers loaded the last eastbound trains with all the *Wehrmacht*'s (German Armed Forces) implements of war. The specially waterproofed tanks of the 18th Panzer Division would never cross Brighton Beach, but in eight months' time they would ford the Lesna River to smash the Soviet Army's defenses near Brest-Litovsk.

Having failed to destroy or neutralize the Royal Air Force (RAF)—an absolute prerequisite for a cross-Channel invasion—Adolf Hitler called off his proposed invasion of Great Britain, Operation SEA LION, on October 12, 1940. German plans now called for Britain to be slowly strangled by unrestricted naval warfare conducted by submarines as well as surface raiders that ranged from heavily armed vessels disguised as merchant ships to the modern battleships *Bismarck* and *Tripitz*.

Construction of mammoth submarine, or U-boat, pens was begun at five Bay of Biscay ports that allowed easy access to the open sea. To protect these vital bases and other key points along the French coast from British sea and air attacks, the Germans emplaced coastal artillery and anti-aircraft guns that were themselves surrounded by minefields, barbed wire, and machine-gun nests. Together with the 11- and 16-inch batteries positioned to interdict British shipping along the narrows of the English Channel, these fortresses were the first elements in what Germany's Nazi propagandists would soon call the *Atlantic Wall*.

Throughout 1941, the Germans labored over defensive works that were massive in size and scope, but widely dispersed along the coast. There was virtually no effort to coordinate the various projects of the Army, Navy, Air Force (*Luftwaffe*), and the massive Todt construction organization, which ostensibly was run by the *Luftwaffe* but in practice operated relatively independently to carry out Hitler's special

"Führer directives." All this changed on December 7, 1941, with the Japanese attack on Pearl Harbor. Four days later, Germany announced its support for Imperial Japan and declared war on the United States. Now, U.S. naval forces would enter the conflict alongside Britain's Royal Navy, and the OKW (*Oberkommando der Wehrmacht,* or High Command of the Armed Forces) immediately issued general orders for the defense of "Fortress Europe" from the French-Spanish border to Norway's North Cape above the Arctic Circle.

A much more detailed OKW directive released on March 23, 1942, was given added urgency by the success of a large-scale British raid five days later on St. Nazaire, which destroyed the only dry dock in France capable of accommodating Germany's largest battleships. Hitler and the senior German generals had always maintained that seaports would be the principal focus of British commando raids because the logistical needs of a full-scale invasion of Nazi-held Europe required the capture

RIGHT: U.S. soldiers prepare to board a troop train that will take them to a port of embarkation for deployment overseas. America's entry into the war made it clear to Germany's leaders that Anglo-American armies would eventually attempt to invade continental Europe, and precipitated a strengthening of the Atlantic Wall.

of a substantial harbor immediately after their landings. The German High Command also believed that those landings would most likely occur in the Calais area, or the Pas-de-Calais, just across the English Channel from Dover. The direct—and disastrous—assault on the English Channel port of Dieppe in northwest France by British and Canadian forces on August 19, 1942, seemed to confirm this. It also demonstrated to the Germans that they needed only to further improve the defensive characteristics of the principal ports and the immediately adjacent areas vulnerable to beach assaults. What the Allies learned from Dieppe was something wholly different. The invasion must be made well away from heavily defended ports.

🎙 *Extraordinary defensive mechanisms, including barrage balloons, were required during the bombing of Britain. John Murphy, a ground crewman, became adept at working with these unusual defenses, which protected against low-flying German bombers.*

As time went on and the bombing of the British Isles became heavier, barrage balloons started to appear. They needed more and more personnel under them. They asked for volunteers to go into the balloon division, which required a good bit of training. Because helium was hard to come by, we had to use hydrogen, which is a more dangerous gas to handle. There were casualties, but on the whole we did our job and protected the cities. Many a German plane was brought down by a barrage balloon and the cable attached to it.

The barrage balloon was on a fixed site. There would probably be a score around the city, flying at various heights to deter the dive-bombers that came over and started picking the targets, like a factory or perhaps a dock or a dock area. Sometimes we flew at four thousand feet (1.2km), sometimes five thousand (1.5km), on down to a thousand (304.8m), depending on the weather.

The weather was a great hazard to a balloon, since it could be blown right off its mooring. You had to become skilled at letting

it out according to the weather and then reversing and bringing it in. When you flew it up to a certain distance, you stopped the winch and put what you called an ammunition piece aboard the wire and then clipped it top and bottom. It had a pin that was extracted before the balloon was released. As soon as that cable was touched by the plane, it ignited explosives in the cylinder. This sent the cable up into the aircraft and cut the wing off or folded itself into the engine proper and brought it down. This worked very successfully and stopped the Germans from dive-bombing. They started flying higher, which was the point of having a barrage balloon. ▪

—John Murphy, RAF Ground Crew, Barrage Balloon and Transport Division, attached to Saskatchewan Regiment, 3d Canadian Division (CAN)

ABOVE: *Wehrmacht* soldiers peacefully tend their bunker-top vegetable garden high above a Norwegian fjord. Thanks largely to a series of deception operations, German Army troop strength in Norway and Denmark never dropped below 400,000 during the war, with Navy and *Luftwaffe* men pushing the numbers even higher. The *Wehrmacht* presence in these countries exceeded 500,000 by Christmas 1944, with some 420,000 in Norway alone, as German forces retreating from a Soviet offensive in Finland fell back into its far northern reaches.

BELOW: Soldiers packed aboard some of the civilian vessels that rescued them from the Germans. The lead boat is filled with some of the 120,000 French troops who were evacuated, returned to France, and subsequently captured by the Germans less than two weeks later.

Wartime Britain was home for nurse Iris Bower of the Princess Mary's Royal Air Force Nursing Service.

I was posted to an airfield hospital in Wales. I happened to be in charge on night duty when we were bombed. Unfortunately, that meant serious casualties because the building wasn't constructed of heavy masonry. One of the Red Cross nurses was with me on my round when this happened. I remember her saying, "Don't run." Still, I ran, knowing there were patients in the ward. The next thing I knew I'd fallen down into a crater. All the lights went out and water rushed everywhere from broken pipes. It was a very hectic night. The patients were evacuated to local hospitals. Although I didn't deserve it more than anybody else—it's just that I was in charge on night duty—I was awarded the Associate of the Royal Red Cross. I went to Buckingham Palace in January 1941, and King George VI gave it to me.

One of my other postings was at the Palace Hotel, which was an officers' hospital. One Sunday morning, the Germans dropped some bombs on the hospital. One was a direct hit. It went right through the building down to the basement. There were many killed and injured. I was lucky to be alive. It was such a sad occasion because we had all those wonderfully brave young men—the bomber pilots and the fighter pilots—the Battle of Britain boys. They were such wonderful young men. Some of them were injured badly and burned. It had been such a happy place because we were all such comrades. It was a tragic end to the place. ■

—Iris Bower, Nurse,
Princess Mary's Royal Air Force
Nursing Service (UK)

On the other side of the "pond," Felix Branham of Virginia enlisted long before December 7, 1941, when he joined his local National Guard unit.

I joined the National Guard in 1939 and remained with them until the end of the war. My company in Charlottesville, Virginia, was originally known as the Monticello Guard. It is one of the oldest units in the Army, dating back to the Revolution.

We went over on the *Queen Mary*. I guess we were one hundred miles (161km) out, and I started looking around and said, "Hey, fellas, where's our escort?" One British sailor said, "Yank, this bloody ship goes too fast to have an escort." I replied that it didn't seem that fast to me. He said, "We'll make thirty-two bloody knots!" I said it still seemed slow to me. We changed course every six minutes because a submarine needed eight minutes to line up its sight. The *Queen Mary* is eighteen stories high. If you stand on the deck and go into the water, that's 180 feet (54.9m) down. We'd been told if anybody goes overboard, nobody's stopping to pick you up. ▪

—Felix Branham, Sergeant,
K Company, 3d Battalion,
116th Regiment, 29th Division (US)

Cut off by German forces during the invasion of France in 1940, Britain conducted a nine-day fighting withdrawal of its Army from the French coast rather than surrender. The Royal Navy had hoped to save 45,000 troops, but, despite fierce German attacks that sunk many ships, almost 340,000 British, French, and Belgian soldiers were successfully evacuated from Dunkirk in the Pas-de-Calais from May 26 to June 4. TOP: British soldiers disembark destroyers docked two-deep at Portsmouth, England. Six other destroyers were sunk during the operation, and nineteen were damaged. BOTTOM: British troops arrive safely in England. Many of these same men would return to France during the Normandy invasion.

In Like a SEA LION, Out Like a Lamb

sion force, including both minesweeping and planting defensive minefields. The *Luftwaffe*, meanwhile, was to prevent British air attacks, engage naval vessels approaching the invasion force, destroy coastal defenses, and annihilate British reserves along the beachheads. To accomplish its missions the *Luftwaffe* would have to destroy the British RAF Fighter Command. Neither the German Navy nor the *Luftwaffe* was capable of such assignments, in view of their own weaknesses and the strengths of the RAF and the British Royal Navy.

The German Army initially had little comprehension of the myriad complexities of a full-scale, seaborne invasion, and imagined SEA LION to be little more than a gigantic river crossing. Early proposals called for up to forty divisions to be landed in waves over several days. This was soon reduced to a slightly more realistic assault wave that would consist of eleven infantry divisions, plus upward of two motorized divisions, supported by paratroopers who would strike across the Channel in mid-August. The Army

LEFT: German Army and Navy personnel laboriously load vehicles one by one during an "embarkation maneuver" at Le Havre, France, September 17, 1940.

After the defeat of Belgium and France in June 1940, the victorious German armies faced an isolated, poorly armed Britain across a Channel only twenty miles (32km) wide at its narrowest point between Dover and the Pas-de-Calais region of France. When the British government scorned German peace feelers, German Führer Adolf Hitler issued a directive on July 16, 1940, ordering the invasion of England.

The operation was given the code name *Seelöwe*, or SEA LION, and the German Army immediately began organizing and preparing for an assault. The real burden, however, would fall to the German Navy and the *Luftwaffe*. The Navy was charged with transporting and protecting the inva-

BELOW: The hulks of destroyed Soviet T-34/76B medium tanks and T-60 light tanks sit abandoned at an intersection in Voronezh, Russia, July 1942. As the number of Soviet casualties soared into the millions and German Panzers drove ever deeper into Russia, Soviet Premier Joseph Stalin demanded that the Western Allies open up a "second front" against Nazi Germany. U.S. and British operations in the Mediterranean Theater failed to draw significant German forces away from the Soviets, and Stalin pressed the Allies for an massive invasion of the continent.

 Walter Bodlander, a second lieutenant of the 4th Infantry Division, had very personal reasons for joining the Army.

I'm Jewish, and I was twelve years old when the Nazis took over. By the time I was fifteen, it was clear that it was very dangerous for Jews to live in Germany. My parents sent me to high school in Switzerland. I was just too young for another war that might have saved the world from D-Day and the Nazis—the Spanish Civil War. I had wanted to fight the Nazis then, but I was too young for that. When I volunteered for that one, I was told to go back home because I was seventeen, and they wouldn't take me. By the time they would've taken me, it was over and the Nazis had won. The Fascists had won. Franco had won. I returned to Germany shortly before the war broke out. My father died in Germany, and my mother got out. I had applied for a visa to the United States, but you had to wait three or four years. During that period I was in France and then later on in Palestine, and eventually I came to America in 1940.

I was very anxious to get involved in this war; I felt it was a very personal battle to fight such a regime. Just after Pearl Harbor,

I volunteered and was immediately taken. By January 1942, I was in California for basic training. They didn't know what to do with me because my English was not very good, and I had a German accent. Everyone else was being assigned, but they still didn't know where I should go. I finally asked why. They said I wasn't a citizen. In May 1942, Congress passed a law saying that all aliens who had volunteered for the Army could become citizens immediately. So I became a citizen the following week. I was assigned to artillery but requested military intelligence. ■

—Walter Bodlander, 2d Lieutenant, Headquarters Battalion, 8th Infantry Regiment, 4th Infantry Division (US)

Why Normandy?

British Lieutenant General Frederick E. Morgan and his planning staff conducted a detailed study of possible invasion sites. Earlier planning had assumed that regimental- and division-size landings would be widely dispersed in order to prevent the German *Wehrmacht* from massing for a counterattack,

but this obviously left open the possibility that the Germans would mass anyway and destroy the Allied lodgments one by one. Morgan's staff immediately discarded this approach for Operation OVERLORD and followed the principle of concentration. The chosen landing site must be able to handle the entire invasion force and be capable of rapid development into the springboard that would propel multiple field armies—more than a million men—across the face of northwest Europe.

The first and most important criterion of invasion planners—that the initial landings be conducted well within the range of Allied fighter bases in Britain—immediately ruled out landings in the areas with the best harbors, Brittany and the Netherlands. Belgium's coast featured a number of very good ports, but a shortage of suitable beaches and the lack of ready access to the interior eliminated both it and the Pas-de-Calais to the south from contention as landing sites. Nevertheless, Calais and the Belgian coast held great promise for future deception operations, and the Allies worked diligently to display an interest in this area to the eager German spies listening at every turn. The Seine River sector also contained inadequate beaches, and forces landing on either side of the river's wide estuary could not easily support each other.

That left Normandy. The Caen sector presented the Allies with multiple beaches spread across a thirty-five-mile (56.3km) front, good roads, and a broad access to the interior of France. Yet another beach, ten miles (16.1km) to the west and beyond a wide estuary at the base of the Cotentin Peninsula, held the promise of quick access to Cherbourg's medium-size harbor a further twenty-five miles (40.2km) to the northwest. Yet even with a beachhead on the peninsula itself, it was clear to Allied planners that the German garrison would still have ample time to wreak havoc on the port's dock facilities. Only the belated approval of the torpedo- and weatherproof MULBERRY harbors would make Normandy a viable option.

Some men found themselves serving in Naval Combat Demolition Units (NCDUs), but they weren't always sure what naval combat demolition was or what they would be required to do. Coxswain Nelson DuBroc figured it had some definite advantages.

We were drinking beer at the beer garden in San Pedro [California] one night. This guy said they were having a meeting and recruiting guys for demolition. Maybe we ought to go see. So we went down there, listened to

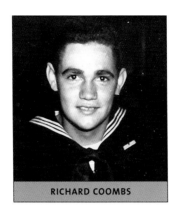

RICHARD COOMBS

BELOW: Dwight D. Eisenhower as a Lieutenant General in his Mediterranean Theater Headquarters before he was chosen to command the Normandy Invasion. Clearly visible is his West Point class ring of 1915 and a lit Philip Morris smoldering in an ashtray.

them, and signed up. I found out then I wasn't going to be stuck in one place all the time, so that sounded pretty good. Plus you got plenty of liberty and it paid well. We had no duties, like KP or guard duty, or fire watches—nothing like that. After the first part of your training, you could go to town every night. We were first in the pay line, first in the mess hall line. We would be exposed to danger but not for long. ∎

—Nelson DuBroc, Coxswain, Naval Combat Demolition Unit (US)

Finding "volunteers" proved to be a challenge for naval recruitment, so recruiters resorted to alternate methods to find men for the hazardous duties of an NCDU. Seaman First Class Richard Coombs was one of those lucky fellows.

I arrived on the *Queen Mary* in Glasgow, Scotland. They put a bunch of us in a room, and this ensign came in, saying he was looking for one hundred volunteers to go into

Navy Demolition. He asked for volunteers, but only about ten hands went up. He said we had to have this, so he said we were going to go from A to C, according to the initial letter of your last name. I was number ninety-seven. That was how I joined Navy Demolition. I had no idea what it was, nor did a lot of the other fellows. The fellows who were already in this outfit had advanced training for nearly six months. When we joined the outfit, we trained a couple of weeks. ∎

—Richard Coombs, Seaman First Class, Naval Combat Demolition Unit (US)

The MULBERRIES

When Winston Churchill was first lord of the Admiralty during World War I, he had eyed the Belgian coast north of Dunkirk as a possible site for a major British amphibious strike behind Germany's broad defensive belt of trenches, barbed wire, and pillboxes. However, the problem of supplying many thousands of soldiers over a naked beach seemed insurmountable. Yet Churchill's nimble mind came up with an ingenious solution, as noted in his memoirs: "[building] a number of flat-bottomed barges or caissons, made not of steel but of concrete, which would float when empty of water and thus be towed across [the Channel]. On arrival the sea cocks would be opened and the caissons would settle to the bottom. By this means a torpedo- and weather-proof harbor would be created in the open sea."

Twenty-five years later, as prime minister, Churchill had his interest in artificial harbors rekindled after the loss of the great British naval base at Singapore to the Japanese in 1942. He came up with more novel ideas: "piers for use on beaches" that "*must* float up and down on the tide," and "pontoon piers of up to a mile (1.6km) in length." Meanwhile, a wide stretch of Normandy beaches had been chosen as the best of six possible invasion sites. Allied planners, however, estimated that the nearby port of Cherbourg would not be captured until roughly two weeks after D-Day, and that repairing extensive German demolitions

and removing mines could well prevent its use for months.

But while this eventuality was painfully obvious to all during the early invasion planning, General Dwight D. Eisenhower later wrote that when the chief of combined operations, Admiral Lord Louis Mountbatten, brought up Churchill's suggestions, he was met with "hoots and jeers." The idea continued to be pressed in the face of firm opposition from the British Admiralty, which argued that building the complex components would consume an enormous amount of scarce resources that should go toward the construction of desperately needed landing craft, and that the frequency of Channel storms would likely wreck the whole project before the artificial breakwaters were completed. The technical and logistical realities of supplying the huge invasion force finally compelled a grudging approval of the MULLBERRIES project with barely eight months to spare before D-DAY in Normandy.

Deception:
Operation BODYGUARD

Germany's third and last summer offensive against Soviet Russia in 1943 barely penetrated the deep defensive belts protecting the road and rail center of Kursk. In the massive Soviet counteroffensive that followed, the German Army was thrown back in some areas as many as two hundred miles (321.8km) by the end of September. With German industry and manpower stretched almost to the breaking point, it was apparent—even to Hitler—that a victory could no longer be gained in the East. And it was now clear that the Anglo-American armies were growing at an alarming rate. It was only a matter of time before the massive force gathering in the British Isles would burst forth upon the continent and drive straight for Germany's principal industrial area, the Ruhr, and then Berlin itself.

ABOVE: Supreme Allied Commander Dwight D. Eisenhower and British Prime Minister Winston Churchill go for a stroll flanked by (left) General Alan Francis Brooke (Viscount Alanbrooke), chief of Britain's Imperial General Staff, and (right) Eisenhower's deputy commander, British Air Chief Marshal Arthur Tedder. Eisenhower—or Ike, as he was invariably called by his colleagues and frontline troops—proved himself to be an outstanding coalition commander and strategist. Brooke, Churchill's chief military adviser, felt that while Eisenhower had "a most attractive personality," he also possessed "a very, very limited brain from a strategic point of view." As Eisenhower's able deputy, Tedder was highly respected by both British and American commanders for his intellect, receptiveness to new ideas, and devotion to Anglo-American cooperation.

TOM McCARTHY

RIGHT: Lieutenant General George S. Patton's continued presence in the Mediterranean following the Allies' successful conclusion of the Sicilian Campaign of July 1943 was intended to give credence to a supposed Allied invasion of Greece and the Balkans. Early in 1944, the flamboyant Patton flew to England to reprise this role, this time at the head of a nonexistent army gathering across the English Channel from the Pas-de-Calais.

As in the Mediterranean deception operation, Patton, whose ill-considered statements and actions had frequently gotten him into trouble, was to make frequent public appearances, but to be "seen, not heard." He was barred from making statements to the press without prior clearance. Here, a congenial Patton greets Bob Hope, Frances Langford, and other entertainers. In addition to newspaper and Army photographers, Movie Tone News filmmakers were also present, and the happy group was seen in movie theaters across the United States and Great Britain.

Because of the relatively short distance between possible invasion sites along the English Channel and the German hinterland, there was no land to trade for time as there had been—and the Germans believed there still was—in the broad expanse of the Eastern Front. Over the years, Field Marshal Gerd von Rundstedt, the German commander in the West, had fought his own rear guard action against calls for troops under his command to shore up the deteriorating situation in the East. Despite an effective German propaganda campaign touting the impregnability of the Atlantic Wall, there had also been few real improvements to coastal fortifications after the British were repulsed at Dieppe in 1942. The result was a pronounced erosion in Germany's western defenses. While this had not particularly mattered in the early days of the American buildup in Britain, the German OKW had watched with growing apprehension as U.S. ground forces in Britain steadily climbed to a stunning eighty-five to ninety combat divisions. Of particular concern were the six new American airborne divisions—the 6th, 9th, 17th, 18th, 21st, and 101st—that along with the veteran 82d, allowed the Allies to strike in force almost anywhere.

🎙️ *Deciding which branch of the service to join was a major question for all enlistees. Berge Avadanian, staff sergeant in the 82d Airborne Division, combined natural interest with practicality in making his choice.*

When I was a very young man on a farm in Bellingham, Massachusetts, we had a hayloft. I used to take one of these old umbrellas that were used on wagons and jump from the upper door of the hayloft onto a pile of hay. Then in the 1939 World's Fair in New York

City, they had one of these guided parachutes that came down. I think it cost seventy-five cents. They towed you way up to the top of a 250-foot (76.2m) tower, then released it.

Immediately after Pearl Harbor, I wanted first to get into the submarines because I figured that's where I could do the most damage. Then they mentioned that there was an outfit called the paratroopers. They paid $50 extra a month. That did it. I became a paratrooper. ▪

—Berge Avadanian, Staff Sergeant, 2nd Battalion Headquarters, 505th Parachute Infantry Regiment, 82d Airborne Division (US)

🎙️ *Jumping out of airplanes appealed to others, including Sergeant Tom McCarthy, also of the 82d Airborne Division.*

I was 5-foot, 5 ½ inches (1.7m), about 128 pounds (58.1kg). I didn't have an inferiority complex, but everything was always an uphill fight. So by becoming a paratrooper, I figured I'll start at the top and work down. If there was something better than that, I didn't know what it was. I considered jumping out of planes as some kind of an adventure. That sounded like a pretty good idea for an afternoon. ▪

—Tom McCarthy, Sergeant, Pathfinders, A Company, 1st Battalion, 504th Parachute Regiment, 82d Airborne Division (US)

Reality hit in basic training for these aspiring paratroopers. Bill True of the 101st Airborne Division found that much of the training involved having both feet on the ground.

Our basic infantry training in Toccoa, Georgia, was aimed at a parachute-type invasion and the kind of combat that we eventually were involved in. We were in training for nearly two years before D-Day. It was basic infantry training with the added dimension of a tremendous amount of physical training. About half of our time was spent in some kind of running, walking, climbing, jumping, to develop our physical attributes as well as becoming basic infantrymen. We had forced marches in basic training of up to 25 miles (40.2km) with no breaks and no water. They were night marches, culminating in our making what our regimental commander claimed was a world record march of 120 miles (193km) in three days, from our camp in Toccoa to Atlanta, where the city rolled out the red carpet and had probably nearly all of the high school bands in town out to march into the city with us. We had a very tough basic training. One night they put us through a maneuver where we had to crawl through the entrails and the remains of butchered hogs to give us a real feel of what slaughter was like. That was about as bad as anything I went through, including combat itself. ▪

—Bill True, Private First Class, F Company, 506th Parachute Infantry Regiment, 101st Airborne Division (US)

A Phantom Army

What the German OKW discovered far too late to save the Third Reich was that much of the *visible* activity in Britain was a chimera, a giant, multifaceted deception designed to keep the bulk of the German Army in France and Belgium away from the Allies' post-invasion buildup in Normandy—Operation BODYGUARD and its counterpart in northern France and Belgium, Operation FORTITUDE. Only two of

Phantom Army Corps and Division Insignia

XXXI Corps

XXXIII Corps

6th Airborne Division

9th Airborne Division

18th Airborne Division

21st Airborne Division

11th Division

14th Division

17th Division

22d Division

LEFT: Complex deception operations were begun as early as 1942 to confuse and mislead the Germans. Their objective was to make Germany spread its forces throughout Western Europe—away from France—and to persuade Hitler that the invasion of Normandy was simply a ploy to draw German forces from the real invasion that would come later in the Pas-de-Calais area. The far-reaching disinformation campaign even involved the august pages of *National Geographic* magazine, which published the shoulder patches of twenty-two nonexistent divisions and two bogus corps among those of authentic divisions on its pages, including the patches shown here. In order to reinforce German perceptions of American reliance on airpower, almost one quarter of the twenty-two bogus divisions were airborne formations. Copies of the *National Geographic* issue were sent to Germany by agents working in the embassies of neutral nations, and the full-color unit symbols made their way into the *Wehrmacht*'s U.S. Army order-of-battle charts in Paris.

BELOW: Rommel (center), commanding Army Group B facing England, and General Johannes Blaskowitz (left), commanding Army Group G in southern France, discuss the upcoming Allied invasion with their superior, Field Marshal Gerd von Rundstedt (right), in early May 1944.

In wartime, truth is always so precious that she must be attended by a bodyguard of lies.

—Winston Churchill

the six new U.S. airborne divisions, the 17th and 101st, actually existed. The others were part of a nineteen-division-strong phantom army (under a very real lieutenant general, George S. Patton, Jr.) and separate airborne corps supposedly gathering directly across the Channel from the Pas-de-Calais.

General Morgan's invasion planners believed that while the weakened German Army in the West might not be able to destroy the invasion force, Germany might well be able to contain it long enough for significant Axis reinforcements to be brought into play. A truncated toehold on the French coast would not allow the Allies to build up sufficient power for

a breakout, and would force them to either fight a prolonged battle of attrition or, as British Lieutenant General Bernard Law Montgomery put it, "be Dunkirked," an allusion to the British Army's nearly disastrous withdrawal across the English Channel after the German invasion of France in 1940. Allied success hinged on the ability to expand and reinforce their lodgment in France faster than the Germans could rush forward divisions to contain it. Intelligence gathered from secret British cryptologic analysis of German radio communications—called ULTRA—provided the key to fooling the Germans long enough to build an unstoppable force on the continent.

ULTRA intercepts in 1942 and 1943 had demonstrated that German intelligence consistently overestimated American strength and that German commanders at all levels were predisposed to believe that the Pas-de-Calais was the most likely invasion site. This belief opened up some interesting possibilities for the Allies. By cleverly reinforcing these misperceptions with false information, Morgan's invasion planners believed that it might be possible to trick the Germans into keeping powerful counterattack forces immobile in the Calais area as they waited for nonexistent American forces to surge across the Channel narrows.

An intricately structured "phantom army," complete with both real and dummy equipment, a fully equipped radio communications setup, staging areas, and even soldiers wearing the patches of bogus divisions, was presented for German intelligence. Meanwhile, the "threatened" areas of Belgium and northwest France received far more attention from Allied air forces than did the real invasion site. Since ULTRA intelligence revealed that the Germans expected the Allies to make an initial landing to draw forces away from Calais, every effort was made to encourage the idea that D-DAY at Normandy was not at all the main invasion, but merely a feint.

British Sergeant Norman Kirby enjoyed an extraordinary vantage point for most of the war.

I was in the Army for six years, throughout the war. I started in the Royal Engineers, and then, when France fell, it became urgent to deal with collaborators and people who might eat away at the security of the Allies. I was then transferred into the Intelligence Corps. At the beginning of my period with the Intelligence Corps, I had a number of rather alarming jobs. For example, for a year I pretended to be a German saboteur blowing up English power stations and gas works. After that I was called for an interview to a place called Southwick Park near Portsmouth. There were twelve of us for the interview.

It was a most disturbing interview. I was interviewed first by a very irate Frenchman who was terribly annoyed. Then he was interrupted by a furious German with a red face and a loud voice who eventually ordered me out at the top of his voice. I thought, Well, that's the end of that. So much for that interview. I hadn't realized at the time that they were deliberately trying to intimidate me. I went over to my motorbike and started revving it up when a voice from the hut shouted, "Where the hell do you think you're going?" I replied that I was returning to my unit. They told me to stay. After the other interviews, they called me back and said I got the job. I didn't know what the job was. It turned out that it was to be in charge of security for General Montgomery's tactical headquarters.

It was a very small headquarters in which there was one of each unit. I was the only Intelligence Corps personnel, but I was not an officer; I was a sergeant. Soon afterwards, we began preparing for D-Day. I had been at conferences in a security role, so I knew that the ultimate destination was Normandy. ▪

—Norman Kirby, Sergeant, Intelligence Corps, Assigned to Montgomery's Tactical Headquarters (UK)

Stiffening the Atlantic Wall

In late October 1943, von Rundstedt issued a report detailing the overall weakness of the western defenses and warning against the danger of Germany's falling for its own propaganda campaign about the impregnability of the Atlantic Wall fortifications. Said von Rundstedt: "It must not be believed that this wall cannot be overcome." Yet even before this assessment, Hitler had accepted that units in the West could no longer be robbed of men and matériel to make up for Eastern Front losses. Through skillful use of Germany's dwindling manpower reserves and a streamlining of

Wehrmacht combat formations, the number of divisions under von Rundstedt's command actually increased, from forty-six at the time of his October 1943 report to fifty-eight by D-Day: thirty-three static, coastal defense divisions and fully twenty-five divisions up to or near "Eastern Front standards" of mobility and training.

How best to employ these forces—some 850,000 men, including support elements—was a matter of intense debate. German Field Marshal Erwin Rommel, who took command of Army Group B, which encompassed all of

BELOW: German officers discuss the upcoming invasion at a meeting in early May 1944. From left: Admiral Theodore Krancke of Navy Group West, who commanded the destroyers and torpedo boats based in ports under von Rundstedt's control; Field Marshal Rommel's chief of staff, Major General Hans Speidel; Panzer Group West Commander Geyr von Schweppenburg, who was in charge of Hitler's counterattack force of Panzer divisions; and a senior *Luftwaffe* officer identified only as Glocker in von Schweppenburg's notes on this photo. Speidel was instrumental in bringing Rommel into the failed conspiracy against Hitler. He later became a principal figure in the reemergence of the post-war German Army, and became the NATO commander of Allied Land Forces, Central Europe, facing the Soviets in East Germany.

Cracks in the Atlantic Wall

The Atlantic Wall was an array of German fortifications stretched along the entire Channel coast and, in places, extended deep into France. By Hitler's description, the Atlantic Wall was "a belt of strongpoints and gigantic fortifications" running from Norway to the Pyrenees, a defense "impregnable against every enemy." In reality, the Wall, much of it built by slave labor, was strong in places and weak in others and never extended as far as Hitler had envisioned.

The Wall, constructed in part from fortifications taken from France's Maginot Line, was dotted by massive reinforced-concrete pillboxes that protected crews manning artillery, machine guns, and antitank weapons. On the beach were antitank obstacles and minefields. Offshore were submerged obstacles designed to snag Allied landing craft. Beyond the beach were more minefields, and weapons ranging from machine guns to railroad guns.

Field Marshals Erwin Rommel and Gerd von Rundstedt both scoffed at the Wall. Von Rundstedt, who had overcome the Maginot Line in 1940 simply by outflanking it, mistrusted static defenses. He called the Wall an "enormous bluff," built "more for the German people than for the enemy." Rommel, however, instituted a massive effort to make it a true barrier to an Allied invasion of northwest Europe, because he feared that if the Allies were allowed to gain a solid foothold on the Continent, their airpower would make it nearly impossible for the German Army to dislodge them.

For the Normandy Invasion, the Atlantic Wall proved formidable but not impassable. The British created a special unit, the 79th Armored Division, to crack the Atlantic Wall along its assault beaches during the Normandy Invasion. The division's plethora of unique vehicles, called *funnies*, included amphibious tanks as well as tanks with mine-clearing flails, bridge-laying devices, and self-contained ramps for scaling the seawall; flamethrowers, for reducing bunkers, and concrete-busting demolition charges; and even tanks capable

ABOVE: Workers employ a battery of concrete mixers during the construction of a sixty-two-mile (99.8km) stretch of Atlantic Wall fortifications opposite the British port of Dover, circa 1940–1941.

units would number ninety thousand combat troops with 650 armored vehicles as well as several thousand horses on which the "mechanized" German Army depended for the movement of most of its supplies.

These plans anticipated virtually *no* losses in landing craft. Also, other than the relatively few tanks and light artillery, no gunfire support would be available to the troops for several days. The largest ships the German Navy would risk in the Channel area would be destroyers. The *Luftwaffe* would provide close air support, as had occurred in previous blitzkrieg campaigns, assuming that the *Luftwaffe* had fully defeated the RAF. It was not long before German military staffs began to grasp the grim realities of amphibious warfare. The size of the invasion was further scaled back again, and Hitler was forced to put off the assault date to September 15.

Both the British and the Germans realized that the key factor was control of the air over the English Channel and southern England. Without complete German control, there would be no invasion. Clouds of *Luftwaffe* fighter aircraft and bombers were launched against British fighter bases and radar stations on August 13. The Battle of Britain had begun, but even after a month of intense fighting, the *Luftwaffe* was unable to defeat the RAF Fighter Command. At a meeting on September 17, Hitler postponed SEA LION indefinitely.

Preparations for the invasion of England outwardly continued until October 12, in a futile attempt to maintain political and military pressure on Britain. With the suspension of SEA LION, Hitler's attention turned east to the Soviet Union, and never again was there a threat of German landings in

southern England. Still, Hitler harbored the belief that, after a rapid, successful conquest of the Soviet Union in 1941, he could again turn his armies west against a British nation isolated and gravely weakened by German U-boats on the high seas.

ABOVE: German troops practiced assault techniques in flimsy, vulnerable boats and pneumatic rubber rafts. The prevailing view among the German leadership that an invasion launched across the English Channel would be little different from a very large river crossing operation lead to amateurish and unrealistic training, but offered good photo opportunities for Nazi propagandists.

LEFT: German soldiers practice scaling the cliffs of Pas-de-Calais at Fécampe, which are similar to those across the English Channel near Brighton, September 19, 1940. U.S. Army Rangers would soon engage in similar training for the invasion of Normandy.

of unrolling a long carpet of bamboo poles over which they would drive to keep from sinking into sand, mud, or soft ground.

The *funnies* were used against Atlantic Wall fortifications on all of the British-Canadian invasion beaches. American forces, however, adopted only the amphibious Sherman tanks for use on D-Day, but were later assisted by British flamethrowing tanks, called Crocodiles, during their siege of the important French port city of Brest. U.S. Rangers also employed special cliff-scaling devices, including amphibious vehicles equipped with hydraulic ladders. Both American and British soldiers trained against replicas of Atlantic Wall obstacles, built from photographs and descriptions obtained from commando missions carried out along the coast.

—NP

ABOVE: German artillerymen draw back the curtains to reveal a 105-mm K333 gun.

BELOW LEFT: A multitiered observation tower made of reinforced concrete and steel rises up from a Pas-de-Calais coastal bluff like an Easter Island monolith.

BELOW RIGHT: German troops scramble up a bluff to a machine-gun nest overlooking the beach near Rive-Belle-Sur-Mer on September 13, 1940. By the time of the Normandy Invasion, such defensive positions were usually either encased in concrete blockhouses or contained within partially buried, prefabricated *Ringständ* emplacements popularly known as "Tobruks."

ABOVE: Sheet metal allegedly captured from the British is used to form the interior walls of a bunker being built a few yards above the high-tide mark at Conbette, France, December 4, 1940.

NEAR RIGHT: Soldiers man a switchboard in an underground bunker.

FAR RIGHT: An 88mm anti-aircraft gun, Flak 18 or Flak 36.

> # The West is the place that matters. If we once manage to throw the British and Americans back into the sea, it will be a long time before they return.
> ## —Field Marshal Erwin Rommel

northern France, Belgium, and the Netherlands in January 1945, argued that all Panzer (armored) divisions must be placed under his control. Von Rundstedt, however, contended that this force should remain a separate command as Panzer Group West under *General der Panzertruppen* Geyr von Schweppenburg. Ultimately, the armored reserve was divided equally, with Rommel receiving the 2d, 21st, and 116th Panzer Divisions while General von Schweppenburg's 1st SS, 12th SS, and Panzer-Lehr Divisions remained an OKW reserve, to be used only at Hitler's personal discretion.

While not everything went Rommel's way at the higher reaches of command, his energy and zeal galvanized even the units beyond his direct authority. Construction projects were given new life, and, in spite of the lack of

design standardization—and, even worse, the great multiplicity of both military and Nazi Party organizations jealously guarding their prerogatives—a remarkable amount was accomplished.

By the time Rommel took command of Army Group B in January 1945, he had already spent several months scrupulously analyzing Atlantic Wall defenses as inspector of fortifications. Rommel knew what he wanted to do, and he immediately implemented a crash program to radically increase Atlantic Wall defenses down to the low-tide level of potential invasion beaches. The program included seeding the wall with obstacles designed to tip over, blow up, or rip open the bottoms of landing craft. One field report captured by the British stated, "In several divisional sectors, more

BELOW: Hitler's generals inspect the Atlantic Wall defenses along a Normandy beach, April 1944. Standing at left, with hands behind his back, is 7th Army commander General Friedrich Dollman, whose fourteen divisions defended the Normandy and Brittany peninsulas; Field Marshal Gerd von Rundstedt of OB West, holding the baton, commanded all German forces in France and the Low Countries, except for the key reserve of Panzer divisions controlled personally by Hitler in Berlin; and Field Marshal Erwin Rommel, behind the officer with the map, whose Army Group B included 7th and 15th Armies defending the areas most threatened by an Allied invasion.

Field Marshal Erwin Rommel

One of the best-known and most capable generals of the war, Erwin Rommel was saluted by foes and fellow Germans alike. In the House of Commons in January 1942, British Prime Minister Winston Churchill said of him, "We have a very daring and skillful opponent against us, and, may I say, across the havoc of war, a great general."

A twice-wounded and highly decorated veteran of World War I, Rommel was given command of the 7th Panzer Division with which he participated in Germany's France and Low Countries Campaign in May–June 1940. His tanks spearheaded the breakthrough near the Meuse, and he almost cut off a large part of the British Army. His rise to world fame began when he arrived in Tunisia in February 1941 to aid the Italian forces that had been chased back from the Egyptian border by the British. Over the next two-and-a-half years, Rommel's Afrika Korps would launch three eastward attacks toward his goal of capturing Cairo and the Suez Canal.

Rommel's attacks never quite succeeded. Each time, stiffening British resistance and the failure of Rommel's supply line brought the offensive to a halt. When he received a telegram from Hitler announcing his promotion to Field Marshal in June 1942, Rommel is said to have remarked, "It would have been better if he had sent me another division." His army was thrown back in retreat by British General Bernard Law Montgomery's meticulously planned second battle of El Alamein in October 1942, and Rommel was flown out of Africa in March 1943 before the surrender of German and Italian forces in Tunisia. Rommel, formerly a relatively

ardent supporter of Hitler, came to despair of German victory, but when appointed to command the forces along the French and Belgian coasts, he immediately began upgrading defenses along the beaches.

—NP

TOP: Rommel as a division commander with his 7th Panzer Division staff, including Hans Speidel to his left, plot their advance through France, May 1940.

BOTTOM: Afrika Korps commander Erwin Rommel offers words of encouragement to his soldiers during the seesaw fighting in North Africa, circa 1941.

mines have been re-laid [*verlegt*] in the last three weeks than in the last three years." These minefields and beach obstacles were, in turn, covered by strongpoints containing bunkered field guns and machine-gun nests. By D-DAY the number of such fortifications on the 870 miles (1,400km) of coastline under Rommel's control had climbed to an astounding 9,300.

Germany's Dilemma

Under Rommel's tireless direction, beach defenses for the 175 miles (281.6km) of the Pas-de-Calais coast, with Boulogne and Calais at its center, had indeed been strengthened to the point that the Allies would no more consider directly assaulting it than the Germans would have considered directly assaulting the French Maginot Line in 1940. The Allies, however, had consistently and effectively worked for almost two full years to guide the Germans into fortifying that area in precisely the way that they did because it robbed other threatened areas—most notably Normandy—of both resources and close-in mobile reserves.

Despite the ever-thickening minefields, the new beach obstacles, and the interlocking fields of fire, German officers at all levels of command frequently were left with the same impression of the Atlantic Wall's lack of depth. "So many knots in a piece of string," said von Rundstedt, while examining a field map of bunkered strongpoints as Major General Wilhelm Richter, commander of the 716th Division, defending the Caen sector of Normandy, described the points of resistance in his sector as resembling "a string of pearls." Von Rundstedt would have been delighted to have destroyed the invasion at the waterline, but believed that Germany had neither the time nor the resources to properly defend each and every area within reach of the Allies. To him, the principal value in a stout defense of the beaches was the delay that it would

impose on the invaders, a delay that would show the Allies' hand and allow the mailed fist of six Panzer divisions to inflict a crushing blow.

To Rommel, the idea of massing divisions in the face of unchallenged Allied air supremacy was worse than folly. If the invasion were not smashed at the waterline, or immediately after the initial landings, Germany's chance for victory would be gone forever. Fortunately for the Allies, the cumbersome and divided chain of command established by Hitler did not allow the *immediate* concentration of armor that Rommel believed was absolutely essential. Few of Rommel's fellow generals had experienced the full-blood, continuous nature of Allied air attacks. To one of the few who had, Lieutenant General Fritz Bayerlein, who commanded the Panzer-Lehr, Rommel wrote, "Our friends from the East cannot imagine what they're in for here. It's not a matter of fanatical hordes to be driven forward in masses against our line with no regard for casualties and little recourse to tactical craft; here we are facing an enemy who applies all his native intelligence to the uses of his many technical resources, who spares no expenditure of matériel, and whose every operation goes its course as though it had been the subject of repeated rehearsal. Dash and doggedness no longer make a soldier."

ABOVE: General Fritz Bayerlein in North Africa's western desert. Bayerlein fought under tank-warfare pioneer General Heinz Guderian during the German invasions of France and the Soviet Union, then under Rommel in North Africa and again in France, where he commanded the Panzer-Lehr division. Bayerlein's *Panzergrenadiers* and *Panzertruppen* would bear the full weight of the Allies' breakout from Normandy during Operation COBRA, and Bayerlein would later fight at Bastogne, the Rhine, and the Ruhr as a corps commander. Unlike his comrade and trusted friend Rommel, Bayerlein would survive the war.

LEFT: Worn but full of fight, a haggard Rommel takes personal charge of Afrika Korps tactical operations during the waning days of fighting in North Africa, circa 1942.

Only the great number of barrage balloons floating constantly in British skies kept the islands from sinking under the seas.
—General Dwight D. Eisenhower

Chapter Two

COUNTDOWN TO OVERLORD

The world had never seen anything like it. On the eve of D-DAY, 1,627,000 "Yanks" lived, worked, and stored their implements of war in 279,204 tents, 398,666 prefabricated huts, and 111,590 buildings, ranging from thatch-roofed cottages and industrial warehouses to grand estates and fashionable hotels. Although this American "occupation" of Britain received the lion's share of attention then and now, the United Kingdom itself supplied 1,750,000 men to the OVERLORD buildup, with some 175,000 Canadians added to the mix, along with roughly 40,000 French, Czech, Polish, and other troops who had escaped from occupied Europe. Added to these numbers on land the British Admiralty counted precisely 52,889 American plus 112,824 British sailors living aboard their ships.

The amount of matériel shipped to Britain was equally stunning—8,000 aircraft, 50,000 tracked and wheeled vehicles, 450,000 tons (4.1 million kg) of ammunition. The statistics seem endless and, ominously, included some 124,000 hospital beds. Upon finding that the island's rail system was woefully inadequate because of its old, undersize, and obsolescent equipment, some 1,000 engines and 20,000 railroad cars were shipped in as fast as American manufacturers could produce them. In all, the U.S. Army Quartermaster Corps in Britain listed some 350,000 different items that it had either acquired from its own "Arsenal of Democracy" across the Atlantic or from Britain through direct purchases and a little-known system of "reverse Lend-Lease." The only key item that the gathering forces did not have until late 1943 was a commander.

Virtually all senior British and American commanders in 1943 believed that U.S. Army Chief of Staff George C. Marshall would be anointed supreme commander of the Allied Expeditionary Force, a move that Churchill had proposed to Roosevelt in 1942 and again in 1943. Roosevelt, however, viewed Marshall's efforts in Washington as absolutely critical to America's war effort, in large part because of the great trust placed in him by Congress.

Others, such as General Henry H. (Hap) Arnold of the Army Air Forces, pointed out that Marshall was Army chief of staff and a member of both the Joint and the Combined Chiefs of Staff. "To be appointed as commanding general of OVERLORD," said Arnold, would make Marshall "just another Theater commander."

The decision was put off, and put off again. For nearly a year, the man in charge of all OVERLORD planning, Lieutenant General Frederick E. Morgan, had acted as the chief of staff to a supreme Allied commander who had never been designated. Morgan urgently pointed out to Marshall and the other combined chiefs of staff that the invasion clock was ticking and that the plans developed by his staff increasingly needed "executive action" to ensure that they were carried out on time. It was December of 1943 before Eisenhower, the

Allied Mediterranean Theater commander, was named to head the Supreme Headquarters Allied Expeditionary Force (SHAEF). With three major amphibious landings under his belt—North Africa, Sicily, and Italy—Eisenhower was an obvious choice for the top spot, and he immediately named Morgan as his deputy chief of staff.

🎤 *George M. Cohan's refrain that "The Yanks are coming! The Yanks are coming!" must have crossed the minds of many British citizens as Americans arrived en masse to train and prepare for the invasion of Normandy. Walter Ehlers and his brother Roland, both of the 1st Infantry Division and fresh from the fighting in North Africa, decided to get a little R and R by visiting London. Ehlers recalls that the excitement was not just at the front.*

We arrived in England in October or November 1943. Our regiment was sent to the Dorchester area, east of Weymouth. Of course, a division's got 14,000 people, so we were stationed all over the place.

My brother and I went in the Army together, and we were in the same company. We obtained passes to go to London, where we experienced our first air raid. The buzz bombs were coming in. You could hear them coming, and then the engine would cut off, and then you'd have to wait and listen to it. But as long as you could hear it, if it wasn't coming right overhead, you were in pretty good shape. When the air raid sirens went off, the citizens of London herded up the GIs and took them down into the bomb shelters. We sat there and listened to the bombs landing. Some of them were pretty close. Dust and dirt came up, and the English people would be sitting there, talking away and chatting just like nothing was happening. As soon as they got the all-clear signal, everybody went about their business. They were so used to it by that time. It was unbelievable. ▪

—Walter Ehlers, Rifle Squad Leader,
L Company, 18th Infantry Regiment,
1st Infantry Division (US)

🎤 *Sergeant O.B. Hill of the 508th Parachute Infantry Regiment was one of the Yanks sent to England to train for the invasion. But his fondest memories of that time are those spent with a Nottingham family.*

I always say we were the luckiest of all the troops who got sent to England. The city of Nottingham was absolutely fantastic. The people there were friendly no matter what we did. On weekends the streets were packed with Americans. We outnumbered the British four to one. We were a loud, boisterous, obnoxious bunch. We'd go into the pubs, and in thirty minutes we had drunk all of the booze allotted for the day. But the British accepted us. We were invited into their homes and mingled with the citizens.

I met the Anderson family in a pub, and they invited me to their home. We became very good friends. I would liberate some things from the mess hall: ham, fruit, flour, sugar—things that they couldn't get normally—and

ABOVE: A group of soldiers leaves a Red Cross Club on a sightseeing expedition of London, with Red Cross worker Louise Alexander acting as tour guide. Americans and Britons—about whom Winston Churchill once quipped were "divided by a common language"—learned much about one another during their close association. For example, Americans stationed in Britain discovered that a "bum" was someone's posterior and that a "fag" was a cigarette. Britons soon found out that their term "rubbers," for waterproof boots, had an altogether different meaning to Americans, who thought they were talking about condoms.

RIGHT: U.S. vehicles, including M-5 prime movers "Hitler's Hearse" (foreground) and "American Band" from a field artillery unit, fill a west-country street as British townsfolk, separated by a thin garden wall, go about their daily business.

take that to Mom Anderson. Occasionally I had apple pie or baked ham, meals like my mother used to make. Many of the guys did the same thing. As a result, I don't think anyone really became homesick. With the Andersons, I felt that they were my family when I was there. After being there the first two or three times, I no longer needed to knock. I lived there. When I had free time, I was welcome to come.

You had to be around the British people to really understand them. They were a different breed. All the rigors that they had faced during the four years of war before we arrived did not seem to have had any effect on them. They referred to the battle at Dunkirk as a little "skirmish." They never allowed their spirits to get down. They always knew in their own hearts that this was all going to come out for the best. ▪

—O.B. Hill, Sergeant, 508th Parachute Infantry Regiment, Attached to 82d Airborne Division (US)

The British people not only welcomed American men into their homes for an occasional meal, but, in many instances, allowed them to move in and become one of their family. First Lieutenant Sidney Salomon of the 2d Ranger Battalion found his job of assigning men to homes made easier by the warm reception they received from their hosts.

Here we lived with the English people, for they volunteered to take us in. That was quite a unique experience. Imagine a soldier from a foreign country, coming up to your door, knocking, and introducing himself. Here he is, a rifle over his arm with a cartridge full of live ammunition. Now he is going to live in your home.

I was a senior officer, so I was taking care of the company. I was given a list telling the address, not the name of the person who lived there, just the address. Opposite the address would be the figure of one, two, or three. I had the company lined up and a clipboard in front of me. I said, "Okay, stop." We'd stop in front of No. 15. I'd look at my clipboard and say, "Two people. Two men are going to live there." So I'd turn around and say, "Okay, Jones and Smith, go up, knock on the door, and introduce yourselves. That's where you're going to live." Now you figure how difficult it might be for some kid brought up on a farm, isolated, not some street-smart kid from New York or some other big city, to all of sudden to have to go up and knock on a door and say, I'm So-and-so and I'll be living here. But the English people were great.

Part of the time we were on the Isle of Wight, a resort area. Of course, the people in England didn't go on vacation during the war years. So we stayed in hotels and boarding-houses there. We had our own rooms. We also ate with the English people. We would receive ration cards that we would automatically give to the people who owned the hotel. That was great, too. For example, there were eight of us who lived in this one hotel. So the proprietor got our eight ration cards. Since they were double ration cards, she and her help could eat better with the combined total of sixteen than just with their own three or four ration cards.

I had a beautiful room. I could lie in bed and see the coast of France on a clear day. This couple had two sons, both of whom were in the service. I had one son's room and the other officer had the other's room. They treated us like sons. We would tell them if we were going to be home. They kept chickens in the backyard and we had fresh eggs every morning, which was a real treat then.

Of course, the Army paid for room and board. Depending on where we were, sometimes we had a room and then used a common place for a mess hall. In Cornwall, we used a public garage for a mess hall. We assembled at the corner and marched through town. This posed a bit of a problem. Being in the Army, we were accustomed to our morning starting with the whistles and sounding reveille. Everybody falls out, then you go to the mess hall for breakfast. Here we were living with the English people. You couldn't just blow a whistle and wake up the English, because we probably got up earlier than they did. Our mess hall was maybe a mile (1.6km) walk to the center of town. The average private generally didn't have a wristwatch, because he was told what to do, what to wear, what to eat, and where to be. This made it a little difficult to line up in the morning. Consequently, we were issued wristwatches. ■

—Sidney Salomon, First Lieutenant, C Company, 2d Ranger Battalion (US)

O.B. HILL

BELOW: A U.S. soldier stands guard at a depot containing lines of M-3 half-tracks along with thousands of other vehicles freshly arrived in England.

Battle of the Atlantic

The free flow of goods and war materials across the Atlantic sea-lanes was the linchpin of Allied strategy in the war against Germany. Without this, Britain would be unable to bring in the supplies it needed for its very survival, and the United States could not take the war to German soil. The bitterly contested struggle at sea was arguably the longest "battle" of the war, as Germany sought to deny the Atlantic to the Allies. Although German aircraft, surface ships, and mines played a significant part in the Battle of the Atlantic, their roles were nonetheless limited, and the principal burden of the fight was borne by Germany's submarine fleet.

The fall of France in 1940 greatly increased the effectiveness of the comparatively small number of operational U-boats (submarines) at the onset of war by providing bases in the Bay of Biscay with direct access to the shipping lanes used by Allied convoys. British and American shipping losses climbed as the U-boat fleet grew. By March 1, 1943, Germany possessed 222 frontline, oceangoing submarines; of those, 114 were at sea in the Atlantic. By the end of the month, U-boats had

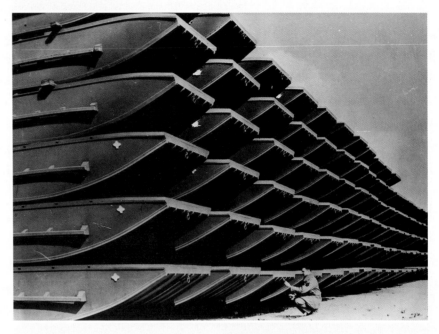

sunk eighty-two ships in the North Atlantic, with another thirty-eight sunk in other areas. With such losses, there could not be a buildup in England for a cross-Channel invasion.

Fortunately, new Allied antisubmarine weapons, long in production, were coming into the battle in decisive numbers. Large numbers of convoy escorts were at sea and fitted with highly effective sonar; long-range bombers,

ABOVE AND BELOW: In May 1943, barely one year before D-Day, the Allies finally turned the tide in the hard-fought Battle of the Atlantic. The fruits of the Allied victory were immediately enjoyed in Britain, where the flow of men and matériel from the United States suddenly swelled to become a flood tide. Above, a mountain of pontoons is held in readiness for bridge-building operations during the invasion of Normandy. Below, Bofors-type M-1 40-mm anti-aircraft guns wait for a crack at the German *Luftwaffe*.

especially the B-24 Liberator, were available in greater numbers; new escort carriers could provide aircraft to close the gap between the land-based aircraft; and Allied code-breaking efforts (ULTRA) were increasingly successful in giving the Allies information on U-boat activity.

In mid-May 1943, a large convoy was attacked by a total of thirty-three U-boats. Not a single merchant ship was lost, while five U-boats succumbed to antisubmarine attacks. From then on, U-boat losses regularly exceeded the number of merchant ships sunk. The floodgates had burst open. The Battle of the Atlantic would ebb and flow for the duration of the war, but men and matériel now streamed across the ocean from the "Arsenal of Democracy." It was only a matter of time before the forces gathering in Britain would surge across the Channel and blast their way into the heart of Nazi Germany.

ABOVE: Corrugated metal-and-canvas sheds protect stockpiles of munitions stored along a country road for easy access.

LEFT: Railroad cars made to British standards were shipped across the Atlantic in parts and assembled in the island's factories.

Soldiers of the Empire who had already arrived and become acclimated to the lifestyle in "merry olde England" now found themselves surrounded by Americans—nowhere more so than in the neighborhood pub. Ken Hanna, a Canadian flying for the RAF, found the English people extremely accommodating.

The airfields were invariably about five miles (8km) out from the small villages. Between the airfield and the village there was usually a corner pub. During blackout periods, which was every night, you could either sit in the mess or your billet or you could wander down to the pub. If you went to a movie in town, the movie got out at nine o'clock, the same time the buses stopped running. So you walked home. They issued us bicycles because the mess hall was invariably a mile (1.6km) or two miles (3.2km) from the airfield, and the airfield was a mile (1.6km) or two miles (3.2km) from where you were sleeping. In early 1944 the Americans started arriving. Americans saturated the place. The little corner pubs that we used to go to in the evening where we'd play darts were suddenly taken over. Places where once we could spend the evening now closed an hour after opening because they had run out of everything. Apart from that, we welcomed the Yanks.

Overall the English people seemed only too happy to welcome these people because they felt that this was the beginning of the end. I can't ever recall too much bad feeling. They stood in long queues waiting for buses. But if a serviceman in uniform appeared, they automatically stood back and allowed them to go to the front of the queue. They were that generous. ■

—Ken Hanna, Pilot,
Royal Air Force (CAN)

Expanding OVERLORD

One of the main concerns of invasion planners had always been that a successful landing on the continent could be rendered a hollow victory if the Germans won the race to build up forces in the lodgment area. The ability of the Germans to do just that was plain for all to see in January 1944, since fully 160,000 Allied troops were irretrievably locked into a beachhead barely twelve miles (19.3km) deep at Anzio near Rome, and would remain so for five more months.

The original D-Day invasion plan had been severely constrained by the perpetual dearth of available assault shipping caused by the global nature of the war. When Eisenhower's ground force commander, Lieutenant General Bernard Law Montgomery, was briefed that only about half of Normandy's fifty miles (80.5km) of useful beaches would be stormed by a bare three divisions, he immediately pushed for a five-division assault over a much wider area. The arguments for such an expansion were sound. A wider area would mean a broader front for the Germans to contend with, could accommodate nearly twice as many vehicle exits leading from the landing beaches, and more Allied divisions could be brought immediately into the battle—eight, in fact, since the number of airborne divisions would also expand from one to three.

But where were the additional Allied sea and air resources to come from? A careful analysis of assault-craft production and their transit times across the Atlantic revealed that enough boats *might* be available for the expanded assault, if draconian measures were also implemented to extract appropriate ships and smaller craft from other areas, such as the Caribbean, West Africa, and the Indian Ocean. However, the biggest gains in existing landing craft for OVERLORD could come from the nearby Mediterranean Theater, if some could be siphoned away from a secondary landing planned for southern France. Known as Operation ANVIL, this was intended to pin down German divisions that might otherwise be sent to Normandy, while bringing additional Allied divisions directly to France from North Africa and Italy. The invasion planners were ordered to move ahead with the new requirements, under the assumption that the additional landing craft would be available by D-Day, May 1, 1944. When it became apparent that they could not reach the required numbers in time, Eisenhower directed that OVERLORD be moved back one more month, to early June.

Dangerous Shortage in Landing Craft

The steadily expanding number of boatyards throughout the United States had already been working around the clock for nearly two years to produce assault craft for operations in the Mediterranean and the two-pronged U.S. drive in the Pacific against Japan. The multiyear buildup for OVERLORD further intensified the Allies' insatiable appetite for these strange little boats with flat bottoms and ramps that dropped forward into the surf, particularly those that could transport tanks and vehicles. So great was the need for such vessels that LCTs (landing craft, tank) designed to carry four Sherman tanks were even manufactured

> The destinies of two great empires . . . seem to be tied up in some God-damned things called LSTs.
>
> —Winston Churchill

ABOVE: Going my way? An LCT hitches a ride to England aboard the deck of an LST. On the deck of the LCT is yet another landing craft, an LCM, and small LCVPs are arranged on the ship's davits. Upon reaching port, a dock crane will lift out the LCM and the LST will head back into the harbor, where it will prepare to release the LCT into the water by allowing it to slide sideways off its deck. The LST does this by purposely inducing a sharp list. All fuel oil is transferred to tanks on one side of the ship while ballast tanks on the same side are steadily flooded and those on the other side are pumped out. Although a 13-degree list was preferred, LCTs were allowed to slip from the greased wooden skids on the ship's deck when the list reached at least 10.5 degrees. The large amount of water thrown up when the LCTs struck the water acted as a cushion to prevent the vessels' hulls from colliding.

in quantity by a boiler-making firm in the heart of the North American continent, in Kansas City. After sliding down the ways into a tributary of the wide Missouri, they navigated the winding, 1,600-mile (2,574km) river route to New Orleans, then made a 6,000-mile (9,654km) voyage across the North Atlantic to Portsmouth, England, loaded onto the decks of cargo ships and LSTs (landing ship, tank).

Although the shortage of LCTs was considered "critical," the situation was even worse with its larger cousin, the LST, which was longer than a football field and capable of landing fourteen fully loaded trucks and fifteen Sherman tanks directly onto a beach. There were never enough of them, and consequently, senior members of Navy and Army commands frequently found themselves personally involved in horse-trading with an array of less-capable alphabet soup vessels in an effort to obtain more of the unique ships. What follows is a greatly abbreviated representation of the negotiations between SHAEF in London and Allied Force Headquarters (AFHQ) of the Mediterranean Theater from January through March 1944. The numbers and types of assault shipping/landing craft involved are real.

SHAEF: We'll overload our APAs and give you six AKAs, which can be used in your calmer Mediterranean waters for twenty LSTs and twenty-one LCIs.

AFHQ: No, we're having our own problems because of Anzio. We'll keep everything in the Mediterranean we have now. You send us the ships you are offering, and we'll divert to you the twenty-six LSTs— with their deckloads of twenty-six LCTs— scheduled for delivery from America.

The disposition of every individual LST and LCT was closely monitored because of the never-ending scarcity, and SHAEF pressed the British, whose facilities were already stretched to the limit with the MULBERRIES and new landing craft construction, to somehow make room to repair the hundreds of landing craft— including valuable LSTs—idled after training accidents. Would there be enough available by D-DAY or would the assault have to be short-changed? A frustrated Eisenhower cabled to General Marshall: "The uncertainty is having a marked effect on everyone responsible for planning and executing OVERLORD," adding that the invasion was already fifteen LSTs short because of Operation ANVIL. Wrote Eisenhower: "I think it is the gravest possible mistake to allow demands for ANVIL to militate against the main effort."

Disaster at Slapton Sands

The March 1944 decision to delay ANVIL and reallocate landing craft to Britain—just long enough to mount the cross-Channel attack—assured that OVERLORD's minimum needs would be met. The additional assault craft also enabled the forces assembled in England to more easily carry out two full-scale dress rehearsals for the D-DAY landings.

Techniques and procedures for the marshaling, loading, and unloading of men and materials had been carefully worked out at the Assault Training Center on the Devon coast of western England, and honed to perfection as elements of the U.S. 1st, 4th, and 29th Infantry Divisions worked their way through the facility's grueling program. Large-scale maneuvers, however, had never been conducted, and

SHAEF developed plans for the rehearsals to take place on the beaches near Dartmouth in southern England. Exercise TIGER, beginning on the night of April 26–27, 1944, would approximate the upcoming landings on Normandy's UTAH Beach, while FABIUS in early May rehearsed the assault on OMAHA Beach.

The opening of Exercise TIGER went off without a hitch, but disaster struck on the second night. A convoy of eight LSTs, carrying mostly Army engineer units, was set upon by German torpedo boats out of Cherbourg. Slipping past a thin screen of British destroyers and motor gunboats, the fast German E-boats struck the three-mile (4.8km) long convoy as it moved along the Lyme Bay coast, sinking two LSTs and heavily damaging a third before making good their high-speed escape. U.S. Navy investigators put the number of dead and missing at 638. Army engineers came up with the much higher figure of 749 for dead and missing. Either way, far more men were lost training for the UTAH Beach assault than would ultimately be killed during the invasion itself.

As terrible as the loss of life was, what the action off Slapton Sands portended for the success of D-DAY was disturbing. The loss of three

BELOW: Members of the 29th Ranger Battalion step up to the firing line during a practice session with the Thompson submachine gun at the British Commando School, Achnacarry, Scotland, February 1943. The unit was formed from select members of the 29th Infantry Division, who were to receive an especially high level of training—and in some cases take part in raids along the French and Norwegian coasts—before being sent back to the division prior to D-DAY to spread their knowledge and expertise. Lieutenant Eugene Dance (stepping forward to fire) took part in an operation near Roydenfjord, Norway, and was tapped to set up a sniper school upon his return to the 29th. He transferred to the 101st Airborne Division immediately before the invasion and was rushed through five parachute drops in one day, so that he could earn his jump wings and take over command of a platoon.

[Ships were being] trapped and hemmed in—like a bunch of wolves circling a wounded dog.

—Seaman Emanuel Rubin, LST 496

BELOW: Assisted by a British tugboat, LST-289 limps into Dartmouth harbor, April 28, 1944. The landing ship was severely damaged by German torpedo boats while heading for an early-morning rehearsal for landings at UTAH Beach. Two other troop-filled ships in the convoy of eight LSTs were sunk during the night attack, killing as many as 749 soldiers and sailors—far more men than the actual assault on UTAH.

precious LSTs reduced the reserve of such ships to exactly zero and raised the specter, said Eisenhower, "of both raiders and bombers concentrating on some of our important ports." There was also growing concern over the great discrepancies in the number of soldiers missing after the Lyme Bay action. Were any of the missing engineer officers privy to D-Day's secrets? And, if so, could one have been hauled aboard an E-boat? OVERLORD would be irretrievably compromised if the wrong man fell into German hands. A second, then third, investigation was initiated to determine what sensitive information might have been known by certain missing personnel.

Lock-down

Luckily, the only assault craft struck in-port by the Germans were a pair of LSTs in a post–D-Day random hit by a German V-1 cruise missile. And no strategic information was obtained or surmised by the Germans as a result of the fighting in Lyme Bay. An official Army historian later put the matter to rest by stating that the "incident" passed without further repercussions. Yet, the heavy breathing at SHAEF over the possible breach of security was not unreasonable.

Immediately after the TIGER and FABIUS rehearsals in early May, the assault divisions

BILL TRUE

LEFT: An LCM crew rendering assistance pulls past the mangled stern of LST-289.

and support troops were essentially "imprisoned" in their staging areas. More than 170,000 British, Canadian, and American soldiers hunkered down for the long, dangerous wait until they began the movement to their embarkation points, which was scheduled to begin as early as May 30 and be completed by June 3. Very few of these men knew anything more about OVERLORD than their own specific tasks, but the fact that they had just completed exercises that closely mimicked the actual invasion, and that they were concentrated in staging areas immediately adjacent to ports far from the Channel narrows opposite Calais, would have been enough to raise alarm among the Germans. Battalions of U.S. and British Military Police (MPs) backed up a specialized force of some 2,000 U.S. Army Counter Intelligence Corps personnel guarding against any unauthorized movement, any breach of camouflage discipline.

Throughout the rest of Britain, millions of soldiers, sailors, and airmen went about the daily business of training, moving supplies, and maintaining the bomber offensive over Nazi-occupied Europe. Built into these routine activities—and unknown to even the most senior

officers—was the ongoing deception that the Pas-de-Calais was to be the invasion's target.

German agents who, in fact, were working for the Allies, dutifully reported troop movements, real and imaginary, as Patton's make-believe divisions filled the airwaves with radio traffic in the same region that four very real British and Canadian corps supplied plenty of authentic activity as they readied themselves to follow up the invasion. German reconnaissance aircraft were allowed an occasional glimpse of a fake buildup of invasion shipping in the Channel ports opposite Calais, but they were never allowed to overfly the real assault force jammed into every harbor, inlet, and river farther west. Meanwhile, Allied bombers and fighters pounded the road and rail net running to the Pas-de-Calais with more than twice as many strikes as were launched against Normandy and Brittany.

Practicing jumps repeatedly was all in a day's work for the paratroopers. But at what point can the jump be over-rehearsed? Private Bill True of the 101st Airborne Division believed that happened to them prior to D-DAY.

INVASION SHIPS AND CRAFT

AGC: Amphibious force flagship

AKA: Assault cargo ship equipped to launch landing craft

APA: Assault transport ship equipped to launch landing craft

DUKW: Amphibian truck (25 troops or 500 lbs. [227kg] cargo)

LB: Landing barge (many types: oil, water, repair, antiaircraft, etc.)

LCA: Landing craft, assault (35 troops and 800 lbs. [363.2kg] equipment)

LCC: Landing craft, control (crew only)

LCI(L): Landing craft, infantry (large) (205 troops or 75 tons [68,100kg] cargo)

LCM: Landing craft, mechanized (30 tons [27,240kg] of vehicles and equipment)

LCT(4): Landing craft, tank (350 tons [317,800kg] of vehicles and equipment)

LCT(5), (6): Landing craft, tank (150 tons [136,200kg] of vehicles and equipment)

LCT(R): Landing craft, tank (rocket) (1,064 5-in. [12.7cm] fire-support rockets)

LCVP: Landing craft, vehicle-personnel (36 troops or 8,100 lbs. [3,677kg] cargo)

LSI(L): Landing ship, infantry (large) (British equivalent of APA)

LST: Landing ship, tank (1,900 or 2,100 tons [1.7 million kg or 1.9 million kg] of vehicles and equipment)

RHF: Rhino ferry (modular, carries 16 to 40 vehicles)

LEFT: A dozen LSTs landing near high tide on OMAHA Beach begin the process of unloading hundreds of vehicles and tanks. The close proximity of vulnerable transports anchored close to the shore indicates that this photo was taken on June 8, 1944 (D+2), or later.

ABOVE: Soldiers position a Bangalore torpedo under barbed wire during a training exercise in England, August 1943. When fired, the explosives-filled metal tube would blast a hole in the obstacle far more quickly than it could be breached with wire cutters, while also minimizing the exposure to enemy fire. A Bangalore torpedo could be lengthened by screwing on additional segments, and the device was adapted to many demolition tasks. It was frequently used to clear paths through minefields during assaults.

Training in England was rugged. We had a number of jumps there as well as maneuvers. It was all hard training aimed at the invasion. There would be particular maneuvers and special situations arranged where we would jump. We had night jumps as well as some daytime jumps. By the time D-DAY rolled around, we were probably past our peak. I think all of the training that we did from about six months on was primarily training aimed at the higher level of officers on how to maneuver troops and communicate. As far as we down at the frontline level, we knew what we had to do and how to do it as well

after six or nine months as we did after two years. We were ready.

Just about a month or so before the invasion, several of the battalions in our division had an opportunity to make a jump for General Eisenhower and Winston Churchill. It wasn't really a maneuver, except that, after we landed, the idea was for us to seize an objective and take up defensive positions. I participated in that. Both Churchill and Eisenhower talked to the troops. That was a highlight of the training in England. ▪

—Bill True

Even with two feet planted firmly on the ground, there was always plenty of physical exercise for the men. Sergeant Felix Branham of the 29th Infantry Division trained relentlessly for the landing.

We trained in the moors. We trained climbing cliffs. We had combined operations with the British and all the people who were to land. Commandos, our Rangers, and we would practice on all the various ships in the English Channel. We practiced getting off and climbing up these cliffs on these ropes with our equipment. They timed us to determine how much time it'd take to get off a landing craft. We trained with the British Royal Marines. We were a cocky bunch and tried to outdo them. We were well dressed and well paid. We were well fed at that time. Anything we wanted, anywhere we wanted to go, first class all the way. The British resented us for that. We'd walk into a dance hall and we'd take the British girls. We'd flash cigarettes, chewing gum, and chocolate bars. British soldiers would have their dates, and they'd leave 'em and come with us.

We were a competitive bunch. We were trained that way. You were better than any-thing that walks. You are it, except one thing—the German soldier is a better soldier than you are. So you learn a lesson. Don't ever think that you're better than he is because, if you do, you'll get killed. And I learned that. The German soldier was an outstanding soldier, no question about it.

We practiced every type of landing. If it was vertical, we trained on it. We had a place called Slapton Sands. It was the American Assault Training Center. We would go to make a landing in the English Channel and come back just like we were hitting the beach. Later it turned out to be OMAHA Beach. We would attack over barbed wire. We would overcome these obstacles. We had demolition people with us. We had mortars. Everything we used just like we were going to do it. It was really a dress rehearsal.

They separated out the officers and the people who couldn't do the job. One day they'd be gone. They just kept picking and picking, like a football team. We were trained and given pep talks. After a while we wondered if we were just going to be an occupation army. Then we started getting visits from Eisenhower, then [General Omar] Bradley. Later, we got visits from Montgomery.

BELOW: Eisenhower's boss, Army Chief of Staff George C. Marshall (right) was General Brooke's counterpart on the Allied Combined Chiefs of Staff, a group made up of the chiefs of staff of the Anglo-American armed forces that advised President Franklin D. Roosevelt and Prime Minister Winston Churchill. Marshall was the principal U.S. strategist during the war and President Roosevelt's most trusted adviser.

ABOVE: Glider troops of the 320th Field Artillery Battalion, 82d Airborne Division, load canistered 105-mm shells into a Horsa glider. The 320th fared the best of the two glider and two parachute artillery battalions that landed on D-Day, with six of their howitzers commencing fire missions near Sainte Mère-Eglise on the morning of D+1. The smaller 75-mm guns of the other battalions were mostly scattered or damaged during the landings. An efficient artillery crew could unhook the tail section of a Horsa and remove its jeep, gun, and rounds within seven minutes.

Anybody that was anybody would come to visit. That convinced us that we weren't going to be an army of occupation because Montgomery and those guys didn't come around to talk and give critiques to noncombat guys. We were going to get something; we were going to be there. We had heard that General Marshall had his eye on the 29th Division based on our performance in maneuvers in 1941. They liked the caliber that they saw in the 29th. But of course that was still just speculation. The division had three regiments, and mine [the 116th] tried to outdo the 115th. We tried to outdo the 175th. We went on a twenty-five-mile (40.2km) hike three times a week. We trained seven days a week, right up to the time we went into the staging area. We competed with the others. If we went on a division march, and the 115th lost forty men, we wanted to come in sooner and lose fewer. We said if we kept doing these things, when a dirty job came along, we were going to do it.

I had volunteered to go on a boat team. The people who came behind us never were loaded near as heavy as we were. This boat team was trained to fight if you got cut off. We had mortars, machine guns, bazookas. Bangalore torpedoes. We had riflemen. They even taught us Morse code. We could signal where we were. There'd be a light to flash.

There never was a better-kept secret than the Normandy Invasion. In April, Bradley had climbed a cargo net right beside me. He had a critique with us and told us we'd be going to France. He didn't say OMAHA Beach, he didn't say where. We'd had our last practice landing at Slapton Sands. Then we went into our marshaling area near Plymouth. ▪

—Felix Branham

 British Army commando Geoffrey Parrett's training was similar to that described by Felix Branham.

When you joined the commandos, your basic training took place in a castle in western Scotland owned by the Campbell clan. Intensive training consisted of different tough slides, including one after crossing the river

TOP: After Allied assault units for D-Day cycled through a series of large-scale rehearsals in late April and early May 1944, the troops were confined to their camps—in some cases for more than a month—until called out for the invasion. Here, Corporal Jack Bramkamp, Company B, 2d Ranger Battalion, gives a special invasion trim to Corporal Elmer Olander as other Rangers admire his handiwork. Note the artfully decorated back of the battle jacket, which serves as a barber's cape. The sixty-five men of Company B landed not at Pointe du Hoc, but on the extreme western end of OMAHA Beach. Almost half, including Bramkamp and Olander, never reached the seawall.

BOTTOM: Sailors aboard a scout LCM seem to agree with Civil War General William Tecumseh Sherman's statement that "War is hell." They subjected their knobs to the shears just to kill time while waiting to cross the Channel.

on ropes. I remember that one particularly because I fell amongst the rocks and it was rather painful afterwards. They had many of these courses which were adopted by the infantry afterwards, and eventually all the units in the British Army were using these methods. We were told we had to be a little tougher and a little faster. We had to climb about twelve feet (3.7m), and then we jumped down into a big pool of mud. This was to make sure that you could land without dirtying your weapons. They had to be good for firing immediately afterwards. You got a bit of a rocket if you dropped it in the mud or let it go under. They used live ammunition all the time.

Using the lakes around there, we would simulate night landings. As we landed, they'd

be firing live ammunition at you. The instructors would try to fire ahead of you or behind you or just over your head. You'd see the traces coming; it was rather pretty. They would seem to be coming straight at you and then they swerved off at the last moment to give you an idea of trajectory. We also did lots of speed marches. I think they wanted us to do seven miles (11.3km) in an hour; fifteen miles (24.1km) in two hours and fifteen minutes. It was pretty tough going and it was always cold and rainy. The wind came from the Irish Sea, making it rather uncomfortable.

After this part of our training, we went to train on various landing craft, the small one being the landing craft assault [LCA]. This was rather a nice little craft. It would bob around, and I rather liked it. I never ever did get seasick, but many did. We would land on the beach on a sort of sandbar and then wade across to the beach proper. Naturally, you were very uncomfortable and spent the next few hours with wringing wet feet. Of course, you didn't stop there but then had to go on and march somewhere or dig slit trenches, foxholes, or whatever. It was extremely uncomfortable. Your boots turned white all the time, and you could never get them black again for parade because of the salt from the sea.

Sometimes you went out in an LST, which was large—almost like a liner—and in place of the lifeboats they had the LCAs. They lowered these, so you had to jump into them. That was probably the most terrifying part for me. I was always frightened of slipping between them and falling into the sea. They would bob up and down, rocking and swaying, so that was the most uncomfortable part of any landing of that nature. ▪

—Geoffrey L. Parrett, 3d Commando,
1st Commando Brigade (UK)

The planned British attack on the Merville Battery required special preparation. The task was given to Lieutenant Colonel Terence Otway of the 9th Parachute Battalion.

A week after I'd been promoted to lieutenant colonel, and had taken over as commander of the battalion in March 1944, I was told to go to a farmhouse near Amesbury in Wiltshire. There I was shown a model and told to study it with a view to capturing the battery. That was my briefing, and I was locked into the room. I looked at the model and there was a battery on it. I got the whole model in my mind and then called in the briefing officer. He was a brigade major, Bill Collingwood. Then he showed a detailed model of the mobile battery. My first reaction was it seems stupid to jump over what they called the "Atlantic Wall" and land outside another fortress. So then I got on with my plan, and in general, it was an assault both outside and inside using gliders.

OPPOSITE: Soldiers clamber aboard LCI-539 in an English harbor, June 1 or 2, 1944. Diminutive LCVPs and LCAs could not safely cross the English Channel because of the danger of being swamped. Troops would often be ferried within harbors by such boats to larger landing craft and ships for the transit to the assault staging areas, where they would either head for the beach in their current vessel or reboard other small landing craft for the run to the beach. The stacks of rations onboard (upper right) were necessary because there were no kitchen facilities available aboard LCIs for the craft's human cargo. The soldier at lower right is clutching the long barrel of a Browning automatic rifle.

LEFT: Army chaplain Edward R. Walters concludes a service for the Army and Navy personnel assigned to LCIs docked two deep along an English pier.

ABOVE: The "hurry up and wait" of life in the closed-off camps that were spread across southern England ended on June 1, 1944, as countless columns of troops and vehicles moved along secure routes to their embarkation points. Here, U.S. soldiers in full battle gear march toward their rendezvous on the coast through an English street devoid of civilians. American forces generally embarked from ports west of the Isle of Wight through Cornwall at the extreme southwestern tip of Britain, while the British and Canadians used ports east of the isle along the South Downs.

All southern England was one vast military camp, crowded with soldiers awaiting final word to go . . . a great human spring, coiled for the moment when its energy would be released and it would vault the English Channel.

—General Dwight D. Eisenhower

My concerns for the attack were the anti-tank ditch, minefields, and concertina barbed wire. Plus the fact that the ratio of the British Army of an attack onto a fortified place like this was six to one. In other words, the attackers should outnumber the defenders by six to one. We were told that there would be a garrison of 150. I was warned that we might get scattered if we had a very bad drop. I was very worried that I might be attacking with a force of less than 150, and it turned out to be true. That was a big worry.

I had a battalion of 600, and then if you added in the specialists, support teams, and support troops, I had roughly 700–750, including engineers. But as it turned out, I didn't have any engineers.

To train the men, the first thing I did was create a small model in the dining hall of the barracks. I had already decided that I had to have a mock-up battery, resembling, as near as possible, the real objective. But in addition to that, after looking at the problem, I decided it must be on similar ground.

Small, Slow, Vulnerable—and Indispensable: The Landing Craft of D-DAY

Allied forces used more than 4,100 landing ships and craft on D-Day. Ranging in size from the diminutive LCVP and its British counterpart, the LCA, to the massive LST capable of carrying dozens of vehicles and tanks, these highly specialized weapons of war enabled men and matériel to be landed directly on an invasion beach. The extreme flexibility provided by this robust amphibious force severely complicated Germany's ability to defend the "Atlantic Wall," because it enabled the Allies to strike almost anywhere from the Spanish border to the Arctic Circle.

The term "landing ships" incorporated oceangoing combatants that were at least 200 feet in length, while "landing craft" applied to smaller boats and craft unable to operate in very rough seas. Together they performed a tightly choreographed assault that landed more than 132,000 American, British, and Canadian soldiers across Normandy's beaches before nightfall on June 6, 1944.

APA, AKA, and LSI assault ships anchored at designated points offshore from where they launched their men and cargoes in LCVP and LCA landing craft. Meanwhile, LSTs and large landing craft such as LCMs, LCI(L)s, and LCTs sailed directly from English ports to the invasion beaches. In an effort to speed the flow of cargo ashore, some LSTs stopped short of the beach and disgorged fully loaded vehicles onto self-propelled RHFs (Rhino ferries) made of pontoons for the final run to land. Throughout it all, LCC crews did their best to guide the array of invaders to the beaches as other specialized landing ships and craft provided everything from emergency repairs to fire support.

LEFT: A Rhino ferry backs up to an anchored LST to take on a load of vehicles.

RIGHT: Railroad tracks are run up into an LST for quick delivery of railroad cars to support the invasion.

OPPOSITE, TOP: An LST and pair of LCT(5)s discharge vehicles onto shore. In the foreground are M-10 tank destroyers from another craft unseen to the left.

OPPOSITE, CENTER: Soldiers disembark from LCVPs as an LST looms in the background.

OPPOSITE, BOTTOM: An amphibious DUKW drives up onto shore as others follow in its wake.

I told the intelligence people that I wanted a patch of ground which was as near as possible exactly the same as the dock [landing] area, the approach from the dock area to the outside of the wire, from the wire into the battery. They must construct a model and find me a bit of ground. They said they can't do it. So I said, Well, I'll do it. So I flew over the area with a brigade major and picked out the ground near Newbury. I said I want the ground leveled and everything done within seven days. I was told my request was impossible. I didn't believe it. It just had to be done. I arranged for earth-moving equipment to be brought in, and we re-created the site with similar topography. The engineers built mock ground mines that went off.

Every single man knew exactly what he had to do and where he had to go, which was very important. It paid off in huge dividends because we expected to be dropped wide, but we didn't expect a drop as bad as we got. It was essential that every man knew where he was, so that he could reach the rendezvous on his own, if necessary, and, if we had moved off, follow us and catch up with us, and take part in the attack. Every man had air photographs and was questioned about his route four or five times. ∎

—Terence Otway, Lieutenant Colonel, Commanding Officer, 9th Parachute Battalion DSO (UK)

Removing beach obstacles was the domain of the Army engineers and the Naval Combat Demolition Units. Lieutenant Colonel William Gara of the 1st Infantry Division's engineers understood that the multiple-task training of his engineers was crucial for them to be successful in their mission.

Our engineer troops were highly trained, perhaps the best in the entire division. It may sound boastful, but it's a fact. Engineer troops are rather well skilled and there is always a high regard for them. It takes a lot longer to train an engineer soldier than it does an infantryman. Infantry goes on the line. Not to detract from the infantryman, but his job is to learn to fire his rifle and use a mortar and little else, whereas an engineer soldier learns to build bridges, install mines, remove mines, and install antipersonnel mines, so he's far more versatile than an infantry soldier.

According to doctrine, when making an assault landing, expect to lose 30 to 40 percent through casualties—wounded, killed, taken prisoner, or in some way unable to complete their assignment. This rate is very high. You come in with forces at least twice the number that you anticipate that the enemy has in place. So an assault landing requires a tremendous amount of training and requires skilled troops. That's why the 1st Infantry Division was used over and over again. When

LEFT: Soldiers find it "standing room only" aboard an LCI. The man at right wears a plastic bag containing a gas mask around his neck, and a gas-detector armband on his left arm. The armband can be more clearly seen on his buddy at the opposite side of the photo, and this soldier also has a standard Navy double-tube life belt affixed around his waist. Life belts would be fully inflated by two CO_2 capsules before the beach assault. The dark look of their uniforms is due to their impregnation with a compound that neutralizes blistering agents like mustard gas.

leaving Sicily, the men said, "We're ready to go home now. We've done our share. Let someone else do it." But they took us back to England, knowing the division would be involved in the Normandy Invasion. ▪

—William Gara, Lieutenant Colonel, 1st Engineer Combat Battalion, 1st Infantry Division (US)

were when you landed. You could recognize buildings and different things like that.

The sealed camps were rather large, and you felt captive because you weren't allowed out. No one was allowed out of those once you went in, for fear of security. I was in a camp run by Americans. They had a cinema, and we used to go and see movies there. I was fascinated by the American food, and I enjoyed trying it. I remember seeing the movie *Going My Way* with Bing Crosby. You couldn't smoke in the cinemas then either. Every now and again the film would come to a stop and the sergeant running the projector would say, "Okay guys. What's it going to be—movies or cigarettes? Can't have both." This happened I think about four or five times throughout the movie. During the waiting, I read American magazines. We played this game Battleship, which was all the rage at that time, using paper and pencil.

They gave us an emergency ration pack which consisted of a tin and inside were cubes of chocolate. I realized later it was probably just baking chocolate, highly concentrated. It said right on the tin not to be opened without the express orders of an officer or the permission of an officer. There were our fellows unscrewing the thing, pulling it out and tasting it, and saying, "This ain't bad, you know." ▪

—Geoffrey Parrett

OPPOSITE: Barrage balloons waiting to be hoisted lie in front of the Weymouth Pavilion as OMAHA-bound soldiers of the 1st Infantry Division board LCVPs that will ferry them to the troop transport USS *Thurston*. Like many other civilian ocean liners, cargo ships, and oilers, the ship taking these men to Normandy, formerly the recently built *Delsantos*, was acquired by the U.S. government, designated AP-77, and renamed. The *Thurston* was returned to its civilian owners in August 1946 after helping to return troops to the United States. The Rangers headed for Pointe du Hoc also disembarked from this spot.

After months of training, now came one of the most difficult phases for the men—the waiting. Still unaware of their exact mission, its date, or place, they attempted to spend their time in relaxation. British Army commando Geoffrey Parrett was glad that the moment for action was drawing near.

It was rather an exciting time, and I was looking forward to the invasion, and I think most people were. It would break the monotony of all the training. We'd been training for a year and half, and you wanted to do something different.

As D-DAY approached, we started to prepare for it. They showed us models and photographs, so you knew exactly where you

Load-out

The great movement began on Tuesday, May 30, 1944, as soldiers and sailors started the tedious process of boarding the seventeen convoys that would carry the Allied Army to the far shore. Britons watching the spectacle grind its way from inland bases and through the ports of Weymouth, Poole, Brixham, Torquay, and a half-dozen other Channel towns did not have to be told that the invasion was finally on. In other ports all along the English coast, British and American warships made their final preparations to put to sea, while paratroopers at inland airfields were issued maps of their drop zones that for the first time

BOTTOM: Elements of the U.S. 4th Infantry Division await their turn to board LCVPs that will take them to a waiting transport in Plymouth harbor. In the distance, giant cranes mark Plymouth's high-capacity wharves, a flotilla of British M-class destroyers are anchored at left, while the USS *Augusta,* flagship of the Western Task Force, lies anchored at right.

included the set names of their targets. The date for the invasion: Monday, June 5.

In his *History of United States Naval Operations in World War II,* U.S. Navy historian Samuel Eliot Morison vividly describes Portland harbor as "the scene of tremendous activity during the loading of the LCTs and LSTs. The harbor was laid out in lanes with large mooring dolphins so spaced that three LCTs could tie up at each and still swing with the wind

and tide. Beaching craft were constantly moving to and from the shore to be loaded on the 'hards,' cement aprons extending into the harbor at the right slope to accommodate these vessels. Soldiers, tanks, and vehicles were arriving in a continuous stream and the 'hardmaster' and his crew were like policemen coping with an endless flow of traffic; but they managed to keep it moving, and into the right craft. It took about half an hour to load each LCT, which at the same time was topped off with fuel and water."

By June 3, all troops had boarded their assault vessels; gunfire support ships were converging from northern ports in England, Scotland, and Ireland; and the diminutive ships that would lead the assault—the minesweepers—were putting out to sea. Invasion convoys began their sequenced movement from the Channel ports on Sunday morning, June 4, and many were already pushing through the winds and high, white-capped waves when at 5 A.M. they were urgently recalled to port. One minesweeper flotilla had already worked its way to within thirty-five miles (56.3km) of the

Normandy coast, and a convoy heading to UTAH Beach under radio silence was only turned back because a trio of destroyers sent to warn it had reached them in time.

🎙 *Finally, the word was passed, the men gathered, and details of the invasion were laid out. Lieutenant Colonel William Gara attended a meeting . . . and no one doubted the wisdom of the speaker.*

In mid-April we were ordered to load on buses and trucks—officers only. We had no idea where we were going. About four hours later we arrived at a theater where we discovered officers from the 1st Infantry Division, who were spread all over southern England. We milled around in the theater. There was a lot of smoking, a lot of talking, and nobody knew why we were there. Then we saw a little guy come up to the stage, stand in the middle not saying a word, just looking around. Somebody spotted him and said, "That's Montgomery." Still he didn't say anything, no yell for attention. After about three or four minutes, the theater grew quiet. You could hear a pin drop.

Montgomery proceeded to tell us about the plans. His talk was solely to instill the confidence in these troops that everything has been handled. "We know what we're going to do and have been preparing for months. We have 4,000 ships, 2 1/2 million tons of equipment and supplies for this invasion. We have 1 1/2 million men, and we're going to take Fortress Europa. Men, here's how we're going to do it." He said, "Fortress Europa reminds me of the London department store Harrods. Because of the war, people haven't had much opportunity to buy goods. So Harrods has placed all of their goods in their window, making a beautiful window display. Fortress Europa is like that Harrods' window display. We're going to break through that window display, and we're going to find they have nothing in the inventory, nothing in the storeroom. Then we're moving all the way to the Siegfried Line by late September." Remember, this is mid-April. We reached the Siegfried Line on September 13. That son of a gun's prediction was terrific.

We felt pretty good about the invasion. We knew the battleships would blast the dickens out of the gun emplacements. Allied planes would bomb the entire front to provide shelter for us when we came in by giving us shell holes to crawl into. Naval men were trained in the removal of underwater obstacles and creating gaps for the boats to enter. We were reinforced. We had trained at various training centers where they duplicated conditions from the aerial photographs. We ran obstacle courses. We were ready! ◼

—William Gara

🎙 *Men of the airborne divisions, including Private Robert Murphy, would land first. Their spirits were as high as the planes that would carry them to Normandy.*

We were at the aircraft on the night of June 4th to jump in Normandy on the 5th, and it was canceled. It was such a relief that we just had a joyous attitude—joking and laughing as we always did. We were very close friends. Fear and anxiety had left us the night before. I have a picture of the Pathfinders, and you can see that everybody's smiling. We were in excellent mental attitude for the jump. ◼

—Robert Murphy, Private, Pathfinders, A Company, 1st Battalion, 82d Airborne Division (US)

🎙 The mood of the camps remained the same initially in the marshaling areas. It was pretty much like any other maneuver, except [there was] more intensive studying of what were we to do. We had sand tables, and there was a lot of time spent in

OPPOSITE, INSET: In a photo taken several minutes later than the bottom photograph and released to the press through the Office of War Information, sky now meets sea as the port and destroyers have become part of a far horizon. An artistic censor left the lower portion of the *Augusta*'s Measure 22 camouflage, which stretched the length of its hull (the long horizontal stripe at upper right), and simply obliterated all other traces of the ship. Public release of these and other censored photos of Channel ports coincided with the rapidly mounting attack by German V-1 "Vengeance" rockets against London. The Allies were anxious to display images of the successful invasion of France, but feared that photos clearly identifying the launch points of the ongoing resupply operations might prompt Hitler to retarget his missiles toward the vulnerable ports.

ABOVE: Generals Bradley (left) and Eisenhower inspect a captured V-1 launch site in France. Nearly two thousand Allied airmen died during bombing raids against V-1 sites.

TOP: Army engineers preparing to embark for the Normandy coast. In addition to their M-1 Garand rifles and the gas masks held in the dark gray plastic bags worn over their chests, the engineers are carrying the tools of their trade: Bangalore torpedo sections, rope, Stachel charges, and reels of Primacord. The upper portion of the vehicle at right—probably an armored recovery vehicle built from an obsolescent M-3 Lee medium tank— has been removed by Army censors, possibly because the close-up photo made it clear that the vehicle's turret gun was actually a length of pipe.

BOTTOM: Men of the 2d Ranger Battalion at Weymouth board LCAs from the trio of small British transports that will take them across the Channel. Lengths of Bangalore torpedoes are plentiful, and all the Rangers carry grenade launchers that can be affixed to the barrels of their M-1 rifles. Attempting to loft grenades to the top of the cliffs at Pointe du Hoc was neither practical nor safe.

OPPOSITE: Hard stands, or "hards," were essentially concrete beaches con-structed to expedite the loading of landing craft and ships. Once grounded on a hard's gently sloping surface, an assault vessel would simply drop its ramp to allow vehicles to drive directly on board. Above, medics of an Engineer Special Brigade file on board an LCT "parked" on a west-country hard. Note that inflated life belts have been attached to the medics' stretchers. This was done so that the stretchers would float in with the surf if the craft was sunk before reaching shore.

studying exactly where each unit was supposed to be, and which crossroads and what gun emplacement we were to be attacking and so forth. So it wasn't too different from a lot of training. But as we got closer and closer to the day, and then when the day really finally came, the mood did change. It settled down and was quieter. There was not nearly the usual banter and joking as the reality of the occasion hit home. ▪

—Bill True

Ike's Decision: "We'll go"

Weather forecasts by SHAEF's meteorologist group, under RAF Group-Captain J.M. Stagg, had been guardedly optimistic all week, and Eisenhower felt comfortable enough with the situation to cable Marshall on Saturday, June 3, that "We have almost an even chance of having pretty fair conditions . . . only marked deterioration would discourage our plans." In just

ABOVE: Canadian troops climb up a troop ship's gangway past a double-deck arrangement of LCAs. The folding davits of the bottom LCA and more behind it will be hauled in after the landing craft are lowered, in order to clear the way for the LCAs above.

the space of a few hours, however, at the evening briefing, a "marked deterioration" was reported as the unnaturally long period of settled weather was found to be breaking up rapidly. Suddenly, the new conditions were "very disturbed and complex." No dependable forecast could be made beyond twenty-four hours.

A decision was made to review the weather situation again at the last possible moment before the ships at sea would have to turn back. The forecast at the 4:30 A.M. meeting of June 4 was little changed from the evening before, and Eisenhower issued the order that recalled the invasion forces at sea; five hours later, the British Admiralty issued a gale warning. D-DAY was now pushed back to June 6, and another meeting with Group-Captain Stagg was scheduled for late that night to see whether yet another delay beyond the 6th was necessary. The question, said the SHAEF commander, was this: "Just how long can you hang

this operation on the end of a limb and let it hang there?"

If the invasion were not launched on the revised date, the required tidal conditions would not return until June 19, but without the benefit of a full moon for the paratroopers. Worse yet, all the fully briefed soldiers in the assault force would have to be disembarked and herded back to their staging areas. The Germans could hardly fail to find out that something was up. With the winds blowing hard outside and the rain pelting the windows, Eisenhower fully expected the worst, but Stagg reported that a hole would appear in the bad weather before closing up again. It would be just long enough for the invasion force to pass through. Said Eisenhower: "I'm quite positive we must give the order . . . I don't like it, but there it is . . . I don't see how we can possibly do anything else." D-DAY would be Tuesday, June 6, 1944.

TOP: Ground crews at an Eighth Air Force base in England watch as P-51 Mustangs return from a mission over Normandy. The stark black-and-white "invasion stripes" were painted on all Allied aircraft, except large four-engine bombers, during the campaign. If an aircraft appeared without the stripes, it was assumed to be hostile and immediately attacked.

BOTTOM: A waist-gunner's view of U.S. Eighth Air Force B-17 "Flying Fortresses" unloading their bombs over a target in German-held Europe. The 500-pounder bombs from the six aircraft in this photo alone add up to some fifteen tons of high explosives plunging earthward. Although Allied invasion planners were disappointed on D-DAY with the results of the tactical bombardment of German beach fortifications by the B-17 and its heavy cousins, the B-24 Liberator and the British Lancaster I, intense "carpet" bombing of a specific area of the stalled American front line was later a key component of the U.S. Army's breakout from Normandy.

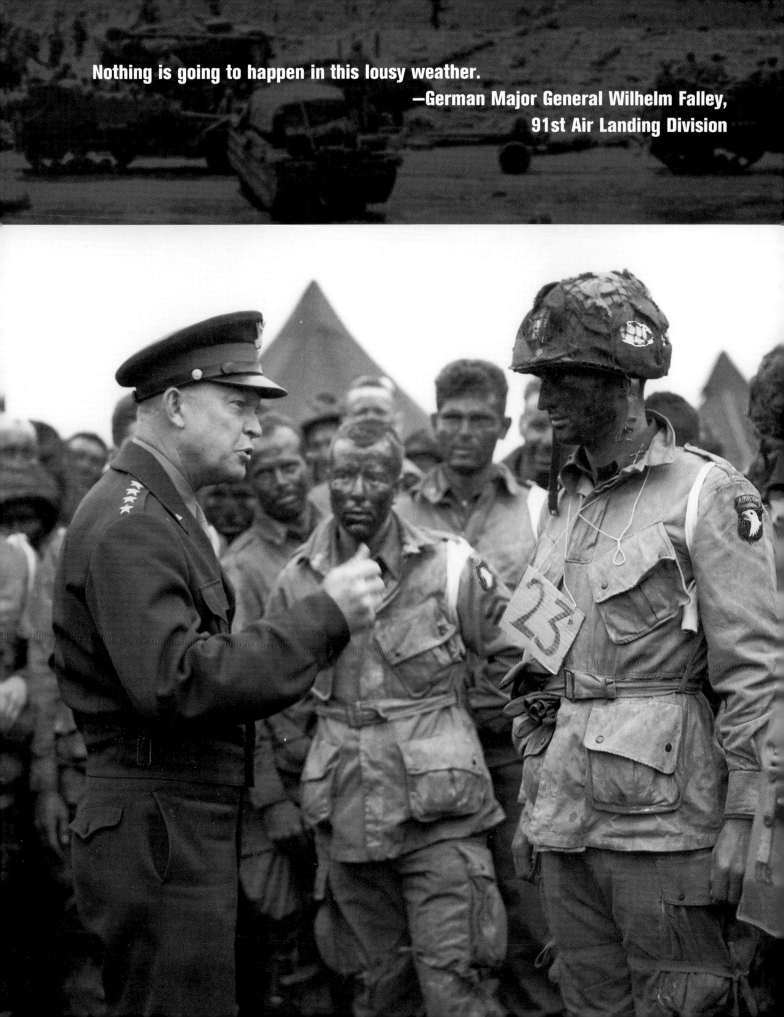

Nothing is going to happen in this lousy weather.
—German Major General Wilhelm Falley,
91st Air Landing Division

Chapter Three

PARATROOPERS IN THE NIGHT

Meteorologists at Field Marshal Gerd von Rundstedt's command center in Paris, *Oberbefehlshaber West* (OB West), also saw the same "hole" in the weather as Group-Captain Stagg did, thanks to reconnaissance aircraft ranging far out in the Atlantic and the weather reports from U-boats. The daily weather update of June 5 detailed projected conditions for the following twenty-four hours and was duly issued to all major commands in northwest Europe. OB West and other major commands also intercepted coded messages to the French Resistance that pre-invasion sabotage operations should be initiated.

The only German headquarters to take any of this information seriously was that of the Fifteenth Army in the Pas-de-Calais, which put its troops on highest alert. Rommel's other army, the Seventh, covering Normandy and Brittany, as well as his Army Group B staff, saw little reason for alarm. The situation was not considered serious enough to notify Rommel, who was home in Germany for his wife's birthday and a meeting with Hitler at which he planned to petition for two more Panzer divisions. The Seventh Army not only canceled a previously scheduled alert, but sent all of its senior and many of its mid-level commanders to attend a *Kriegspiel*, or map exercise, far to the rear at Rennes. Its subject? A theoretical Allied invasion at Normandy.

The reaction of the German commanders seems remarkable today, but the gale sweeping the Channel was so severe that even the nightly torpedo boat patrols out of Cherbourg—the same ones that had caught the LSTs off Slapton Sands—were canceled. After being on constant alert for a week, the entire German chain of command breathed a collective sigh of relief as the foul weather seemed to offer a much-needed respite. All previous Allied landings had occurred only when extended periods of clear weather were forecast, and the approaching calm would only hold for, at best, twenty-four hours. Rommel's frequent admonition that "You shouldn't count on the enemy coming in fine weather and by day" was largely forgotten—even by Rommel. When *Luftwaffe* wing commander Colonel Josef Priller protested the repositioning of his unit during the apparent lull in the invasion threat, his air group commander slapped him down: "Listen, Priller. The invasion is out of the question. The weather is much too bad."

Meanwhile, the Allies were preparing.

Throughout the southern coast of England, troops gathered for their embarkation to France. Each person carried away distinctive memories of the send-off.

At one point, our convoy came to a standstill, and a woman coming right up to my ambulance held my hand and wished me luck. Later, the convoy came to another stop. There were houses on both sides and people waving to us. They gave us tea and gave the men hot water for a shave. I remember a woman giving me a tin of peaches, which was very precious in the war, and I ate it sitting on the pavement. It was this terrific feeling of comradeship knowing the civilians were with us so much. ■

—Iris Bower

We walked by a section of the Canadians who stood in a row and put their heads down. Their hair was cropped like a coconut, but when they put their heads down you could see the letters V-I-C-T-O-R-Y cut in. These were things to take your mind off the actual operation. ■

—Leonard Charles Daniels, Sergeant, 9th Battalion Parachute Regiment (UK)

After the Pathfinders received a briefing on June 5 and returned to their compound, some of the guys got really wild. They took grenades and threw them out in the fields. So here they are jumping around, throwing them down on the bottom of the truck, so we wouldn't get blown up. These guys were wild. Of course, they were all hopped up because they knew we were going on a pretty dangerous mission. But it was all in fun. ▪

—Francis M. Lamoureux, Lead Radar/Radio Operator, Pathfinders, G Company, 3d Battalion, 508th Parachute Infantry Regiment, 82d Airborne Division (US)

Long convoys went to Plymouth and Portsmouth for the embarkation areas, as we had before. The population along the route were so used to American invasion forces training. We had embarked many times with no particular concern. Yet this time the people were lining the roads, waving flags and handkerchiefs. I don't know how, but they knew. ▪

—Walter Bodlander

We had a good chaplain. In the last service he gave before we disembarked, he said something like this: "Tomorrow is a big day. We're going to engage the enemy this time and all the games are over. And all your praying will be over, too. Tomorrow I do all the praying. If I catch anybody kneeling down on the beach and praying within reach of my foot, he's going to get a boot from me." ▪

—Charles Klein, Staff Sergeant, F Company, 5th Ranger Battalion (US)

We spent the rest of our time blackening our faces, making that final little polish of the guns, and then we spent a lot of time sharpening our jump knives. I don't know why that became a bit of an obsession. The guys spent endless time getting a blade sharp enough to cut hairs. Perhaps it was just a way of passing some time in a tense situation.

We suited up in terms of what we were going to take with us early in the evening, after enjoying a really great and wonderful last dinner. We then walked out to the planes

where our chutes had been pre-arranged out on the tarmacs near the planes. We started the final preparations at probably seven or eight o'clock at night. It was still light because England had double daylight savings time, so it stayed light until, I think, midnight.

It was tough to get everything securely attached, including our parachute, because we were really loaded. We had never carried so much equipment and ammunition. I was in a 60-mm mortar crew. In addition to my own rifle, cartridge belt, a couple of bandoliers, and grenades, I had to carry some rounds for the mortar. When you included the weight of the parachute, which of course you would dump once you had landed, we figured we weighed around 300 pounds (136.2kg)—this is a 160-pound (72.6kg) guy who now weighs 300 (136.2kg). We weren't able to board the planes under our own power. They had to help us up the steps.

ABOVE: A paratroop officer makes final adjustments to his chute before loading onto his plane. He wears a life vest and carries a binoculars case around his neck. The holster for his .45-caliber pistol can be seen extending below his dispatch case.

OPPOSITE: An 82d Airborne Division paratrooper heaves himself into a C-47 on the evening of D–1, June 5, 1944. Within two hours, he will leap out from this same door to begin the liberation of France and the defeat of Nazi Germany. Aircraft carrying Pathfinders on D–1 lifted off when the sky was still light. No paratrooper began the invasion with less than 90 pounds (40.8kg) of gear and weaponry, and some men with specialized equipment such as radios, EUREKA transponders, or pieces of disassembled mortars frequently carried loads topping 130 pounds (60kg). In addition to the thirty-six-foot (11m) parachute harnessed to the soldier's back, a smaller reserve chute is attached to the bellyband wrapped around his torso. If the main chute fails to open, a hard pull on its ripcord's red D-ring (visible under his elbow) will release the backup. The weapons he carries include a Thompson submachine gun with fourteen (20-round) bullet clips in an M-6 bag and one in the gun; four hand grenades in jumpsuit pockets and six in another bag; a switchblade knife in one of the zippered pockets below his collar; and a trench knife in the scabbard tied under his heel, around his ankle, and above his calf.

Not being able to even climb up into that airplane without help was really different. This was for sure the real thing.

After we boarded the planes, the message from Eisenhower was given to each of us to read: "Soldiers, sailors and airmen, we are about to embark on the great crusade . . . The eyes of the world are upon you." That was very moving. The atmosphere continued to be very quiet, no bantering. There wasn't a joke passed of any kind, as I recall. Each of us thinking his own thoughts. Here we are after two whole years of training. It really was to do something. ▪

—Bill True

I looked down and there were ships and ships and ships forever. I thought about how big this was, and reality was beginning to come to me. This is the biggest thing that's ever happened. And now what? What really are we getting into? ▪

—Tom McCarthy

Piccadilly Circus

As midnight approached on the night of June 5–6, an overwhelming armada of more than five thousand ships and landing craft began to form up opposite their assigned beaches. So great had been the blanket of sea and air protection—and so severe had been the gale—that these ships had remained undetected throughout the day as they rendezvoused at "Piccadilly Circus" off the Isle of Wight, then pointed their bows toward Normandy. Filling the Channel as they churned south along ten four-hundred-yard-wide lanes, carefully swept of mines and marked by 245 minesweepers and motor launches, were battleships and cruisers; destroyers, frigates, sloops, corvettes, and troop transports; hospital ships, repair ships, ammunition ships; ships to direct the landings, ships to coordinate air cover, ships to be sunk as artificial breakwaters; and assault craft of every description. The force seemed unstoppable—almost like an element of nature. But Eisenhower and his lieutenants knew better.

A hundred things large and small could go wrong and help the Germans either defeat the Allies outright, or so degrade operations that OVERLORD would fail in its strategic purpose. Montgomery's principal fear was that the Germans would not be fooled into believing that D-DAY was a diversion; that they would recognize it for what it was and release the powerful Fifteenth Army from the Pas-de-Calais area instead of waiting for an invasion that would never come. If Operation FORTITUDE failed to lock most potential reinforcements in place for two weeks, and if a large enough area was not secured during the initial stage of the invasion, the lodgment could be overwhelmed. Everything rested on the forces moving across the Channel being able to surge inland with the greatest possible speed. It was the job of three comparatively light Allied airborne divisions and an American Ranger battalion to make sure that this happened.

Bridges and Batteries

Like the British Admiralty, Montgomery was not completely sold on the idea that the MULBERRY artificial harbors would work. UTAH Beach was Montgomery's insurance policy. Well to the west of the other targeted areas and across a wide estuary, it was added to the OVERLORD plan to expedite the capture of Cherbourg, because even a port largely destroyed by German demolitions was better than no port at all if the MULBERRIES failed to live up to expectations. UTAH was also not as heavily defended as the other four invasion beaches, and for good reason. It was a terrible site for a mass landing.

Just inland from the wide, gently sloping dunes flanking the Varreville lighthouse on UTAH was a flooded expanse ranging from one to two miles (1.6–3.2km) wide. The only way to exit the assault area was to cross four long causeways, and the initial beachhead itself would front only one of them. To make UTAH Beach work, an airborne division would have to be dropped east of Sainte Mère-Eglise to seize

ABOVE: Invasion convoys
of LCIs stream across the
English Channel on their
way to Normandy. Tethered
to the landing craft are barrage balloons intended to
deter low-flying German
attack aircraft.

the causeways and a critical water-control lock
at La Barquette, then block German reinforcements approaching from the south across the
Douve River. Further study of the terrain made
it clear that yet another airborne division
would be needed farther to the west, to both
hold the newly arrived German 91st Division at
bay and to capture bridges across the Merderet
River, which had been flooded to a width averaging a half-mile (0.8km). The airborne divisions
chosen for these missions were respectively the
101st and 82d. If all went according to plan, they
would control the ground nearly halfway across
the Cotentin Peninsula by nightfall on D-DAY.

Some fifty miles (80.4km) to the east lay the
targets of the British 6th Airborne Division.

Originally this force was to take Caen, from
which a vital network of roads radiated out in
all directions. Montgomery's addition of a
third division assaulting the beaches near the
city seemed to guarantee that it would be
captured early, enabling the paratroopers to
be shifted to other missions. The 6th Airborne
was now to secure the water barrier hemming
in the British left flank—the river Orne and
its parallel canal—and to bar German reinforcements from approaching the area by
destroying bridges five miles (8km) farther to
the east on the Dives River. Elements of the
division were also to destroy a heavily fortified
German battery at Merville near the mouth of
the Orne.

German gun batteries were sprinkled all along the Normandy coast. Some were no threat because the approach lanes for the invasion shipping were well beyond their range. Others, although thickly casemented by many feet of reinforced concrete for protection against aerial bombs and naval gunfire, were poorly sited. Engineering marvels, they were nevertheless constructed too far forward, too close to the beaches, where they were vulnerable to precisely aimed naval gunfire. British and American warships could—and, on D-Day, did—fire directly into the casements' embrasures to destroy the guns and crews. Only two batteries could not be effectively bombarded. The Germans had failed to oblige the Allies by pointing the Merville Battery directly out to sea and thus ease its destruction. Instead, it was both inland and sited in such a way that its four guns had a clear field of fire across the shallow approaches to Britain's SWORD Beach. The other worrisome battery position was under construction, back from the cliffs at the high Pointe du Hoc jutting out from the coast between the OMAHA and UTAH beaches.

The Allies believed that each position would fall to determined, battalion-strength assaults. At Merville, British paratroopers would hammer their way through a thick outer ring of land mines and machine-gun nests to storm the casements from the rear, spike the guns, then withdraw to carry out other missions assigned to the 6th Airborne.

At Pointe du Hoc, specially trained American Rangers would land on a thin, rocky beach; launch grappling hooks directly from their DUKW amphibious trucks; then scale the nine-story-high cliffs. After reaching the top, they would fight their way down the two lines of gun positions spreading back from a casemented fire-direction center at the head of the Pointe, destroying the dangerous weapons as they went. But unlike the battalion attacking the Merville Battery, there could be no safe withdrawal for troops from this position. The Rangers, reinforced by a second battalion, would hold on to a tight defensive perimeter until relieved by forces from OMAHA Beach on their left.

Meanwhile, other British soldiers were landing at the Merville Battery. Lieutenant Colonel Terence Otway of the 9th Parachute Battalion was the commanding officer of this operation. Much of his force was scattered in the landings. He quickly brought order to the chaos.

When I arrived at the rendezvous, my orderly got there first and told me there were only 50 men out of 700-plus. And we didn't get up to more than 150. The alternatives were either go on or give up—there was no halfway. I had to reorganize, and, instead of having four companies, I made it into four platoons. We left at the proper time. I crossed my fingers and hoped that it would work, which it did.

There wasn't one man who displayed any excitement or worry about it at all. They just accepted it; they knew we had a job to do and accepted the reorganization. I was astonished. I think this was due to the training.

I only had one fixed machine gun and no engineers. How the hell do I get through the wire? And having got through the wire, how the hell do I get into the casements? We didn't

BELOW: Paratrooper Richard "Dick" Thorne grins for the camera in the most famous shot in a series of photographs taken aboard his transport aircraft by Albert Krochka. Behind him is Frank Sayers, a Native American affectionately known as "Chief." Both 101st Airborne troopers are loaded down with the bulky gear worn in combat drops, and Sayers has one of the dreaded Griswold bags hanging from the front of his chute's belly-band. The photo was taken just before the C-47s in this group came under intense anti-aircraft fire.

BELOW: German gunners
are put through their paces
on one of the Merville
Battery's four 100-mm
Czech cannons built by
Skoda before the war.
Much of the equipment
used by the static divisions
defending the Normandy
coast had been captured by
Germany during its early
string of victories.

get through the wires; we went over the top of them. We got into the casements by doing what the Germans didn't expect—going round the other side.

It was pitch dark. The Germans did not appear to be reacting in any way at all. I'd sent out some scouts ahead. One came back and said that there was a German patrol heading our way. We counted them as they went by, about sixty men. We, being the large battalion of about a hundred and something, went into shell holes. They didn't hear us. So there was no German reaction at all on the ground between us and the battery. We didn't

meet any real resistance until the following day, and then it was half-hearted.

I told them to cross the wire by getting some volunteers and telling them to lie down on the barbed wire, so the others could run over their backs as a bridge. They all volunteered. All of them. They considered it an honor to go in first. A direct frontal infantry attack. We were all volunteers; we knew what we had to do. We knew what our chances were, which weren't supposed to be very high.

I think we took 23 prisoners out of 150 at the garrison. The rest were killed or wounded. The German commander is on record saying he had only 12 unwounded men who were

capable of firing guns, out of 150. So that basically gives the scale of our success.

I had arranged for a bugle to be blown. We were outside, down outside the wall. Very quietly we took up position, ready to assault over and through the wire. We were going to blow two gaps instead of the original four because of the shortage of Bangalore torpedoes. As soon as they went up, the men were to go through those gaps and over the inside wire. We did not have enough to blow the inside wire, but we did blow some gaps of inside wire, so the assault troopers went through first. The support company followed.

I was in the gap, with the leading troops, and I stood in the gap while the others passed me. I was criticized for that because, as a commander, people said I should have been at the head, to which I replied, What the hell use would I have been if I'd been dead as a commander?

The troops then spread out, and one part went round to the seaward side while the other part went to the gun side. One party went to the entrance, which was on the landward side, throwing in grenades. The other party went round to the open side where the guns were firing toward the sea. They attacked in there with Sten guns. The Germans there were killed or wounded. But the great number of them were actually down below because they had chambers underneath each gun. Those remaining emerged with their hands up. Once that part was done, I sent the success signal up, and an RAF aircraft went over waving its wings, which was the acknowledgment signal.

My signal officer then produced a pigeon from his inside pocket. I wrote out a message, and that pigeon actually landed in Whitehall.

We took breechblocks out and threw them away, right out into the fields. You can't fire a gun without a breechblock. My orders were not to destroy the guns but to neutralize

them. That word has been consistently over-looked. And if you can neutralize the guns and stop them from firing, you've done your job even if you don't have explosives to blow the things up. We did put grenades down them, so that would cause a bit of trouble because they would have to get all the metal splinters out of the guns before they put any shells in. That's all we could do because we didn't have the explosives.

I then had to regroup with what little I had and go on to the next objective because they had given me an awful lot to do. I was supposed to attack another post nearer the coast. By then I had about fifty men left. ▪

—Terence Otway

More gliders landed with additional troops for Lieutenant Colonel Terence Otway's operation on the Merville Battery. The gliders' landing left many shaken as well as injured. Private Frederick Glover discovered that one could be wounded before ever hitting the ground.

As we came over the battery in the glider, we wouldn't have been necessarily aware that we were actually over the battery at that point. But we were made very much aware of it because we came under fire from the 20-mm flak guns we knew were inside the perimeter wire. There were many sparks and bangs.

I felt a blow to my left leg and almost immediately to my right. I knew that I had been hit. Regrettably, of course, we had not received the signal from the ground, which was supposed to be a flare. That was to indi-cate that the battalion was in position and we should go in. Consequently, the glider pilot came down as low as he dared, and, get-ting no recognition signal at all, lifted the glider over the minefield, and we crashed in an orchard outside the battery.

The glider pretty well disintegrated and we tumbled out. I went into what must have been the bomb crater. Looking up, I saw the tail section of the glider. A friend of mine, Ron Sharp, was still sitting in the back struggling to get out, and the frightening thing was he

ABOVE: In spite of the apparent pounding of the Merville Battery by the RAF, few bombs actually fell within the central position containing the casemented guns, and none of those penetrated the reinforced concrete. Although one bunker received some minor flooding when a pump was destroyed, all were operable at the time of the paratroopers' assault, which came from directly behind the array of bunkers.

FREDERICK GLOVER

OPPOSITE: 82d Airborne Division gliders from the D-DAY assault lay strewn across the fields outside Les Forges, a village south of Sainte Mère-Eglise, on the morning of D+1, June 7, 1944. The upper fields had dried sufficiently since the rains of D−1 to raise a dusty haze from these follow-up landings, and C-47s with more gliders orbit as they wait their turn to release their tows. With the exception of some Horsas at the extreme left, all the other gliders in this photo—in the air and on the ground—are Wacos. Sherman tanks of the 4th Infantry Division had only just reached this area, and can be seen on the road in the middle distance.

had a flamethrower down on the floor by his legs. He did get out without getting hit. There was a German patrol moving up to reinforce the battery, and they were firing at us. The next thing that I can clearly recall was that I hadn't had any opportunity to do anything about my legs at all because this happened in split seconds. Then a comrade who I didn't know and was possibly one of the Pathfinders grabbed me and said the battery's this way.

I could walk fairly well, which surprised me. As we got to the perimeter—the outer perimeter wire—the action inside the battery ceased. The survivors were withdrawing from the battery. I could see that they'd taken heavy casualties because I could see people lying around. They were withdrawing in good order. It seemed evident to me that they had actually gotten into the casements and the attack had been a success. They were moving away from the battery, I presumed, in the direction of the battalion objective.

At that point we met up with the patrol led by Captain [Bill] Brown, which had been in the second glider and had crashed about half a mile (0.8km) away. We tried to keep up with the patrol as they moved off, but didn't get particularly far because by that time my legs were seizing up. Another paratrooper was in a similar condition. We were then left in a ditch by the corner of a field with two wounded German soldiers. One had been shot through the legs and the other one had been hit in the chest and was in a bad way. We administered morphine. We stayed there then for some hours, expecting eventually that we would simply be picked up by one of our own patrols or one of the special service patrols coming up from the beach.

Walking along the top of this ditch came a Red Cross man with medical equipment. He was a member of what we called the non-combatant corps who had parachuted in. They were conscientious objectors insofar as they would not bear arms but would administer first aid. He came upon us, dressed our wounds, and then at that precise moment we could hear shouting, and across the field came a patrol in extended order moving toward a farm building. We recognized that

the language was German. We used to carry a yellow triangle for identification purposes, and the Red Cross man got up on the top of the ditch and waved it in the air. He placed himself at considerable risk.

The patrol swung around and came toward us. They looked at us. I could tell by their insignia they were an SS unit. One of them came over to me and looked down. I realized we carried a fighting knife, which did not comply with the accepted laws of war. It was a stiletto-type weapon with a nonfolding blade. He called his colleagues over, and they didn't sound too pleased about it and took it off. They also noticed that I had some plastic explosive and some .45 ammunition. The situation worsened at that point.

Then, this young German soldier spoke to them and pointed to his comrade. He was still alive. We had written in indelible pencil on his forehead the time that the morphine had been injected. The whole atmosphere changed completely. They became quite friendly at that point. We were lifted into the back of an ambulance and taken to a small village. ▪

—Frederick Glover, Private,
I Company, 9th Parachute Battalion (UK)

One of the men who encountered Glover and the other wounded soldiers that night was Gordon Newton of the British 9th Parachute Battalion.

In each glider there would be two flame-throwers. Being the "big boy" of the company, I was the dead ringer to get the flamethrower.

The intention was that, at the height of the battle, when the 9th Battalion stormed the battery, three gliders would land in between the attacking force and the defending force. So it was a rather dangerous operation, and we hoped that the attacking force would recognize the people in the glider force. Accordingly, we were given luminous paint to paint the skull and crossbones over our left-hand breast pocket. We could be recognized, but it wasn't really adequate and probably proved a good target center for the Germans.

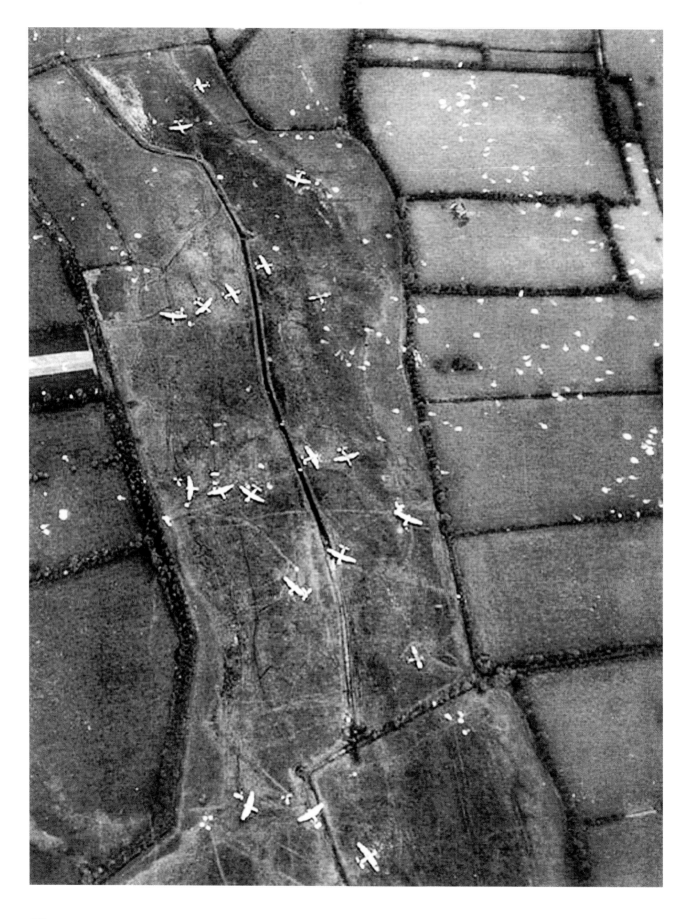

We left about half past twelve in the morning. It was rather strange in the blackness where there was no light at all—all you could see were numerous skull and crossbones. The flight wasn't a particularly comfortable one; it was a little bit bumpy. The mood was very quiet. They were all pretty hyped up and tense, waiting to get on with this job. We were fearful that we might make fools of ourselves.

The glider pilot said the glider suddenly stopped in midair. It actually stopped. He wondered, What on earth's happened? He couldn't see anything unusual, but the rear gunner in the tug in front of us said we had a parachute streaming out the back of our tail. So the glider was drawn down toward the Channel, down to about a hundred feet (30.5m). The glider pilot came through and asked us for a knife. We searched through our equipment, got him a jackknife, and he went through and cut it loose. The glider then rose with the tug, but it was very badly strained, and very difficult to fly up that way.

Unfortunately, the battalion had experienced setbacks in rendezvousing and getting to the battery. There were no radar signals to lead us in, no star shells, no lighting. Nothing. It was complete blackness down there. We had no idea where the other two gliders were. The tug pilot was getting a little bit edgy because he was being hit. Suddenly a flak shell came through the floor, out through the roof, and hit the flamethrower. Fortunately, it hit the air supply, not the liquid supply. It was quite harmless.

At one time we got into a searchlight. It was quite an eerie sensation. The whole glider lit up like daylight. We heard from the commanding officer in our glider that we'd been given the option to either cast off or go home, and he'd said cast off, as we thought he would have done. We came down, but there was nothing at all to lead us.

We came down to where there was a fire, and of course it wasn't the battery; it was a village of about a kilometer and a half away. We knew something was wrong, because as we looked out the window, we could see trees. We knew full well that we weren't on

the target. Rommel had flooded the area, and we had landed in the floods. The water was about waist deep, and the corn was lying flat on the water. But there was a silver ribbon going through it, which we assumed to be a road or a lane. Instead, it was an irrigation ditch. We were very shortly lying at the bottom of this ditch; the flamethrower was still attached to my body—it was going *blub, blub, blub* where it had been hit in the air tank. We made our way to dry ground, which wasn't far away.

As we got to dry land, all hell broke loose. This was the battery being attacked. Looking up, the second glider arrived, and I saw it cast off, lift its nose, and go down onto the battery. We started to make our way toward that area, but were intercepted by enemy troops. After a short gun battle, they very gentlemanly put their hands up and were taken prisoner. One had been wounded.

We now had these prisoners. We went back to the glider and destroyed the specialized radar equipment. We had brought sandwiches, but had been too tense to eat. We now shared them with our German prisoners. We were really lost.

Then down a little lane came two figures—both badly wounded. One was limping, he'd been shot in the ankle. His name was Glover. The other was a corporal, McCord, who'd been very seriously wounded in the arm. So we were hampered even more. Eventually, we had to leave the wounded German and Private Glover, in the hope that they'd be picked up by other British or German troops. As it was, they were picked up by German troops, and Glover was taken prisoner.

Our main problem was we didn't know whether the invasion had been a success. We could hear bombing. The whole ground shook, and great big holes appeared which would take a house. They were really large bombs. ■
—Gordon Newton,
9th Parachute Battalion (UK)

GORDON NEWTON

OPPOSITE: Discarded parachutes, Horsa gliders, and a single smaller Waco glider are strewn across Landing Zone E west of Ste. Marie-du-Mont on D-Day. Skid marks gouged into the French fields mark the twisting paths that some gliders took before grinding to a halt.

In the pale glow of the rising moon, I could clearly see each farm and field below. How peaceful the land looked. . . . I felt that if it were not for the noise of the engines, we could hear the barnyard roosters crowing for midnight.
—Major General Matthew B. Ridgway, 82d Airborne Division

ABOVE: Major General Matthew B. Ridgway commander of the 82d Airborne Division.

The Big Drop

The main landings of the three Allied airborne divisions did not occur at once but were made in sequence: the British 6th Airborne at fifty minutes past midnight on June 6; the U.S. 101st Airborne at 1:30 A.M.; and the veteran U.S. 82d Airborne at 2:30 A.M. This timing was designed to both minimize congestion in the skies above Normandy and to whipsaw the German defenders, who would theoretically be well along in planning a response to the first landing when news would arrive of the second, with the process repeating itself again during the third major drop. To further confuse the situation, thousands of one-quarter-life-size dummy paratroopers called "Ruperts" were dropped where the Germans could not miss them—at Caen and Rouen to coincide with the British landings—and at Avranches during the American landing. In this way, various German headquarters would immediately he made aware that not all the reports of parachutists behind every bush could be trusted. With a little luck for the Allies, German indecision over which air drops were bogus and which were a genuine threat might well delay a forceful response long enough to allow the real parachutists—some 20,000 in all—more time to seize and consolidate their objectives.

Immediately before the drops, Pathfinders forming the tip of the airborne spear were dropped behind enemy lines. High winds, a thick cloud bank, and German anti-aircraft fire blunted that tip almost immediately. At the three British drop zones, Pathfinders generally landed close to their intended objectives, but were unable to mark their drop zones properly in the bare fifteen minutes before the rest of

their division arrived overhead. The British troop transports approaching from the east were also thrown off stride by headwinds and anti-aircraft fire, which resulted in some British paratroopers being dropped before they were over their zones and then blown even farther to the east, into the flooded reaches of the Dives River.

On the Cotentin Peninsula, few American Pathfinders landed on their targets. Complicating matters during the approach of the main American force was a cloud bank several miles inland. Pilots instinctively loosened up their tightly packed formations to avoid midair crashes and threw off the time-to-target counts that started at the coast. But while the cloud bank was just thick enough to break up the formations, it was not thick enough to shield the aircraft from the eyes of anti-aircraft gunners below. Fire erupted all along the flight paths, further disrupting the drops as aircraft maneuvered radically to avoid the flak.

U.S. transport aircraft coming in from the west overshot the two zones farthest inland from UTAH Beach, roughly nine miles (14.5km) from the shore and on the far side of the Merderet River. Brigadier General James Gavin, assistant division commander of the 82d Airborne, was one of the few soldiers to come down there, and he soon saw the assembly lights of the two regiments he was to land with appear on the wrong side of the river with the division's third regiment. The 101st Airborne had one of its regiments hit their drop zone fairly well, but the other two were hopelessly scattered. Even with the help of the dawn light, the 6th and 101st Divisions were able to gather up only about 40 percent of their men, while the 82d scratched together less than one third of its force.

While many men desperately yearned to regain their sea legs, many spent the night in gliders or airplanes crossing the night sky. Major William Kirkpatrick was a pilot and training officer for the 82d Airborne Division.

By the time I got there, the first planes were marking the drop zones for the 101st, which were farther east on the peninsula than the drop zones for the 82d. I was the lead plane for the elements that were going to drop the Pathfinder paratroopers for the 82d Division. By then I could see ahead of me that the East Coast was a wall of fire. I decided the heck with that. So I dropped my speed down as low as I thought I could. When you have a big formation, it gets very tough. You have all the prop wash from the planes ahead of you buffeting your plane around. You're down at just above stalling speed. The minute those guys get out of the plane, you can feel the plane jerk as each paratrooper jumps. You count, and the minute the last one goes out of the plane, you put your nose down and give it the

gun, because you've got to get your flying speed back. That means you're going to lose some altitude immediately. Then I turned with my group.

As luck would have it, we wound up right over that machine gun. My right wingman, who was on the low side of the turn, got a few bullet holes in his wing, and that was about all that happened to us. The thing I feared most was the small-arms fire. I had acquired a piece of armor plate from a wrecked fighter plane that fit right under my pilot's seat, so I would have some protection from underneath.

When I made my 180-degree turn and climbed up to several thousand feet, it was a beautiful, clear night. There was a ground fog, and a cloud bank that had built up. It had grown much bigger and had moved farther inland, even in the time that it took me to climb and go back over. If there'd been a German fighter in the air that night, he could have looked down and seen a river of airplanes against a black sea. The real problem for our guys was when they ran into the fog.

BELOW: British 6th Airborne Division troops hook up a trailer filled with supplies to their jeep after unloading their Horsa glider. An even larger glider, the Hamilcar, weighed 14 tons (12.7t) when fully loaded with a Tetrarch light airborne tank. Hamilcars landed three deadly 17-pounder antitank guns, their tow vehicles, and munitions in the opening glider landings. A fourth never arrived due to a broken towrope over England.

WILLIAM KIRKPATRICK

Flying in formation in a fog is something you can't do well. The guys on the end of that big formation were having a terrible time, because any little adjustment in throttle setting that the lead plane made telegraphed back. Consequently, it became more exaggerated as you got toward the end of the formation. It was not the ideal way to drop troops.

Although the pilot controlled the plane, you listened to your navigator. He told you what heading you should be on, how far out you were, when they should be getting ready to jump. He said when to drop them, then you turned on a switch in the cockpit, which turned on a green light by the rear door. ■

—William Kirkpatrick, Major, Pilot, Operations and Training Officer, 9th Troop Carrier Pathfinder School (Provisional), 82d Airborne Division (US)

 Another member of the 9th Troop Carrier Command was Vito Pedone. He, too, was piloting one of the lead aircraft.

Many pilots of the C-47 were not used to flying pretty low and people firing at them. They gave us flak suits. I was fortunate to get about twenty more flak suits by trading them for a case of scotch. When the day came and we loaded on the airplane, Colonel [Joel] Crouch comes up to me and he says, "What are you doing with all those flak suits?" I said, "I'll show you in a minute."

I took the front part of that airplane and made a beautiful blanket of flak suits on it—a double layer on it. I said that's just there to protect your butt and my butt when it comes on fire.

As they hit the English coast, the lights went off. The only identification that they had in formation flying was a blue light on the top of the tail. They had to watch that to keep in formation. And that was one of the reasons they couldn't fly on instruments through the clouds.

We got right on the drop zone. Being the lead crew, it was much easier for us because we didn't have all this distraction. We just

made a bend around the cloud and headed to the drop zone. However, for the guys behind us, bedlam hit. First, the low cloud scattered the airplanes, then the anti-aircraft guns became very, very strong. So between the bad weather, the low clouds, the guns being fired, and the planes being shot down, that's when you had a problem of discipline. This was the first time anybody had experienced those things. When I was over the drop zone in Normandy, behind me was this conveyor belt of 1,500 airplanes that was 300 miles (482.7km) long. I would say for 95 percent of those crew members, it was the first time they were going into combat. ■

—Vito S. Pedone, Pilot, Staff Operations Officer, 9th Troop Carrier Command (US)

 One of the Pathfinders dropping that night was Lead Radar/Radio Operator Francis M. Lamoureux of the 82d Airborne Division. His portable EUREKA radar beacon was vital to signaling the forthcoming paratroopers.

My particular role was to set up and operate the EUREKA as soon as I hit the ground. Then, when given the word, send the code for the drop zone: N—dash dot, dash dot. That's what they would see, and know they were flying in on our signal for the correct drop zone.

I made a soft landing and was soon ordered to start signaling. What was going through all of our minds was, What happens if they called off the invasion tonight and no one comes? We waited and waited until finally we heard the drone of our planes. It grew louder and louder until chutes opened and guys dropped down on us. We shouted for joy. This group of paratroopers was the first wave. There was supposed to be a second wave of planes, so we waited. Nothing happened. A third wave was supposed to come. Still nothing. My lieutenant said he didn't think any more were coming. Our orders were to set the EUREKA to self-destruct.

Now we had to go out and fight the war. But we didn't go very far because German personnel carriers were patrolling the road. One of the guys who had jumped out on top of us started shooting with a Tommy gun and we threw grenades at them. They disabled the truck, but one of the guys got away. That was the first kill. Since I carried the EUREKA, I couldn't carry a rifle, but I did have a Colt .45 and ammunition. I was to take the first rifle I found from a dead American. ■

—Francis M. Lamoureux

BELOW: An American soldier lies dead among the splintered ruins of a jeep-carrying Horsa glider that smashed into a hedgerow. The frequency of such mishaps earned gliders the nickname "plywood coffins" among airborne soldiers.

Sergeant Tom McCarthy of the 82d Airborne Division "geared up" with his small team of Pathfinders and boarded their C-47.

My personal assignment was security. I was to engage as quickly as I could if we had any opposition and keep them occupied until the radar could get under way.

As we flew over, I looked down and I saw the armada in the Channel. There were ships and ships and ships. You thought about how big it was, and reality began to sink in. As the mainland began to show up, it appeared like a dark spot against the horizon. That was a dark night. The unfortunate thing was the full moon.

By the time we jumped, it was [as bright as] daylight. That full moon lit up everything. I said some Hail Mary's, some SOBs, some more Hail Mary's, and hoped that ground showed up pretty soon. I looked right down at the guys shooting at me. Some were fairly accurate because one of them put a crease across my left temple. I don't know whether he scared me or made me mad, but I knew I was all right. In the beginning, they used to give us an envelope for your rifle. We quickly learned that didn't work. We jumped our rifle on our shoulder with the sling. Normally you came in feet first, so chances were you wouldn't smash your gun. At the same time, that gun was ready to go. All you had to do was push one in the chamber. Being ready to go was rather important.

It was just fight and stay alive. There were two guys banging away at me coming in. I got out of the chute, moved into the high grass, and watched them. They came searching for me, and I let them search. They came by and when they were about ten feet (3m) away, I fed them a grenade. I was supposed to occupy, so I "occupied" them.

ABOVE: This lean and mean paratrooper is Brigadier General James Gavin, assistant division commander of the 82d Airborne Division. Shortly after D-DAY Gavin, at age thirty-seven, was tapped to lead the 82d, becoming by far the youngest division commander in the U.S. Army. Late in the war, when he encountered Soviet senior officers north of Berlin, the generals at first refused to believe that the "baby-faced" Gavin was indeed a division commander.

RIGHT: Lieutenant Colonel Benjamin Vandervoort of the 82d Airborne Division, left, in St. Sauveur-le-Vicomte, broke his leg during the drop near Sainte Mère-Eglise and fought the invasion on crutches. During movements across country, Vandervoort (played by John Wayne in the movie *The Longest Day*) was loaded onto a wheelbarrow by his steadily growing band of lost paratroopers from both divisions and ferried from battle to battle. Note that the paratrooper behind him is carrying a German submachine gun.

The problem was the light. There was no way to move or stand in that kind of light without being silhouetted. You would get your head blown off because you didn't know where they were, but you knew they were there. So I spent some time in the dark grass trying to locate anybody. I moved toward a hedgerow for better protection and kept it behind me for a shadow. I did see some of the lights, over in the field, but they were too far away for me. I know we had missed. A second in an airplane could take you quite a ways. The next thing I knew was the wonderful feeling when I heard the drone of airplanes above. Soon there were chutes. I said, "Oh boy, they're here!" Once they hit the ground, I was watching them. I was with the 504th [Parachute Infantry Regiment], but I didn't have a problem going over and joining a smaller unit from the 507th. I didn't know who it was, but I didn't care. By now, I just wanted a little bit of company.

The first contact I made was rather funny. The guy was green all right. He was laying on the side of the hedgerow, and I sneaked up on him. I was afraid not to because I didn't know how he was going to react. The next thing I knew, he was challenging me with the password. He said the first part a couple of times before I finally answered him. I just stood looking at him. He was relieved. I said, "You're

lucky, kid. You'd have been dead as hell if I was a Kraut." We moved out together and tied up with a small group from the 507th. I eventually got bandaged.

Later a colonel did the one thing that you don't do in command of a parachute unit: he set up a CP [command post] instead of going right on the attack. I was asked to help set up the perimeter. All of these guys coming in were carrying a colored scarf for identification. These kids from seven [the 507th] still had them. We were setting up the position. I was spotting a couple of machine guns because there was an open field in front of us. I wanted to be sure that if the Krauts came across, we would have a raking fire. You had to keep it low and take them down because once they get in, if there were too many, they get in on you. You're in trouble.

Across the small field come three guys out of the woods. I had just finished with these guys, telling them to get rid of the damn yellow flags. I said, "You're fighting the Krauts. They already know you've got them. All they'll do is get you in trouble." Sure as shooting, they jumped up and started to wave the flag. I hadn't dug a hole yet. Another guy, Cates, was with me when the Germans laid in a barrage like you've never seen. Mortars. There's nothing more dangerous in the world, because they come down and land in your pocket. We were

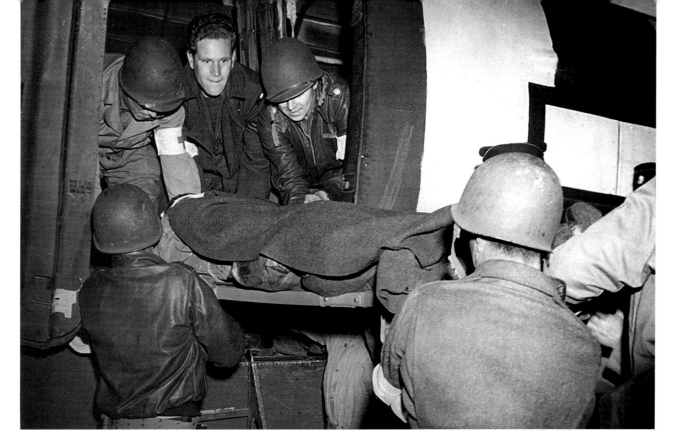

caught in the open field. We went down. It flattened me, and I was out for a while. They filled me up with lead from my head to my back and legs. I was bleeding. When I woke up, Cates was there and had gotten it bad in the leg. I looked at him. I said, "We're not going to get any help here. We've got to get out of here. Maybe we can get back to the CP. There will be some medics, so we can get patched up." Cates couldn't walk too good. Although I was hurting, I lugged him part way. He was bleeding from his bad leg, but we made it in. ∎
—Tom McCarthy

Pegasus Bridge

The Allied capture and successful defense of the Bénouville bridges over the Orne River and its parallel canal would allow a quick expansion of the British beachhead and force any German unit bent on attacking the lodgment into making a six-hour detour through Caen. Unlike the 6th Airborne's assault on the Merville Battery, an amply fortified position requiring a substantial attacking force, the Bénouville bridges could be taken "on the

cheap" by a comparatively small number of men if total surprise were achieved. The British plan was for three gliders, carrying a platoon each, to silently sail right up to each span shortly before the great mass of the aircraft hauling the main force crossed the coast and alerted German defenses throughout the area. As soon as the plywood fliers ground and splintered their way to a stop, their human cargoes would burst out shooting and immediately seize the bridges just ahead of the 6th Airborne's main airdrop.

Glider operations during OVERLORD and other operations are often blamed for misdirected flights, destroyed cargoes, and catastrophic troop losses from crash landings. However, during the Orne River assault, the release times from the tow planes and the precisely scheduled turns during the descent—all done in the black of night—were carried out masterfully. A stream of three Horsa gliders swept down on the thin sliver of ground leading to the canal bridge. Smashing through treetops, then crashing and grinding along the ground through the perimeter wire, they came to a halt—one, two, three—with the nose of the first glider just forty-seven yards (43m) from the target.

ABOVE: An aircrewman and medics from a follow-on airborne echelon remove a severely wounded paratrooper from a damaged C-47. The soldier became one of the first casualties of D-DAY when he was struck in the head by shrapnel or small-arms fire on the way to his drop zone.

BELOW: A taut cable
stretches out from a glider
to its tow-plane during
a follow-up to the initial
airborne operations.
The smaller coiled line is
a telephone cable for
communications between
the two aircraft.

At first there was little movement from the stunned soldiers inside the gliders. The pilots of the lead glider were thrown through the plexiglas windshield, and the second glider had broken in half as it bumped over a ditch, but there were few casualties in the landing. The bridge was quickly taken and nearby anti-aircraft positions fell after hand-to-hand fighting. The bulk of the fifty-man German garrison made a short-lived stand in the Bénouville village quarters where they were billeted. The battle at the canal was over in fifteen minutes, and the troops at the river bridge five hundred yards (457m) away found it undefended. Their gliders had come down three hundred yards (274.3m) and seven hundred (640m) yards, respectively, from the objective, with their third glider mistakenly landing five miles (8km) to the east at a pair of bridges on the flooded

Dives River. The canal bridge at Bénouville was later renamed Pegasus Bridge after the winged symbol of the 6th Airborne Division.

Some British troops arrived early to capture key gun emplacements and bridges. They were busy long before daylight broke across the English Channel. Wally Parr of the British 6th Airborne Division recalls the blend of serious and humorous activities that busy night.

I was in the number-one glider, 25 Platoon, with Lieutenant Denny Brotheridge, Major John Howard, and his radioman. I was in charge of the back door. We sang all the way over, all sorts of stupid songs until we cast off over Cabourg, about twenty miles (32.2km) from Bénouville. It was planned that three

The whole sky is a fantastic chimera of lights and flak, and one plane gets hit and disintegrates wholesale in the sky, sprinkling a myriad of burning pieces.

—Guy Byam, BBC correspondent with the 6th Airborne Division

gliders landing on the Orne River Bridge should do a figure eight in that direction coming from Ouistreham. The other three gliders, making for the Caen Canal Bridge, should do figures of eight and come in. This was to save six gliders coming in together accidentally, especially in the dark.

When I looked out that door as we came down lower, the damned trees looked about six inches (15.2cm) underneath me, and they were moving up ninety miles an hour (144.8kph). We got the order to link up, and we hit the ground with a crash. The glider took off again, crashed again, did another slight takeoff, hit the deck, and slithered straight across toward Pegasus Bridge, as it's now called. John Howard had asked the glider pilots to put the glider as near the barbed wire as possible. They put the glider straight through the barbed wire. The only thing that stopped them going any farther was a rise in the ground. The pilots, still tied in their seats, were thrown through the front of the glider. The whole front of it collapsed, the floor was ripped up, the skids went. I saw the wheels go past the door I was looking at. When it finally stopped, it just went silent. There was dust and then a moan and then somebody yelled, "Out, everybody out!"

We jumped out, and Major Howard had his men line up. The bridge was only fifty yards (45.7m) away. If you'd carried that glider and put it there, you couldn't have put it any closer. John Howard just said, "Charge," and me and Charlie Gardner run straight past. Our job was to charge over this side, across the bridge, over the other side of the road, and knock out two German dugouts. This we did.

A machine gun opened up from over there in the hands of a young sixteen-year-old German soldier. When the glider crashed, he

thought it was a plane shot down. So he called the sentry to take the crew prisoners. Then he's faced with thirty screaming black-faced maniacs. We missed him and his mate. They ran down the canal bank in the opposite direction, hitting the bushes, and watched the battle take place all day. At ten o'clock that night they gave themselves up. He now runs a hotel in Hamburg, and every 6th of June, we meet, shake hands, and have a drink. He still says he's the luckiest man alive—and he was.

I opened the door of the first dugout and hit him with a hand grenade. Charlie, with a Sten gun, repeated a second, then a third one. As we came past, we heard a moan, so I took out a phosphorous grenade. Then we went up the bridge on the side. That's when the real battle started.

Our job was to take that bridge. The 7th Parachute Battalion was to make their way as fast as they could to Bénouville, to the bridges, to surround it and help us to hold the

BELOW: Royal Marine commandos reinforce the glider troops who stormed the Orne River bridges. Although the 6th Airborne Division's bridgehead was relatively thin—extending only two miles (3.2km) east of this point—it was never seriously in danger during the German counterattacks that occurred through D+6, June 12, 1944.

lot until Lord Lovat and his commandos could reach us by midday the next day. They fought around Bénouville all day. They lost over three hundred men.

Ham and *Jam* were the code names for the two bridges. Ham for the Pegasus Bridge, which was the canal bridge, and Jam for the Orne River Bridge. It was the radioman's job to try to pick up brigade radio with the biggest set, and brigade would send the message back to England. He kept shouting, "Ham and Jam," "Ham and Jam," to indicate that both bridges had been captured intact. In sheer desperation, John Howard said, "Oh, haven't you got them yet? For God's sake, man." Suddenly he got them and yelled, "Ham and bloody Jam!" "Where the hell have you been?"

At one point, I ran across the bridge, after I'd done my job, to the café, and asked where Den Brotheridge was. We were supposed to rendezvous with him, some thirty yards (27.4m) past the café, in the ditch on the left. Nobody had seen him. I saw two men wounded lying on the bridge, and a dead German lying in the middle of the road there. I started to run, and I ran past what I thought was another dead German and stopped, turned around, and it was Den Brotheridge. I knelt down beside him and he said something. His eyes were open. I said, "I'm sorry, I can't hear you," so I put my hand under his head to lift him up and he just closed his eyes and bled everywhere. He was the first man to die in the invasion.

When we landed and opened fire on that bridge, D-Day was sixteen minutes old. We were the first to actually open fire on German opposition. The first all-out attack of the greatest invasion in military history was the Pegasus Bridge. Fifteen minutes after midnight. There was one hour difference between our times. Local time, it was quarter past eleven that night on the 5th of June when we landed.

I had to get back over the other side of the bridge, and by this time people were spreading out everywhere. In the fields there was a bit of phosphorous smoke burning near the front of the café. We started to go up the road

when we heard a noise. We walked over, looked, and found a woman with two children. We said, "Go inside," "Go inside," "Liberation." I was afraid a grenade was going to roll down there. The mother never said a word but just stared up at me. I was shouting, "Liberation," "Go inside," *"Allez," "Allez,"* "Get out quick," "Let's get up there." Then I reached in my pocket, and the older of the two children took the bar of chocolate. That was the liberation of the first two children and their mother. It was just after midnight.

Charlie and I ran up the road and heard tanks. They came across from Bénouville going toward Caen. Somebody came running back to me and said, "For God's sake, get the PIAT [Projector, Infantry Anti-Tank, a weapon similar to the American bazooka]," still in the glider. I left my rifle then. I went back down to the bridge, John Howard was standing there, and told him we got tanks. I ran back to the glider to retrieve some PIAT bombs. I soon found they had been damaged in the crash and were now useless. I ran up with the grenades, and the only thing I could think of was get up behind the hedge, because this time the tank was really coming back down toward the bridge. I started running, when all of a sudden there was a God almighty bang and an explosion. B company had waited until that tank was twenty yards (18.3m) distant and hit it dead on, and there was the biggest fireworks display we'd seen for a long time.

There was a certain amount of activity then. Just as it was getting dark, a boat came up from Ouistreham. We all lined up on the bridge. John Howard said, "When I blow the whistle, fire," and he blew the whistle (for victory [*da, da, da, dum*]) all night. I think this thing was about fifty yards (45.7m) away, coming toward us, and it almost stood still. Everything hit it, and it went into the bank. So we fought our first naval engagement. We brought off what was left of the crew.

It started getting light, then we put out fluorescent strips—yellow and pink—right across the bridge. Then appeared the first glorious sight of planes flying in. They came from over the side of Bénouville. It was a flood of Spitfires flying down over the bridge.

TOP: A British soldier perched high on a ladder keeps a close watch on the far side of the Orne Canal and River bridges for enemy activity. The nearly flawless approach and landing of the British gliders, seen on the opposite bank of the canal, enabled this critical objective to be seized in less than fifteen minutes.

BOTTOM: Without stopping to consolidate, British troops went straight from their rough landing to a direct assault on the Bénouville canal bridge, part of which can be seen through the trees at center right. During subsequent German efforts to retake the key site, part of the assault force was cut off in the buildings on the opposite side of the canal.

ABOVE: British infantry move to reinforce the east side of the canal. Elements of the German Fifteenth Army attacked the very shallow British bridgehead across the Orne River, which was located near the western tip of their defense sector, from June 10 to 12, 1944. That the Fifteenth Army never again made an effort to take the Bréville Ridge east of the Bénouville bridges genuinely surprised British Second Army commander Lieutenant General Sir Miles Dempsey, since the vulnerable ridge over-looked the coast as far as JUNO Beach and the huge logistical build-up all along the inland plain.

As they passed over the bridge, each one did a victory roll.

I got my job then. I sat behind the 50-mm cannon and fired at everything that moved down the canal bank. The Germans were trying to attack from the direction of the Bénouville château in the Caen area. After a while, John moved his command post there and says, "Parr, for Christ's sake, keep the bloody gun quiet. I can't hear a thing I'm saying on this [radio] set."

About half past nine, somebody spots two blokes on top of a water tower down on the left-hand side. I put three shells through the water tank. They disappeared over the back, and the water supply disappeared for a lot of other people in the area.

About ten o'clock, a German plane came screaming over to destroy that bridge. I didn't see but I heard the plane. The fellows saw the bomb coming down, they thought they were dead. It struck the side of the counterweight of the bridge, bounced off, hit the canal bank, and toppled in without exploding. That was the biggest stroke of luck we had.

Another amusing sequence occurred at about ten o'clock. A couple of fellows came walking across the bridge, rather scruffy individuals with long French shovels. These two fellows came along, but nobody could make out what they were or who they were. Then somebody said, "They're Italian." One fellow who knew a bit of the language asked what they were doing. They said they were recruited labor and their job was to dig the holes to put in the poles [Rommel's asparagus] to stop the gliders from landing. John Howard said, "Tell the silly buggers to look over there. There's the gliders." They did look, but then proceeded to walk on, insisting that the Germans told them to carry on digging the holes to put in the poles to stop the gliders from landing. You can imagine the comments from some of the blokes. "Hey, they're over there, Mate." When the battle was going on, they went down the bank and started to dig more holes. They had their job to do.

About eleven o'clock, coming up from Caen and at a steady rate, was a boat. We spotted it, and Major Howard ordered, "Don't let that damn boat get anywhere near this bridge." It came just past the château, which was eight hundred meters. I let fly the first one. It dropped short. Big wave came up, it turned. Second one hit it broadside up, and I'm firing armor-piercing shells. It then turned away and started to chug up around the curve. I put three more up its back side. That was that.

The one big mistake I did make was one of the things we were told was not to fire at the château, because it was the local maternity hospital. There was a corrugated tin roof on top of this gun pit that when you traversed the gun, it went around with it. And by this time there was a load of bullet holes in it, believe me. One of our fellows told me to look at the windows in the upper right-hand corner. You could see them firing from there, rifle fire from that one, machine-gun fire from that one. I eased it around, nice and careful, took aim, set it at eight hundred, and put three shells straight through the windows. As I finished, John Howard came out, and I thought he was going to shoot me. "Parr, the maternity home! The maternity home!" He's never forgiven me for that to this day. There was a machine gun up on there, and that's the truth. ▦

—Wally Parr, Corporal, 25th Platoon,
6th Airborne Division (UK)

Elsewhere, others were awake and bustling about in anticipation of the day ahead. Sergeant Felix Branham anxiously awaited feeling French soil under his feet, thinking it was the first step toward returning home to Virginia.

We went aboard the USS *Charles Carroll* on that 30th of May. We were cooped up on that ship. We griped because we were razor sharp and wanted to get out. We said we've got to go through France. It was our stepping-stone home. They paid us. Four dollars for the enlisted men; twenty for the officers. Actually, we were paid in invasion franc notes. One of our officers said we were being paid so nobody had to die broke. Then we played poker. I won a five-hundred-franc note the night before we landed. I asked all the members of my boat team to sign it. Thirty men signed it.

They woke us on June 6 at 1:20 A.M. Three hours later, our landing craft was being lowered to the water. We were told we were twelve miles (19.3km) from shore. Everybody was in good spirits. They were tired, but wanted to get off the ship. One of the guys said he hoped that wasn't Slapton Sands again. ▦

—Felix Branham

BELOW: Armed with a Thompson submachine gun, a 101st Airborne paratrooper guards captured grenadiers of the German 91st Air Landing Division as they dig graves near St. Côme-du-Mont for fallen members of their unit and the 91st's 6th Parachute Regiment.

ABOVE: Paratroopers of the British 6th Airborne Division roll past a worse-for-wear Horsa glider. The ability of the large Horsas to deliver jeeps and even field guns to a landing zone greatly enhanced the power of the mostly-infantry Allied airborne divisions.

RIGHT: British paras dig in along a Norman road.

Descent into Hell

The approach to the 101st Airborne's northern and center drop zones was completely disrupted by the cloud bank and German anti-aircraft fire. Whole planeloads of paratroopers floated down to their death in the wide, flooded area behind UTAH Beach, but most were sprinkled randomly across the countryside and had no idea where they had come to earth. And those were the lucky ones. . . .

The nature of the countryside added to the chaos. Beyond the targeted drop zones—one of which was completely missed—the land was a crazy patchwork of irregularly sized fields enclosed within hedgerows, thick embankments overgrown with tall, tangled hedges. With the help of a simple child's toy, a clicker that had been issued to many paratroopers before the mission, soldiers alone or in small groups slowly formed larger bodies with some capacity to actually carry out their missions. Not only did the regiment that landed relatively intact in the southernmost of the 101st's three drop zones seize all its objectives along the Douve River, but the understrength collections of soldiers from different units that coalesced farther north secured all four targeted causeways leading to UTAH Beach.

The two full regiments of the 82d Division that overshot their drop zones were so badly dispersed that they teetered on the brink of being "combat ineffective." Paratroopers from thirty or more aircraft came down in the flooded Merderet River, and great numbers died in only a few feet of water as they struggled to free themselves from their parachutes, weapons, and other gear weighing from 85 to 130 pounds (38.6–59kg). Unbeknownst to SHAEF planners, the recently arrived German 91st Air Landing Division had moved even closer to the coast and was now positioned west of the bridges that the 82d was ordered to take. Almost miraculously, small groups of determined paratroopers managed to seize and hold the bridges west and southwest of Sainte Mère-Eglise. That key crossroads town itself was taken by the regiment that had landed comparatively intact nearby, but not before the garrison decimated a group of unlucky paratroopers who floated down into the town square, their parachutes brightly illuminated by the light from burning buildings.

The widely scattered airdrops, the "Ruperts," the movement of lost paratroopers looking for their units or objectives, all created a chaotic situation on the ground that made it extremely difficult for the Germans to discern exactly what were the ultimate Allied objectives in Normandy. The German command structure was also handicapped because virtually all of its senior officers in Normandy were at the map exercise in Rennes and not with their units. The only German divisional commander not at the exercise was Major General Wilhelm Falley of the 91st, who had started out late and decided to turn back because of the constant air activity buzzing all around him. He and his logistics chief arrived back at his headquarters, in a château north of Picauville, only to be gunned down by a group of lost U.S. paratroopers who briefly captured the site before they, in turn, were wiped out.

Following the Pathfinders were the paratroopers. Private First Class Bill True of the 101st Airborne Division witnessed the German firepower that tore the night sky.

I can still vividly remember when the anti-aircraft started coming up. Just as we flew over the coast of Normandy, the tracer bullets and the other anti-aircraft was coming up, and I was sitting where I could look out the open door. It really looked like the tail of our plane was on fire. There was that much anti-aircraft going on. I can vividly remember how surprised I was that there were people down on the ground trying to kill me—and possibly succeed. It really struck home with me in a startling way.

We finally stood up and hooked up; the buzzer finally went at 1:20 A.M. There was never a happier time to get out of an airplane. People say, "How can you jump out of an airplane?" But staying in an airplane was the terrible thing as far as we were concerned. I bet we poured out of that airplane as fast as we did on any training mission.

ABOVE: French civilians give directions to 101st Airborne Division soldiers who landed near St. Marcouf.

Just as I went out of the plane, I remember seeing a fire. I thought it was the Pathfinders who had been dropped ahead lighting signals telling us where to go. But as I saw it I realized it really was a fire. I later learned it was a house burning in Sainte Mère-Eglise. We landed just outside in a field surrounded by hedgerows, right next to a nice peaceful cow that glanced at me rather unconcerned.

I looked up and saw the tracers were going up while rows of parachutes were still coming down. I got out of that parachute as quickly as I could. On that jump, our rifles were partially disassembled in a pack. It was a moonlit night and quite bright, so I wanted to get out of the field, over to a hedgerow, and assemble my rifle. I was doing that, when somebody was heading straight for me. My first thought was, My first German spotted me landing. Now he's coming after me, and I couldn't get my gun together in time. All I could do was throw it in his face, and maybe I could knife him. Then I heard "click click" and I knew it was one of my buddies. He had clicked his little cricket issued to identify each other. I'm forever grateful that they thought of that little cricket because he and I maybe would've killed each other—or one of us might have been seriously injured as a result. That was a tremendous relief. We got our

rifles together. We eventually joined other fellows from our group as we headed toward the beach. The Germans were firing at us and we fired at areas we never really saw. But over the next few hours we managed to finally get down to the beach area. There were probably twenty or twenty-five of us together by that time.

All that time spent with sand tables, studying the exact place we were going to go and how we were going to get there, went for naught because we were all spread all over the place. It worked having each of us in the wrong place, because the Germans were faced with utter confusion. Every way they turned there were paratroopers, so I guess our missions were largely accomplished. Maybe each of us didn't do what he was supposed to, but what needed to be done got done. ■

—Bill True

Alone and lost, Sergeant O.B. Hill of the 82d Airborne Division was finding that landing in floodwaters while under enemy fire was an unpleasant experience.

We were supposed to land near the Merderet River alongside Chef-du-Pont and take the bridges. When we did jump, I looked down and I could see the river. However, I landed in the floodwaters and they came to just above my waist. On the way down, the Germans were shooting at me, and they hit the gas mask on my side, spinning me around. I don't know how high we were, but it wasn't very high because it didn't take long to get to the ground, although it seemed like forever with tracers coming up at you. They were still shooting at me when I hit the water and stood up, so I went back down, and had just my nose and my head sticking out to try to breathe. It was a difficult experience. The shooting at me in the water continued for ten to fifteen minutes. It seemed much longer, but I don't think it was. Evidently they assumed that they had gotten me because I didn't make any moves. When everything quieted down, I waited what I considered to be an appropriate amount of time, then started moving toward the shore.

As I was walking in the direction that I thought I should be going, I heard noises coming from my left, so I stopped and laid down on the ground. When I laid down, I realized I was right by a ditch, and I could hear the sound of people walking. Not knowing whether they were ours or theirs, I didn't make a sound. As they passed right in front of me, one of them spoke to the other in German. I assumed that they could hear my heart beating. After they passed, I got up and jumped this ditch, and continued on in the direction I started. Suddenly I was challenged with the word of the day, which was *flash*. But I couldn't think of the password, so I just said, "Oh, shit." Bill Brown, one of my corporals, started laughing. We continued our way toward Chef-du-Pont. Ironically, in the pre-invasion briefing, the password *flash* and its response *thunder* had been beaten into our heads to make sure no one would forget.

Colonel Mendez, one of our best officers, revealed at a reunion that he, too, had forgotten the password. This was to be used if we didn't click our cricket.

About an hour later we ran into a bunch of Germans at a crossroads. By now we had about ten guys. We were outnumbered but still managed to drive them off. We continued and picked up a few more strays. Another firefight occurred at another crossroads. Again we drove them off and made our way to a little town named Bougeville. We discovered that, instead of the Merderet River, we had landed on the Douve River. There were some Americans on the other side of the road and behind the buildings in this town. Germans were on both sides of us, to the right and to the left. We had a bit of a firefight with the Germans on the right side of my crew. Then we crossed the road and drove them off. ▪

—O.B. Hill

LEFT: Paratroopers prepare to move out from St. Marcouf to their assigned objective near UTAH Beach. The vehicle in the foreground is a French infantry supply carrier pressed into service by the Germans. It is similar in both design and function to the British Universal, or "Bren gun," carrier. The paratroopers' "Screaming Eagle" shoulder patches have been censored.

101ST AIRBORNE DIVISION

The U.S. 101st Airborne Division parachuted into Normandy and suffered extensive losses as it secured the vulnerable exits from UTAH Beach. Reinforced by its glider elements, the division quickly moved against German paratroopers defending the strategic crossroads town of Carentan. Fearing encirclement, German forces withdrew from the town on June 11, 1944, after several days of heavy fighting. The 101st then defended the area against persistent counterattacks until it was relieved on June 27. The division was then sent to Cherbourg to mop up isolated resistance and garrison the fallen fortress.

LEO CORDIER

RIGHT: On D-Day afternoon, paratroopers of the 82d Airborne division take a well-earned break in a French town before moving on to the next objective.

Many Allied troops that night arrived in flimsy gliders, including Leo Cordier. While the flight could be eerily quiet, the landing usually was extremely rough and often deadly.

The ride of a glider after you cut off from the tow is very smooth and quite enjoyable. It's the closest to being like a bird.

We flew directly over the battleship *Texas*. It was firing its big guns toward UTAH Beach coast, and we could actually see the shells disappearing into the haze and heavy smoke at the beach. We flew on for about another two miles (3.2km), and then we encountered the greatest sight that I could imagine—the invasion fleet.

We landed in a field with a couple of horses, figuring they wouldn't be there if the area was mined. We went to clear the trees but were a little too high, meaning we had to dive toward the ground in order to make it; otherwise we would have crashed directly into the trees. We got on the ground, applied full brakes, put the glider up on the skids, and at about sixty miles (96.5km) an hour, we plowed right into the embankment where

hedgerows were. I tried to cock it to the right so the wing would hit first, to absorb some of the shock. Instead, we just slid directly into the embankment. My feet punched through the nose of the glider. The control column came back and hit me in the face. Fortunately, no one was seriously injured. ■
—Leo Cordier, Second Lieutenant, Glider pilot, Attached to 82d Airborne Division (US)

Not everyone that night arrived at the intended destination. Some planes missed their targets and lost their way in the confusion of fog and enemy anti-aircraft fire, and one Pathfinder plane never came near its destination. Captain Harold Sperber had to make a snap decision that night that affected the fate of his crew.

We left England and flew over Land's End. It was dark, but everything was going along fine. We went in between the Guernsey and Jersey Islands and the peninsula. We had just started into our climb from low-level water flight to avoid radar when we got hit. We didn't know what did it, but it knocked out an engine. Then it was decision time. A very short decision time. We had to think, Can we crash straight ahead? How can we avoid killing everybody on board?

To keep flying, the other engine had to go full speed, but the plane was extremely heavy, since each paratrooper weighed about three hundred pounds (136.2km). So we made a turn, got down over the water, hoping to keep altitude over the water, but you could hear the prop hitting the waves. There were over 820 planes that night carrying around 15,000 men. Here we were turning around, going against the grain at a low altitude. Meanwhile, we had to throw out everything that was heavy and nonessential. They even tossed out a land mine. Since we were so low, they threw out their parachutes. That made the airplane a little bit easier to control. Now we had to decide where to land. In the Channel was a British destroyer, the HMS *Intrepid*. We decided to try to ditch near it. By now the engine was overheating so much we hardly needed a light in the cockpit. We told the paratroopers to prepare to ditch.

We dropped into the water with our landing light on. A wall of water came over the top and that's all I remember for a bit. I temporarily lost my eyesight, but I could hear the airplane moaning and groaning as though it were tearing apart. Then all I could see was green water. I got out and flashed SOS with my flashlight.

This big destroyer sailed within ten yards (9.1m) of where we were, stopped right alongside us, really blanking the winds and the sea from where we were. A fabulous bit of seamanship. They threw a landing net over, and a man on top tossed me a line.

I was able to hold the airplane against the destroyer while the guys got out of the back of the airplane. As the last guys climbed out, I was still holding the line. A destroyer does not want to just sit in a combat zone. They rely on speed, and they want to be up to twenty to thirty knots to avoid everything. They started up the screws. The airplane started sinking underneath me, and I quickly decided I lacked time to go through the back way. As the screws of the big destroyer turned, it just sucked the airplane underneath, and it was

gone. Just in time, I swung over and caught my leg in the landing net. They pulled me along for a little while. Some of the men were reeling in the landing net. Apparently, one of the seamen thought the net seemed especially heavy, and he looked down. "Blimey! There's a Yank down there yet!"

Everybody then was checked. All were safely aboard. I was handed a big white Navy mug of hot buttered rum. Boy, it was good! But I gave it to my navigator. Later in the morning we watched the invasion. It was fantastic. Then about noon a PT boat came and took us back to England. We saluted and said, "Goodbye, *Intrepid*." ◾

—Harold Sperber, Pilot, Pathfinders, 50th Troop Carrier Squadron (US)

HAROLD SPERBER

Merville and Pointe du Hoc

The principal water barriers on both flanks of the D-Day beachheads were in Allied hands before first light, but dangerous German coastal guns still threatened to wreak havoc on the assault waves. Less than a third of the 500-man British battalion assigned to destroy the Merville Battery had been assembled, and time was running out. The attack on the outer perimeter was to occur as gliders carrying an additional 60 men smashed down into the middle of the position, and if the four guns were not spiked by 5:50 A.M., the Royal Navy was to do its best to silence them with gunfire. With only a scant 150 paratroopers, the battle began.

The men opening the attack through the barbed wire and minefields were relieved to see two of the three gliders appear right on schedule. Then, dumbfounded, they watched as the aircraft whooshed on past into the darkness. The strike had to be carried out with the few troops on hand, and the battery was taken in confused, bloody fighting among the casements, bunkers, and trenches. At least sixty-five of the British were killed or wounded, but the position was captured.

ABOVE AND OPPOSITE: Rangers who landed along the rocky shoreline (obscured by smoke and extending right to the Pointe) found only decoys made of telephone poles and shredded camouflage nets (above) in the unfinished gun positions, and still more telephone poles pointing harmlessly out to sea from the two finished casements. The layout of the site led Allied intelligence analysts to correctly deduce that it had been designed to support long-range guns of up to 155-mm. It was assumed, when the Rangers found the guns in a concealed location nearby, that they had been moved back from the Pointe, but the French intelligence chief for the Grandcamp Sector maintained that they had never been moved forward and installed at the unfinished position.

Then came a big surprise. The massive German casements held not the expected 150-mm guns with a range of nearly 15,000 yards (13,716m), but unfamiliar howitzers that the assault party initially judged to be just 75mm. The sting of losing so many men to destroy such puny weapons was soothed somewhat when closer examination after the battle revealed that they were actually old—but still deadly effective—100-mm Czech howitzers. Fearing that a prescheduled naval bombardment was about to strike the battery position, the raiders spiked the guns and hastily withdrew. At least two of the guns were soon repaired by the Germans and raked the landings on SWORD Beach.

Four beaches to the west, the Rangers at Pointe du Hoc were in for their own surprise. The Germans had not anticipated a seaward assault by a large force, so casualties during the scaling of the cliff were light. Upon reaching the top, the Americans found that the camouflaged position containing two finished casements, four partially constructed gun positions, and myriad ammunition bunkers, trenches, and anti-aircraft positions had been thoroughly pummeled by naval gunfire and bombers. So thorough was the damage inflicted by the 14-inch shells from the battleship *Texas* and an air attack a half-hour earlier by B-26 Marauders that it had rendered the whole area a lunar landscape of cratered rock and earth. Everything except the casements and a large observation post was now unrecognizable, making it difficult for the Americans to get their bearings. Rangers mopping up scattered resistance in the desolate terrain quickly discovered that the German camouflage had concealed decoys: the six long-range, 155-mm guns sited to cover both OMAHA and UTAH beaches were nowhere to be found.

Small teams of Rangers immediately spread out into the countryside to find the battery, which could train its guns on the invasion fleet from well inland with the help of artillery observers. They found them expertly hidden in an orchard seven hundred yards (640m) from the German observation post at the tip of the Pointe. Meanwhile, other Rangers discovered that the observation post itself had survived the bombing, and was still functioning. (It successfully held out against the Americans until D+1.) At the camouflaged battery site, the guns were sited toward UTAH Beach with ammunition at the ready, but miraculously were left unguarded as the gun crews organized themselves a short distance away.

Taking advantage of the fantastic stroke of luck, two small parties of Rangers disabled the big guns then quickly "got the hell out of there." The Rangers' hastily formed defensive perimeter was manned only by the three companies that had made the original assault, because the follow-on battalion, believing that the operation had failed, had proceeded to OMAHA Beach. The Rangers on the Pointe would fight off a series of fierce German counterattacks until they were relieved two days later.

Some of the first Americans to storm ashore were Army Rangers. Their ranks would all-too-soon be thinned, but, undaunted, they continued their assigned tasks. Among them was First Sergeant Leonard Lomell of the 2d Ranger Battalion.

We went toward the Pointe and suddenly realized that the British coxswain was headed for the wrong cliff, not Pointe du Hoc. After Colonel [James E.] Rudder called attention to this error, it meant turning right parallel to the cliffs about three hundred yards (274.3m),

Actual location of Battery
along tree Line

Battery observation post

ABOVE: A-20 Havoc light bombers pummel the German
battery position at Pointe du Hoc with 500-pound bombs.
Pre-invasion strikes by the Ninth Air Force had been conducted far apart on April 15, May 22, and June 4, 1944, in order to
conceal the invasion plans. From the middle of April to
D-DAY only about 10 percent of the total bomb tonnage
was directed against coastal batteries, with two out of
every three of those strikes occurring away from Normandy,
in the Pas-de-Calais area, and some as far away as Brittany.

INSET: Sixty years later, the indelible scars of the D-DAY
attack by B-26 Marauder Medium bombers and 250 shells
from the 14-inch guns of the battleship *Texas* still pit the
plateau behind the pointe. The thin, rocky shore below the
nine-story cliffs at right was the site of the Ranger landings.

then going for three miles (4.8km) running a gamut of fire because Germans all along the top of those cliffs were firing at us. Then a quick left turn to assault a small, narrow beach with one of these hundred-foot (30.5m) cliffs. Of course, the Germans fired down as we came ashore. That coxswain's mistake cost us thirty precious minutes on our landing, enabling the Germans to prepare for us. If we had landed as planned, we would have caught them by surprise.

My company, D Company, was supposed to go around that cliff and approach from the west side because we had three gun emplacements assigned to us to destroy. Because we were late, everything was messed up, as far as we were concerned, with the original plan. One of my boats was sunk, taking my company commander, the executive officer, and some of our key men down with it, so I only had two boats left. We jammed our two boats in between E Company and F Company. There was room, making it rather crowded, but the idea was to get up that cliff as fast as you could, find those guns as fast as you could, destroy them all as fast as you could.

I was an acting platoon leader. The men went straight off the ramp from right side or left, fanned out, and went for the ropes at only fifty yards (45.7m) away and started climbing. In my case, I was the first one wounded. I didn't realize I was wounded at the time. I got this burning sensation through my right side, spun me around, and as I went off the ramp I went out of sight, over my head in water because of a shell crater there that I didn't see, and the guys pulled me out. Fortunately for us, we could run in and out of shell craters and the like to make our way to check different positions. A wonderful benefit that the boys at OMAHA Beach didn't have, because no shell craters or bomb craters were found on OMAHA Beach. They had nothing to hide in. But we did.

Some of the lines weren't successful. The Germans were up there cutting the lines. They were rolling bullets over the end. They were dropping grenades on us and machine-gunning us, and riflemen from the flanks in the side of the cliff were shooting at us where

they had open range of fire. But still my men were successful. Everyone had to grab a rope that was going to support them, so I think our success would indicate that it was a good way to get up those cliffs, because we got up there. Some of our special expert riflemen picked off the enemy as best they could.

When we landed, we had certain guys in every landing craft who were especially powerful men. We called them monkeys. They were fast. They moved up those ropes with a BAR [Browning Automatic Rifle] on their back like it was nothing. They reached the top to keep the Germans off the edge of the cliff, so the rest of us could climb up. Many were successful, but others weren't. But if one died, the next guy grabbed his BAR and took over.

Out of the 225 men that landed that morning, 108 of us got up the cliff. ■

—Leonard G. Lomell, First Sergeant, D Company, 2d Ranger Battalion (US)

The German guns at Pointe et Raz de la Percée, halfway between the Pointe du Hoc and the main OMAHA Beach landings, were the objective of the 2d Ranger Battalion's C Company. The tide swept some of the landing craft past the target—but not that of First Lieutenant Sidney Salomon.

On D-DAY, my company had its own mission. We were to land at Raz de la Percée. Go over to Crestla Beach and climb the cliff. There we would find a fortified house with artillery

Three old women with brooms could keep the Rangers from climbing that cliff.

—Naval intelligence officer discussing Pointe du Hoc mission

firing down on Vierville. The maps we used appeared to come from a tourist agency. And we soon learned that the intelligence we had been given was faulty. That house was a farmhouse, not "fortified" at all. There were German soldiers living in the house.

We landed and waded through the waist-high water to the beach. There I started running. I hadn't run more than maybe ten yards (9m) when a mortar shell landed right behind me. It knocked me flat, and I went facedown on the sand. I thought I must be dead. Then sand started kicking up in my face, and I thought, I'm not dead. I figured some machine gunner's got a bead on me and he's getting the range. This was no place to lie down, so I got up and ran to the base of the cliff, a distance of about one hundred yards (91.4m). A medic took some shrapnel out of my back, sprinkled sulfa powder, and put a patch on it. I put on my shirt and jacket and said, "Let's start up."

Twenty men of C Company died in the first ten to fifteen minutes crossing the beach. When we got up on top of the cliff, the only thing I did was gather all my men together—only nine men out of the thirty-seven men in my landing crew reached the top. Only two of those nine had not been wounded. And the other seven, including me, were lightly wounded but able to climb up there. The seriously wounded remained below.

With only nine men, I figured there was no point in continuing our mission. We were not an effective fighting force. I was laying in a shell hole. The other platoon leader came in, too, peered over the edge, viewing the trench ahead of us, when he suddenly fell back. He was killed instantly.

Then I turned and grabbed two men. I told them to follow me. We ran across to that trench and began clearing it out. I threw a grenade, waited a minute, then ran and sprayed the inside. We proceeded cautiously and found something like a manhole. On the wall were targets on the beach with elevation and settings matching the flags on the beach. We knocked out the mechanism and moved on. Coming around a curve was a German from the opposite direction. He was more startled than I was and stopped dead in his tracks. I grabbed him, thinking maybe we ought to take one prisoner to get some information.

Since nine men couldn't win the war, I decided that the best thing for us was to hold on to this ground up here, since we didn't have any communication with anybody. Our radios were gone in the drink. We stayed at the top for the rest of the day and made certain that nobody came in. We dug slit trenches and spent the night. ■

—Sidney Salomon

The job of Staff Sergeant Charles Klein and the 5th Ranger Battalion was to fight their way along the coast and relieve the Rangers at Pointe du Hoc and Pointe et Raz de la Percée. But first they had to storm OMAHA Beach.

The situation for landing was not very favorable. The Channel was very angry that day. There were maybe fifty yards (45.7m) between crests, so a vessel would be riding up one steep wave and plunging down into the valley of another. Whereas in the open ocean, the crest of the waves are very far apart. That's why the vessels were taking so much water—the rising and falling in the waves at a very steep angle.

CHARLES KLEIN

When we were going in toward the beach, we started taking on water, so the coxswain who was the captain of that little vessel ordered us to start bailing. They had two hand pumps and men were operating the pumps to bail out water. Then he informed us that that wasn't enough because we were still taking in water and taking it fast. If we didn't do something else, we'd soon be on the bottom of the English Channel. Before long, everybody was standing up in the boat, bailing that boat with our helmets in addition to the two pumps that were working. It was not according to the book, but that's what we had to do to get there.

We sailed by the battleship *Texas*. Actually, we were several hundred yards away from it, but that's such a big vessel it was very visible even in the darkness. There was the *Texas* with all her guns turned on the beach, firing broadside. When she let a salvo go, she lit up the sky. I didn't think there could be anything existing on the beach afterwards. She actually rolled from the recoil when she fired. It was a tremendous thing to see. She put on quite a show.

One reason we landed so early was to arrive at low tide. At that time, the obstacles would be exposed, so landing craft could avoid them. Although it was low tide, the seas were so high that the crests of the waves were covering these piles. Our vessel was riding on a wave. The wave was traveling faster. Then, just before we reached this particular pile, the wave dropped out from under us and we were in a trough and ran into one of these piles. But happily for us, we struck this pile below the mine and didn't contact the mine.

The coxswain ordered us to push off. I happened to be the first man in the middle row. I jumped up and put my shovel to it and I was pushing, trying to push us free of this thing. My first sergeant was on my left—he jumped up to assist me, but even the two of us couldn't push it off. A man on my right side had the presence of mind to use the butt of his rifle as a crowbar, and he put it between the pile and the ramp of this vessel that we're on. A landing craft has a ramp on the front that's the bow of the boat when

you're cruising in the water. But when it hits the beach, the ramp comes down, and then you're supposed to race off it and engage the enemy. The ramp crimped onto this pile. Fortunately, when the soldier on my right put his rifle butt in there, he managed to pry us off.

Concurrently with that effort, the coxswain had the landing craft in reverse and its tow engines were pulling at high power. So when we disengaged ourselves from the pile, the boat raced backwards, and then the coxswain maneuvered the vessel so we were able to go between these piles. Then we grounded on the beach. Actually, it was a sandbar before the shoreline.

At that point, the coxswain tried to lower the ramp, but it wouldn't go down for us because it was jammed, and we couldn't get it down. Now, most of us were riflemen, so we could handle that. But others had Browning Automatic Rifles and 60-mm mortars and ammunition. They're rather heavy to carry. We needed to get off the boat in a hurry. The coxswain ordered us to jump on the gunnels of the landing craft and jump. People who were carrying these heavier weapons couldn't climb up and jump off at the same time with these weapons. Riflemen stood on the wide gunnels. The heavy weapons were handed off, the men jumped, and the riflemen handed them the heavy weapons to take ashore. During this time the Germans were shooting at us, since we were in a very exposed position. I think the only reason that we survived was that there were so many targets for the Germans to shoot, with so many crafts landing simultaneously with us. With so many targets, I don't think they took enough time to take aim. Otherwise, I'm sure at the range that they had, more people would have been hit. Up to this time, we had not had any casualties from our landing craft.

Earlier I had asked the coxswain if we would have a dry landing. He assured me we would. All of us had waterproofed our rifles, meaning they were in a plastic bag. I wanted to get that thing off so I could shoot. I stripped the waterproofing off my rifle, jumped overboard, crossed the sandbar, and immediately sank in deep water. I treaded water to get ashore, and, of course, my rifle was completely submerged.

The beach was a very unusual one. It wasn't a sandy, hard beach like you're used to finding on our American shores. It had very round, smooth stones—pebbles, you might say. It was like running on a bed of marbles that would displace as you ran on it, and the footing was very bad. You couldn't dig a slip trench because the stones would just slide right back into the hole. You couldn't find any shelter for yourself on that beach.

We were supposed to land on OMAHA DOG GREEN beach. Fortunately for us, we had a very experienced battalion commander, Colonel Matt Schneider. He saw the intense fire that was laid down by the Germans on OMAHA DOG GREEN. And he thought our job was to survive, not to perish under that slaughter. So he moved us to the left of DOG GREEN, where the fire was less intense. Earlier companies that landed on the first wave had blown holes in the barbed wire, allowing the rest of the battalion to go through.

When we reached the top of that hill, all of us were panting and coughing from inhalation of that smoke. I was lying down on the shoreside of the crest. It gave me a little shelter from small-arms fire. Down on the beach an LSI [landing ship, infantry], a very large vessel, had grounded. They lowered the ladders. I guess the men were just about to leave. Apparently, they weren't quite firm yet, so it took a little bit of time. Before the men started to disembark, a shell hit that ship, and I have never seen anything go so quickly. I don't think there was a living soul that managed to get away from that vessel alive. It went up just like a charcoal fire. Poof! It was a mass of flames. I don't know how many men in the LSI perished, but by the size of that ship, there must have been about two hundred men on that vessel. We lost two hundred men in one instant. ▪

—Charles Klein, Staff Sergeant, F Company, 5th Ranger Battalion (US)

BELOW: A huge rockslide caused by the Allied bombardment of Pointe du Hoc ultimately expedited the taking of the German position by both shortening the Rangers' climb and providing a protected gouge along the cliff face where German heavy weapons could not reach. It is from this point, well to the east of the German observation post at the tip of the Pointe, that the main Ranger penetration was made. In addition to the extension ladder, there are a number of ropes running up the cliff, and a bundle of supplies can be seen being pulled to the top.

RIGHT: Captured Germans, at top, are marched to a holding area near the Ranger command post on D+2. In the distance at upper right is the jutting rock feature that gave the site its name. The German observation bunker lies just over the lip of the high ground at the top of the photo with the fixed—and empty—gun positions extending back in a great "V" from the Pointe. The American flag was draped across the rocks in the hope that it would help prevent an accidental bombardment by supporting Allied ships, and as a guide to landing craft.

Sergeant Leonard Lomell and the other men of the 2d Ranger Battalion scaled the cliffs at Pointe du Hoc only to find that their targeted gun emplacements were empty. Lomell's two-man patrol, however, soon found the guns well inland from the cliffs and ready to fire on American troops arriving on UTAH *Beach.*

When we finally reached the top of the Pointe, the place was decimated. You could look across that Pointe and it looked like the face of the moon with all the thousands of holes and craters and the like. The concrete emplacements were several feet thick with steel rods inside, but they were blown to kingdom come. No guns. Some telephone poles or timbers stuck out of some emplacements, which might make you think there were guns, but they had never been there. To have gone through all of the fighting to finally achieve our position only to find the guns not there was disappointing. However,

we were prepared for that and had alternate positions. Our guys were quick thinkers— very resourceful and determined.

You looked across that landscape of forty acres (16.2ha), flat with nothing but shell craters and blown to pieces. So we looked inland and saw trees and only one road out of the Pointe. There were minefields on each side, and I figured there's men there. They come and go, so they must come and go by that road. They had a machine gun covering it, and another emplacement covering a billet nearby where they slept above ground. We neutralized the machine gun, killing them. Next we decided to go out to that road and get to the coast road that ran between UTAH Beach and OMAHA Beach.

We came upon this sunken road between two hedgerows. We didn't know much about hedgerows. It was a frightening sight. When an American boy looks at a hedgerow, it's maybe three feet high (0.9m). These were fifteen feet (4.6m) high, with trees growing out thirty to forty feet (9.1–12.2m) in the air. You could hide a column of tanks in this and never be seen from the road. Going from the blacktop into that sunken farm road between pastures, we saw that something heavier had cut up the dirt.

We had twenty-two men when we started from the cliff. By the time we got to the coast road, there were only twelve of us left. The rest had become casualties—killed or badly wounded. The two staff sergeants took the ten men to set up a roadblock on the blacktop road. My acting platoon staff sergeant, Jack Kune, and I went patrolling. We leapfrogged. This means I stood, making myself invisible, trying to stop breathing so no German could hear us. Jack would run up ten, fifteen, twenty yards (9.1m, 13.7m, 18.3m), hoping that he could get to that spot where he wanted to make his observation. I covered him while he did. Then I went by him another thirty yards (27.4m). He covered me and we leapfrogged, protecting one another going inland.

We had gone in about a hundred yards (91.4m), and it just so happened on my leap around him to the hedgerow, I looked over and there before me was a swale, an indentation. Back from the edge of the cliff, the land started to fall in the rear down to the lowlands. I looked over and in an apple orchard were guns all set up, ready to be fired on UTAH Beach, and no men that we could see. We did spy about seventy-five to eighty men a hundred yards (91.4m) away from where we had just been when we were leapfrogging. We saw a German combat patrol of about fifty men heavily armed within twenty feet (6m) of us while we hid in a ditch. We did not fire, because our orders were to stop anybody coming from UTAH Beach toward OMAHA Beach. These men were coming from the opposite direction. They were going toward UTAH Beach, so we didn't feel that we should give up our position. By then, we were about a mile (1.6km) inland.

We saw these men and that patrol going west on the blacktop road in a field behind a wall. Then they came out and crossed over a half a mile (0.8km) west of us, and went on parallel to the road that Jack Kune and I were

going. It appeared to us that some German officer or noncom [sergeant] was standing by his vehicle talking to these men. I don't know what he was talking about. We couldn't hear him, but figured he was giving them an update on the invasion. By now it was about 8:00 A.M.

I said, "Jack, hop up there and cover me. I'm going in and do the best I can with a thermite grenade." They're about the size of a little lager beer can. When you opened the can, the air hit, and it became molten metal that poured out. It seeped down into crevices of gears, tubes, breechblocks, etc. As it cooled, it locked everything, rendering them inoperable.

Both of us had machine guns. I told Jack if they looked my way, drill the first one, so I'm warned to get out of there. I put two guns out of action, then wrapped my field jacket around the butt of my submachine gun and smashed as best I could the gun sights of all five guns. I returned to Jack and told him we've got to get more grenades, because I had three more guns.

So we ran back some hundred yards (91.4m), and each guy gave me his grenades. We stuffed them in our jackets and shirts. No leapfrogging this time, just running as fast as we could. No Germans. They apparently hadn't noticed the damage. Instead, they were still talking. Fortunately, we were at the right place at the right time—a lull in the battle. We used the thermite grenades to finish off the guns. As I'm coming out of the swale, having destroyed and rendered inoperable the five guns, Jack said, "Come on, Len, let's get out of here!"

We were both nervous at that point. I crawled up the embankment of that hedgerow, when a big explosion occurred. We couldn't hear each other, so we just ran like a couple of scared rabbits as fast as we could back to the blacktop road where our ten men were at the roadblock. Our ears opened, and we started rationalizing. I thought it was the *Texas* or the destroyers trying to get those guns; that they may have had a short round. Jack's theory was that some of the incendiary compound dropped into the powder bags. It was a textbook raid. ▪

—Leonard Lomell

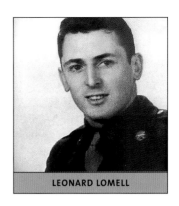

LEONARD LOMELL

I wake up at night and see the Channel floating with bodies of the cream of our youth.

—Winston Churchill

Chapter Four

THE MAIN ACT

The Allied minesweepers assigned to OMAHA Beach had already cleared an anchorage for the troop transports and were opening a channel for the bombardment group when their sister ships finally arrived to start mine clearance off UTAH at 2 A.M. These forces, and three more belonging to the British, had worked their way from "Piccadilly Circus" near the Isle of Wight, opening four-hundred-yard (365.8m) wide paths that included both "fast" and "slow" lanes through the German minefields. In the full moonlight, the finely choreographed moves of Operation NEPTUNE—the naval component of OVERLORD—almost resembled a peacetime review off Spithead or New York, as battleships and cruisers sailed in line behind the tight V-formations of mine-sweepers. The bombardment groups were followed by the transports and large landing craft carrying the men and equipment that would begin the liberation of France.

The most modern British warships were kept in Scotland to guard against a sortie by the German surface fleet through the North Sea, but ample muscle to support the landings was provided by two massively

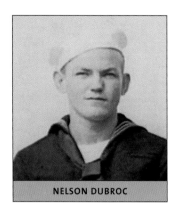

NELSON DUBROC

PAGES 110–111: Heavily loaded reinforcements splash ashore on Omaha Beach from LCT-538 about 11:30 a.m. on D-Day. The white, crescent-shaped symbol painted on their helmets indicate that these soldiers belong to either the 5th or 6th Engineer Special Brigade. Although their job was to construct roads and supply dumps inland, the beachhead had to be first won and secured. All are heavily armed, and some can be seen carrying boxes of .30-caliber machine-gun ammunition.

Silhouetted against the water at the photo's left is the long tube and conical mesh flash deflector of a bazooka rocket launcher, for use against German tanks and bunkers. The soldier at left is probably the bazooka's loader and is carrying half of the two-man team's supply of twenty armor-piercing rockets. Helmets displaying a white crescent extending all the way down to the lip are those of the 1st Engineer Special Brigade at Utah Beach, while short red crescents signify membership in the 6th and 7th Navy Beach Battalions.

OPPOSITE: The center gun on the USS Nevada's "A" turret recoils after firing a 14-inch round at a German target in Normandy.

gunned British monitors, *Erebus* and *Roberts,* and the elderly battleships *Ramillies, Warspite* (a veteran of Jutland), *Arkansas, Texas,* and Pearl Harbor survivor *Nevada.* Nearly two dozen cruisers were assigned specific beaches and coastal batteries to pound, and more than half of Neptune's 101 destroyers were arrayed roughly three thousand yards (2,743m) from the shore, where they could supply direct fire on specific targets. Before D-Day was over, some of these diminutive "tin cans" would provide the most critical gunfire support of the invasion as they risked grounding to shoot at deadly German fortifications from as little as eight hundred yards (731.5m) from the high-tide line.

The U.S. and Royal Navies handled operations very differently in their respective sectors. American forces began their landings in the west at H-Hour—6:30 a.m.—when the tide was low, believing that it was better to force their way across the extra two hundred yards (183m) of mortar and machine-gun fire than risk having landing craft pile up like sitting ducks on Rommel's thick belt of obstacles hidden beneath the surf at high tide. Because of reefs in the British sector, their landings on the flanking beaches of Gold and Sword were made on the rising tide almost one hour after the Americans', and even later in the center at Juno, where the risk from shoal waters was greatest.

The British and Canadian troops also made their runs to shore from transports anchored seven miles (11.3km) out and adjacent to the gunlines of warships pounding German targets from nearly as far from land. American and other Allied warships operating in the U.S. sector conducted their fire missions from roughly two miles (3.2km) closer to the beaches, but launched their small assault craft from transports anchored fully eleven miles (17.7km) away from the Utah and Omaha beaches. Operating this far out in the Channel increased the effects of wind and tide on the invasion craft and resulted in unintended consequences at both American beaches.

Even as the first shore batteries came tentatively to life after dawn and began to shell the shadowy targets offshore, the guns of the inva-

sion fleet lay silent. The first waves of soldiers bound for the American beaches churned against the rough seas and the manning of the small landing craft for the British beaches was well under way when, just before 5:30 a.m., a rolling thunder began to boil up from the western end of Normandy and roll inexorably east. By 5:45, some ninety warships were firing up to ten tons (9,080kg) of shells per minute at targets in an arc from Barfleur on the Cotentin Peninsula to Villerville at the mouth of the Seine. "You could see the ripple of flashes along the gray horizon," said a British seaman, "and you had to force yourself not to duck as the great shells tore overhead with the sound of tearing canvas."

Among the first to arrive on the beaches the morning of June 6 were the men of the Naval Combat Demolitions Units, or NCDUs. Their expertise was necessary to remove obstacles that would hinder the upcoming landing craft. Carrying out their mission, however, would be far from easy. Their accounts, including those of Coxswain Nelson DuBroc, Chief Petty Officer Jerry Markham, and Seaman First Class Richard Coombs, describe the horrors found on the Utah and Omaha beaches.

When we arrived at Omaha Beach, nobody was there. It was just us and the Germans. We were the first guys. We were the pointed end of the stick. Our primary objective was to clear a fifty-foot (15.2m) gap through the obstacles. Then when the tide came in, we could guide boats in through the gaps, and then they could get the infantry in much easier.

We came in about 6:30. Not one unit landed, I don't think, right on time, or at the specific place where they were supposed to land. It didn't make too much difference because the beach was all the same, all obstacles were the same. The rubber boat filled with explosives was too heavy to pick up, so we just grabbed up as much as we could carry, and just jumped in and started putting them on the obstacles.

They had Army people in the front of the boat. I guess they maybe were there to protect us. When they dropped the ramp, guns fired right into our boat. So these guys were just laying there and we had to climb over them to get out.

It seemed that the Germans had their machine guns synchronized. They would pass in front of the boat, and then they'd come back, and come back again. After we put the stuff on the obstacles, you could look and you could see the bullets hitting the sand. Then you'd run to that hole or past that, and you'd stop, trying to hide behind something or the bodies that were there already. And then when it came back again, then you'd go some more. They would sweep the beach, back and forth. Plus you had the 88-mm artillery shells coming in, falling all over the place.

As soon as we came out of the landing craft, we started putting the charges on the obstacles. They had what they called Belgian gates, a barricade. They had stuff that looked like the jacks that the girls played with on the beach. They had posts with mines on top of them and stuff like that. You had to rig the explosives with stuff flying all over the place. Some of these gates were about four, five, six feet (1.2m to 1.8m) high. The ones way out in the water, we'd put charges all over them. When that stuff started flying around, there was no place to hide. You just laid there and hoped it didn't come down on you.

We got a bunch of it rigged, right on the water's edge, then we were going to blow it up, pull the fuse. Later I learned we didn't blow everything because things were snafued by then. The Army was coming in on top of it, and you couldn't blow the thing with the Army coming in, or you would have blown them up. Soldiers cut the fuse, and then we returned later, and put it back in there. We cleared men out of the way by hollering, "Fire in the hole." They got out those that could. Some of them were dragged out because of wounds.

For those of us who weren't killed, it wasn't because we were better soldiers or better trained or more efficient. We were just lucky. Everywhere you looked, you could see the fire coming somewhere from the beaches.

There would be a flash like a blast furnace from the fourteen-inch guns of the *Texas,* that would lick far out from the ship. Then the yellow-brown smoke would cloud out and, with the smoke still rolling, the concussion and report would hit us, jarring your ear like a punch with a heavy, dry glove. "Look at what they're doing to those Germans," I leaned forward to hear a GI say above the roar of the motor. "I guess there won't be a man alive there," he said happily.

—Ernest Hemingway, war correspondent

Ste. Marie-du-Mont

Vehicles headed to exit 1

RIGHT: The tide is receding from the high-water mark in this early-afternoon shot of UTAH Beach and the air-drop zones. Although the stretch of beach running north from Exit 3 was the designated landing area, the initial assault waves had fortuitously landed opposite Exit 2 and slightly north, where defenses were weak. However, even the stronger German positions were not deep, and U.S. troops took Exits 3 and 4 (not pictured) by simply rolling up the German strongpoints from the flank.

By the time this photo was taken, a stream of men and supplies were headed across Exit 2 toward the fighting around Sainte Marie-du-Mont. A trickle of vehicles can also be seen moving up the beach to the recently opened Exit 3, and inland across its causeway. More vehicles are moving down the beach toward the virtually unde-fended Exit 1. LCIs and LCTs from follow-on waves have been directed to a portion of the beach between the intended and the actual landing sites, where pools of water left by high tide have yet to drain back to the sea. The artificially flooded Douve River extends across the top left of the photo, and the flooded Merderet River—where many paratroopers lost their lives—can be seen flowing into the Douve at top right. The dark spot along the center of the photo is a low-lying area flooded by the Germans, but the large, dark patch in the vicinity of Sainte Marie-du-Mont and the irregular dark areas at center left are the shadows of a cloud remaining after most of the morning's overcast has cleared. Paratroopers holding Sainte Mère-Eglise and a key bridgehead across the Merderet would not be reached by troops fighting their way from UTAH until the following day, D+1.

And then on top of that, you had the artillery coming in, too, which, in a way, helped us. When they hit the beach, they'd blow some of the obstacles away, creating holes where you could jump in.

By around noon or so, after the tide had come in, you started to see all these bodies and body parts floating around. You knew this was serious business. One memory I have of that day was seeing a soldier who must have had his helmet strapped on under his neck. They blew his head off. He was laying on the edge of the water, and the tide would flip his neck back and forth, back and forth. I guess it got to one of the guys. He picked up a wooden ammunition box, inverted it, and put it over the guy's neck, so you wouldn't be looking at that. ▪

—Nelson DuBroc

Each man had about forty pounds (18.2kg) of plastic explosives carried in a little canvas bag called a Hagensen pack. We then carried extra explosives in a rubber boat that we threw out in the water from the landing craft, which was hazardous because the mortars were hitting nearby. One whole unit, Number 13, was killed by one.

To prepare for D-DAY, we were assigned men of the Army Combat Engineers. Our job was to clear the obstacles from the low-water mark up to the high-water mark. Starting about midway and continuing on, the Army would come in, cross the beaches into the ravine exits, and blow the mines, booby traps, and such. There was no fine line distinguish-ing our section from the Army's. Gap teams had different-sized sections as well. My offi-cer and I carried the detonators under our armpits, taped under there for security pur-poses. It didn't matter if it hit you there and you got it. My job was to carry the reel of electrical Primacord to go behind and tie every man into this single firing line. Primacord had a firing rate of 22,000 feet (6,706m) a second. You had a simultaneous explosion when you detonated it with a deto-nator cap.

The understanding with our Army guys was that they would go halfway up, 150 yards

Flooded Douve River

Merderet River

Ste. Mere Eglise

Exit 2

Exit 3

Intended Landing Beach

Initial Landing Area

German Beach Obstacles

The task of destroying the dangerous obstacles lining the invasion beaches of Normandy fell to Naval Combat Demolition Units (NCDUs). These special units trained on replicas of the defenses and also contained U.S. Army engineers. Ensign Nathan Irwin of NCDU Team 139 describes many types of German beach obstacles and the methods used to eliminate this threat to Allied landing craft.

Every man was designated a job. We had certain men placing the charges. We had other men who were in charge of stringing this detonating cord down the row of charges. And we had a couple of men in charge of electrically setting off the charge. We had men just carrying a certain amount of explosives, so that we could work. Of course, this posed a danger for our boat as well as the men coming into UTAH Beach. Any hit could have sparked an explosion. Still, this was the only way we could have done it; you couldn't expect to simply find your explosives lying on the beach when you arrived.

The reconnaissance people kept us informed as to the type of obstacles we would encounter on the invasion, and we prepared accordingly. We used men's socks for the charges. Starting with a composition C2 plastic explosive that resembled laundry bars, you pushed them into the socks, then lengthened them and then tied a detonating cord, Primacord, of about twelve inches on each end. Every man carried about twenty or twenty-five of these, averaging two pounds apiece, in a knapsack. These charges would be laid on the base of the obstacle, and then the ends lashed together, tying it around the base. These obstacles were all in a line down the beach. One man with a reel of Primacord started at one end, tying all these loose ends to this detonating cord. It was like Christmas lights on a Christmas tree. Finally, all we had to do was place a fuse at one end, and detonate it. It would carry the charge and detonate every individual charge along the line.

There were several kinds of obstacles that could stop a small boat, especially when the obstacles were a little bit under water, and the boat passed over them. You'd have hedgehogs of three steel beams welded together. You could have stakes, sharpened stakes, either steel or wood, pointed towards sea. The boat comes over, the stake or hedgehog would rip the hull and render that craft useless. Another type were called tetrahedrons, which were steel triangles, welded together. You could have wooden ramps facing inland. So when the boat hit the ramp, it went up the ramp and tipped over.

BELOW: The diagram depicts typical terrain and obstacles on OMAHA Beach. The tide at OMAHA had already been coming in for an hour and a half when the first landing craft ground to a halt at 6:30 A.M. A sandbar at OMAHA's extreme western end and the uneven surface of the low-tide beach resulted in some LCVPs coming to rest on gentle rises in the sand that had been hidden by the surf. Ramps frequently dropped forward into water that was far deeper than expected, and many heavily laden men were drowned. Soldiers and sailors of the joint NCDU Teams were tasked with blowing lanes through the still-uncovered beach obstacles, but heavy losses prevented most of the targeted obstacles from being destroyed before they were submerged by the incoming tide, which crested between 9:54 A.M. and 12:45 P.M.

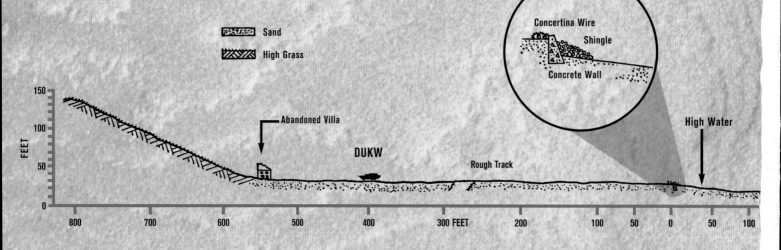

Sand

High Grass

Concertina Wire

Shingle

Concrete Wall

Abandoned Villa

DUKW

Rough Track

High Water

FEET

150

100

50

0

800   700   600   500   400   300 FEET   200   100   50   0   50   100

LEFT: Construction teams scurry for cover during the approach of an Allied reconnaissance aircraft. Stakes are arranged in bands near the low-water mark, and the heavy stakes between the ramps are intended to steer landing craft toward these ramps, causing them either to tip over or to slide into the shorter, mine-tipped stakes. Obstacle type and placement varied, depending on beach conditions and local resources.

BELOW: A Teller anti-tank mine clamped atop a stake. Although mines of this type were not entirely waterproof and deteriorated quickly due to exposure to sea salt in the air and water, they only had to be operable long enough to provide an effective barrier through the spring and summer "invasion season" to have served their purpose.

Obstacles with mines would be among the nastiest. Fortunately, we didn't seem to have any problem with them. We just went ahead and placed charges on the base of these obstacles. When we landed at Normandy on June 6, we were working against a tide that averaged around twenty-three to twenty-five feet (7.0m to 7.6m). We had planned the invasion so that the obstacles would be exposed. We worked on dry land parallel to the beach, and toward the sea.

We didn't have much time. When we hit the beach, we were told to do about fifty feet of a row. They figured that was all we'd have time for. The tide was coming in as we were working. The whole invasion was planned to take cognizance of when these tide conditions were. We wired up whatever we could in that small space of time, about an hour before that water came in. Once the tide came in, we couldn't do any work. ◼

—Nathan Irwin,
Ensign, NCDU, Team 139 (US)

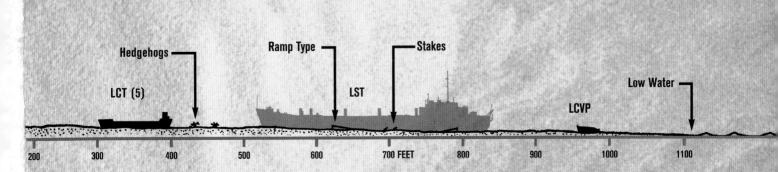

Hedgehogs   Ramp Type   Stakes

LCT (5)   LST   Low Water

LCVP

200   300   400   500   600   700 FEET   800   900   1000   1100

BELOW: Canadian soldiers examine the blasted turret of an obsolete French tank installed atop a prefabricated "Tobruk" emplacement near Dieppe. The obstacles visible on the beach include (a) tetrahedrons, (b) hedgehogs, sometimes known as Czech hedgehogs, on concrete footings, (c) unmined stakes driven deep into the beach, (d) element "C," often called a Belgian gate, (e) portable stakes, on concrete foundations, and (f) unidentified obstacles composed of three stakes on a concrete foundation, which were apparently not manufactured in any appreciable quantity because they could easily be upended. Some of the stakes once had mines strapped to their tips, and the Belgian gates are angled to deflect landing craft away from shore and to encourage collisions with other landing craft.

(137.2m), and start. Then, if we were successful in clearing from the low-water mark and caught up with them, we would continue helping them clear all the way up to the high-water mark. Then maybe go inland [to trip] the booby traps, if we had enough explosives left. That was the plan. It didn't work that way in reality because everybody was shot to hell in a basket on OMAHA. There were only five gaps blown out of sixteen that morning, plus two partials. I merged two units together, what was left of them. Over 50 percent of my unit was killed.

For us, things started going badly about 4:00 in the morning. We were three or four miles (4.8 or 6.4km) off the shore of Normandy when the LCT began sinking pretty fast in the stern. I went to the coxswain who was captain of our LCT. I said, "I think we're taking too much water."

He said, "No, I'll take a look." He returns and says, "Yep."

So I call my officer, who is green from seasickness and unable to do anything. I tell him, "I'm getting another landing craft. We've got to get off this thing, because it's going down." So we got the landing craft to come alongside, got the crews off, and she went down.

When we hit the beach, the Army guys were out first, going up the line with the gap team. We came along afterwards. I was in the rear because I was carrying the firing line, tying all the explosives as they were placed, and some of my seamen were handling this rubber craft with the extra explosives. As we got it out into the shallow water, a mortar come over and hit near the craft, and it blew it all to hell and gone. I saw half of my seaman's head blown off. That's when I knew that we were playing for keeps. All those explosives were gone.

I turned and started falling. The Army guys were scrunching down, hiding behind the mined obstacles to get out of the line of gunfire. There's my officer laying facedown in the water. So I turned him over to see he was dead. He'd been killed by a heavy piece of shrapnel. I began to move along the lines, looking for my men. They had scattered as preplanned to different sections. I would

see some of them down—some of them wounded. After about an hour, it was a matter of survival. We couldn't work. The fire was too intense. Three guys had a dugout in the sand behind the beach wall. A mortar came over and hit the sand and buried them. I jumped and ran and dug their heads out really quick so they wouldn't smother. The movie *Saving Private Ryan* captured the intensity of the battle, but think of those first nineteen minutes actually lasting four hours.

The crosscurrent tide swept some of the other units into ours. Since another unit was having its own problems with casualties, I merged the two and used their explosives with what little I had to blow a partial gap in those obstacles. It was the best we could do. And it was the only thing we could do other than just lay there and get killed. As we progressed, we tried to carry the wounded with us. The water temperature was fifty-eight degrees (14.4°C). It was horrible. But we did get a lot of the wounded onto dry beach.

Waves of soldiers continually arrived, and this hampered our job. We were able to finally load a portion of these obstacles with explosives. We couldn't blow them because the soldiers coming in were hiding behind the mined obstacles. I told these guys to get the hell out of there. But by the time we got one bunch out, another bunch would come and hide in it. So this thing was just a rabbit hutch.

I didn't deliberately blow any obstacle or guy, although I had to scare the hell out of a lot of them. You crawled over a guy and took out a red smoke bomb, threw it down, and said, "You've got two minutes to get your ass out of here or you won't have to get out. It's going to be blown out of here!" and then you started moving away real fast. He knew you weren't kidding and moved too. So I was running up and down trying to get them out. After awhile, they seemed to know to stay away from us because we were drawing a lot of fire. ▪

—Jerry Markham, Chief Petty Officer,
NCDU, Team 46 (US)

JERRY MARKHAM

D-DAY'S Lost Fleet

German beach obstacles, mines, and shore batteries took a fearsome toll on Allied landing craft and small warships during the first few days of the invasion. Some 55 LCVPs were sunk or destroyed at OMAHA Beach and 26 more at UTAH; 35 LCTs and LCIs were similarly lost in the American Sector plus 49 more damaged; and at JUNO, 90 landing craft—a third of the assault force—were sunk or damaged. But this was only the beginning. The hulks of more than 200 ships and large craft sunk during the invasion are strewn across the ocean floor off Normandy.

Even thought Hitler and his High Command withheld powerful land forces that could have attacked the Allies because of their belief that the main invasion was yet to come in the Calais area, German Naval Command Group West threw all of its rapidly diminishing might against the invasion. Nightly battles erupted between the principally British screening force and German E-boats operating out of Le Havre and Cherbourg. The fast E-boats succeeded in sinking two LSTs and several small merchant ships plus other craft, including tugboats towing MULBERRY components. Attrition was high, however, and much of the deadly force of the small German raiders was soon destroyed during massive raids by the RAF on their bases at Le Havre and Bologne on June 14 and 15.

A sortie by German destroyers out of Brest was beaten back, but "human torpedoes" piloted by German frogmen succeeded in sinking three minesweepers and so badly damaged a British cruiser that it was added to a MULBERRY breakwater rather than salvaged. The capture of Le Havre on September 8 effectively ended surface raids, but the *Luftwaffe*—absent on D-DAY—proved to be far more troublesome and destructive, particularly when it scattered pressure-sensitive mines along the shallow sea bed. Twenty-six warships, large craft, and a troop transport were sunk by mines and conventional air attacks during the first ten days of the invasion, but by far the most terrible loss came many months later, when the Belgian troop ship *Leopoldville* was torpedoed by a U-boat on Christmas Eve, 1944. More than 800 men drowned within sight of Cherbourg's harbor, 762 of them belonging to the American 66th Infantry Division.

Argentan

Falaise

H.M.S. *Swift* ■ June 24

H.M.S. *Magic* □ July 6

Human torpedoes sank the *Magic* and the *Cato*, both British minesweepers. Of 26 human torpedoes in the attack, nine were destroyed.

Merville Battery

Ouistreha

H.M.S. *Pylades* □ July 8

German "human torpedoes" sank the British minesweeper *Pylades* and damaged the Free Polish cruiser *Dragon*, manned by Polish patriots. The *Dragon* was later scuttled for a breakwater off GOLD BEACH.

Varaville •

Dives-sur-Mer

Riva-Bel

Lisieux

Cabourg

H.M.S. *Svenner* □ June 6

Three fast German *Schnellboote*—called E-boats by the Allies—sank a Norwegian destroyer, the *Svenner*. The British destroyer *Swift* picked up nearly 100 survivors, but 34 men were lost. A mine then sank the *Swift* on June 24.

Villers-sur-Mer

Deauville-les-Bains

Honfleur

Seine

to Paris

HIGH-TIDE MARK

Cap de la Hève

Le Havre

Montivilliers

Épouville

GERMAN HUMAN TORPEDOES
These were one-man torpedoes, midget submarines that ran partly above the surface. Operators were not on a suicide mission, as the Allies suspected. The pilot would aim and fire his torpedo—then hope for pickup by an accompanying ship.

British 3rd Infantry Division

LST Landing Ship, Tank. These were 328 feet (100m) long and capable of landing with 500 tons (453.6t). After unloading their cargo, versatile LSTs became hospital ships, bringing 41, 035 wounded men back to England.

LCVP Landing Craft, Vehicle, Personnel. These were about 36 feet (11m) long. They were called Higgins Boats after inventor Andrew Higgins, who, said General Eisenhower, "won the war for us."

LCP(L) Landing Craft, Personnel (Large). These were also 36 feet (11m) long and were capable of carrying 36 men or some 8,000 pounds (3,628.7kg) of cargo. Several of these were "smokers," used to produce smoke screens during the invasion.

LCT Landing Craft, Tank. The largest version used on D-DAY ran 119 feet (36.3m) long. These could each carry three 50-ton tanks or 150 tons (136.1t) of cargo. Some LCTs carried two tanks side by side, set to fire over the bow toward the beach.

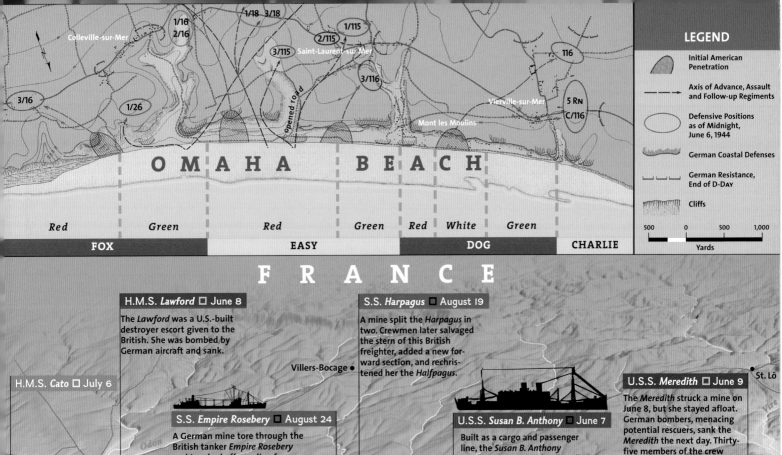

LEGEND

- Initial American Penetration
- Axis of Advance, Assault and Follow-up Regiments
- Defensive Positions as of Midnight, June 6, 1944
- German Coastal Defenses
- German Resistance, End of D-Day
- Cliffs

500 0 500 1,000

Yards

1/16
2/16
1/18 3/18
1/115
2/115
3/115
1/116
3/115 Saint-Laurent-sur-Mer
3/116
Colleville-sur-Mer
116
5 RN
C/116
Vierville-sur-Mer
3/16
1/26
Mont les Moulins
opened road

O M A H A   B E A C H

Red	Green	Red	Green	Red	White	Green

FOX	EASY	DOG	CHARLIE

F R A N C E

H.M.S. *Lawford* ☐ June 8

The *Lawford* was a U.S.-built destroyer escort given to the British. She was bombed by German aircraft and sank.

S.S. *Harpagus* ☐ August 19

A mine split the *Harpagus* in two. Crewmen later salvaged the stern of this British freighter, added a new forward section, and rechristened her the *Halfpagus*.

Villers-Bocage

U.S.S. *Meredith* ☐ June 9

The *Meredith* struck a mine on June 8, but she stayed afloat. German bombers, menacing potential rescuers, sank the *Meredith* the next day. Thirty-five members of the crew were lost.

St. Lô

H.M.S. *Cato* ☐ July 6

S.S. *Empire Rosebery* ☐ August 24

A German mine tore through the British tanker *Empire Rosebery* and touched off gasoline fumes. The blast hurled the lifeboats into the sea. The ship, ripped in half, went down with 13 men.

U.S.S. *Susan B. Anthony* ☐ June 7

Built as a cargo and passenger line, the *Susan B. Anthony* became a troopship fondly called Susie. On June 7, she lay in two pieces, sundered by a mine. Every one of the more than 2,000 men aboard was saved as she sank.

U.S.S. *LST-523* ☐ June 19

Caen

Benouville

Lion-sur-Mer
Luc-sur-Mer
Saint-Aubin-sur-Mer

Courseulles-sur-Mer

Bernières-sur-Mer

SWORD

JUNO

Arromanches-les-Bains

GOLD

Bayeux

Longues-sur-Mer

Port-en-Bessin

Colleville-sur-Mer

Widerstandsnest 62
Saint-Laurent-sur-Mer
Vierville-sur-Mer

Grandcamp-les-Bains

OMAHA

Pointe du Hoc

Bay of the Seine

Canadian 3rd Infantry Division

British 50th Infantry Division

U.S. 1st Infantry Division

U.S. 29th Infantry Division

U.S. 4th Infantry Division

LCI(L) Landing Craft, Infantry (Large). These were 160 feet (48.8m) long. They could land 188 men on lowered bow ramps or carry 75 tons (68t) of cargo. U.S. Coast Guard coxswains manned many LCIs, including some at British and Canadian beaches.

LCF Landing Craft, Flak. These ran up to 196 feet (59.7m) long. A converted LCT, the LCF was armed with anti-aircraft guns to shield troops from close-range air attacks. At Utah Beach an LCF may have brought down a German aircraft.

LCM Landing Craft, Mechanized. Up to 56 feet (17.1m) long, the LCMs were the smallest landing craft capable of carrying a tank. Early in the invasion, LCMs delivered troops and demolition teams to destroy German beach defenses.

RHINO FERRY This was a wide pontoon raft, 176 feet (53.6m) long, used to carry LST cargo to shore. Members of the Navy's Construction Battalions, known as Seabees, invented and built these dependable, slow moving craft.

I saw a lot of things that day which I don't even want to talk about. Guys yelling for help. Guys going to their mates. I saw one fellow go out and try to rescue another, and an 88 landed. The two of them went up in the air and came down like a rubber ball.

A little time later, we went up the hill inside the white tracer markers. By that time, some of the soldiers started to get up the hill. They were beginning to knock off the Germans in the bunkers. I went up inside our unit's white markers. There we found what was left of our outfit. Originally, there was maybe 250 or 300 guys, and I only saw maybe about 20 or 30 up there. The commanding officer at the time was Commander Cooper. So we just got up there, and we sat down. The next thing I know Cooper yells, "Vernon! Coombs! Take all these wounded men down!" It must have been some of our men and some of the Army guys. They were all bandaged, and anybody who could walk. Now we had to go back through it again—back to the beach to board a hospital ship. Vernon took the front; I took the back. We had them all put their hands on their shoulders, and we went down in the white tape marks. As we

marched them back down, 88 mms were still landing on the beach. We had to get them out to the LCIs pulling in. We marched them up the ramp, but they made us stay with them.

I found out later, there was about seven or eight of them from our outfit who got through to the obstacles. One chief petty officer and the five Army men from our boat never got out of the water.

We didn't have any backup. Imagine all the tanks that were coming in, floating in the water; I didn't see one tank make it. They sank with the men in them. So we didn't have any tanks on the beach firing up at the hill, protecting us. It was a real rough day. Thank God there were no German planes up that day. All I could see were American planes going over, and they looked beautiful.

It was a very bleak, stormy day. My most vivid memory of that day is staying low. I never knew there was so much firepower like that. You can't imagine bullets hitting the sand, 88s going over your head. Explosions. Everywhere is the smell of death. You heard moaning, guys screaming, the smell of gunpowder in the air. ■

—Richard Coombs

RIGHT: Invasion forces from ports all across southwest England gathered at a staging area dubbed "Piccadilly Circus" in the English Channel south of Portsmouth and sailed to the Normandy invasion beaches along a corridor called "The Spout," which had been cleared of German mines. Some 5,000 ships and landing craft took part in D-Day operations, and the number grew to nearly 7,000 within the next ten days.

Europe June 6, 1944
(1939 boundaries)
- Axis-controlled area
- Allied-controlled area
- Neutral country

0   300
0   300

THE ALLIES AND THE AXIS
Adolf Hitler and his Nazi Party took over Germany and, in 1939, started war in Europe by attacking Poland. They conquered Norway, Denmark, Belgium, the Netherlands, France, and Balkans. England stood alone. In 1940 Germany, Italy, and Japan formed the Axis. Then in 1941 Germany invaded the Soviet Union. The Russians were on the offensive by 1944. With D-Day, Hitler was forced to fight in the west as well as in the east and in Italy: the Allies had taken Rome on June 4.

U.S.S. _Tide_ ☐ June 7

S.S. _Norfalk_ ☐ July 20

H.M.S. _Minster_ ☐ June 8

S.S. _Charles Morgan_ ☐ June 10

U.S.S. _Corry_ ◼ June 6
Within minutes after hitting a mine, the _Corry_ broke amidships. The crew was ordered to abandon ship, and spent two hours dodging artillery shells in the frigid sea. Of the _Corry's_ 284 men, 260 survived.

Carentan

• Isigny-sur-Mer

HIGH-TIDE MARK

UTAH

• Ste. Mere Eglise

U.S.S. _Glennon_ ☐ June 10

U.S.S. _YMS-304_ ☐ July 30

Saint-Vaast-la-Hougue

Valognes

S.S. _Leopoldville_ ☐ December 24
A Belgian steamer formerly in the Congo service, the _Leopoldville_ sunk after being torpedoed by a U-boat. Although 802 men were killed, another 1,653 were ferried ashore before the ship sank or survived their ordeal in the frigid waters.

Cherbourg

S
E   W
N

GERMAN MINES
Mines sank or damaged some 40 Allied vessels off Normandy. It could have been worse. German bureaucratic squabbles limited mine laying, and most mines in crucial zones had timers that left them duds by D-Day.

Barfleur

Pointe de Barfleur

Scale varies in this perspective. Distance from Le Havre to Cherbourg is 80 miles (129 km).

Scale for landing craft silhouettes
0 ft   100
0 m   50

DUKW The "Duck" was a 31-foot (9.5m), six-wheel amphibious truck that could carry 25 fully equipped soldiers or 5,000 pounds of cargo. Slow at sea, it could hit 50 miles an hour (80.5kph) on roads. High seas and overloading swamped many Ducks on D-Day.

Allied invasion wrecks June 1944–December 1945
(Remaining as of March 2002)

Type of ship
- Cargo ship
- Destroyer
- Landing ship
- Minesweeper
- Troopship

Cause of sinking
- ☐ Enemy action
- ◻ Mine
- ☐ Torpedo

Land key
- ◼ German artillery

Other type of loss
- ○ Barge
- ○ Landing craft
- ○ Pontoon
- ● Ship
- ○ Tank
- ○ Other

Scale for ship silhouettes
0 ft   100
0 m   50

SOURCES: SHIPWRECKS BY BERTRAND SCIBOZ AND MARC VIOLET, EUROPEAN SUBAQUATIC RESEARCH CENTER; BATHYMETRY BY NATIONAL INSTITUTE OF SEA SCIENCE AND TECHNOLOGY (FRANCE); LAND RELIEF BY SCOTT GOWAN, WORLDSAT INTERNATIONAL INC.; CONSULTANT, JACK A. GREEN, U.S. NAVAL HISTORICAL CENTER
NATIONAL GEOGRAPHIC MAPS

TOP: The minesweeper USS *Tide* burns after striking a mine near the northern end of the Carbonnet Bank on D+1. The bank extended southeast from the Îles St. Marcouf and ran generally parallel to Utah Beach, astride the boat lanes between the transport area and the shore. The *Tide* is flanked by a torpedo boat, PT-509, at left, and another minesweeper, the USS *Pheasant,* both of which have rushed to her aid. The *Tide* sank while under tow to England.

BOTTOM: LCI-85 had nearly reached Omaha's Fox Green Beach when she was snagged by a Belgian gate while still in water too deep to disembark her passengers. German field guns near the Colleville draw immediately took the LCI under fire. She was struck repeatedly and set ablaze, and the gangways were blasted from the bow. Pulling free from the obstacle only widened the gaping hole in her bottom. The LCI was doomed, but its crew managed to transfer all the casualties to another vessel before it sank. LCI-85 was transporting much of the 16th RCT's medical battalion personnel, including its forty-four-man platoon of litter bearers. On the far left of the deck a medic clings to a life raft while beside him another lies wounded on a stretcher and a third sprawls dead against the craft's superstructure with an unrolled stretcher extending over his shredded upper torso. On the right are some of the LCI's Coast Guard crew. A Navy censor painted out the face of the wounded medic, and at the lower right a long strip of deck was airbrushed over to obscure the faces of the dead and severely injured awaiting transfer.

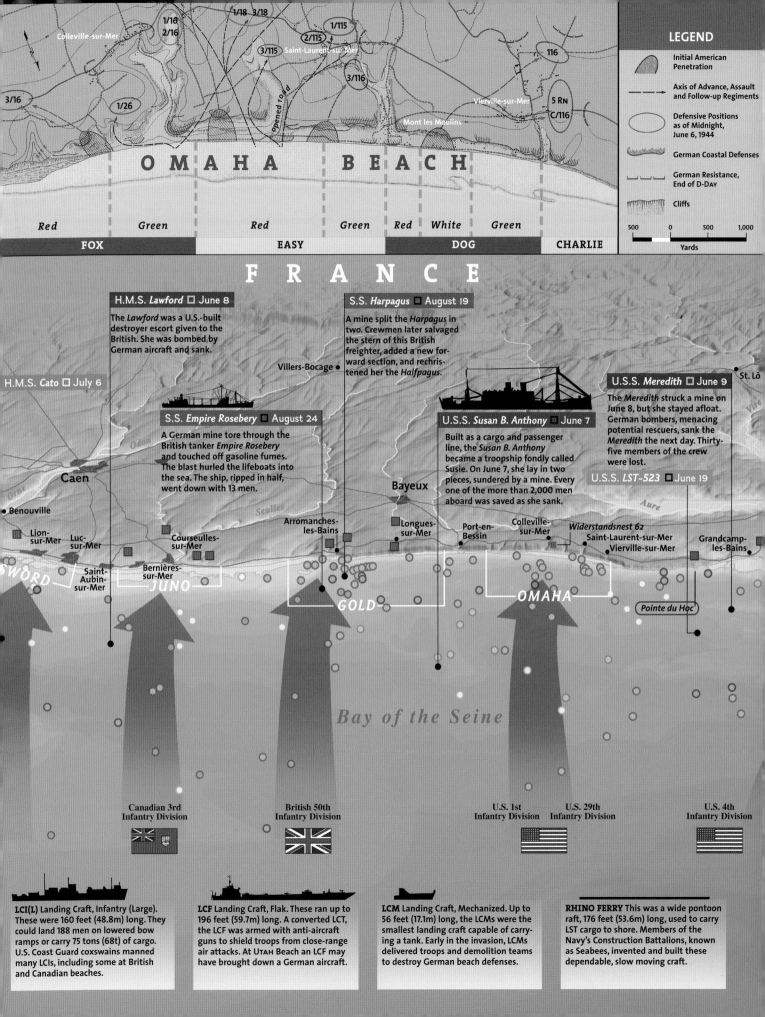

OMAHA BEACH (map)

Colleville-sur-Mer • 1/16 2/16 • 1/18 3/18 • 1/115 2/115 3/115 • Saint-Laurent-sur-Mer • 1/116 • 3/116 • 116 • Vierville-sur-Mer • 5 Rn C/116

3/16 • 1/26 • opened road • Mont les Moulins

O M A H A   B E A C H

Red | Green | Red | Green | Red | White | Green

FOX | EASY | DOG | CHARLIE

LEGEND

- Initial American Penetration
- Axis of Advance, Assault and Follow-up Regiments
- Defensive Positions as of Midnight, June 6, 1944
- German Coastal Defenses
- German Resistance, End of D-Day
- Cliffs

500 0 500 1,000
Yards

F R A N C E

H.M.S. Lawford ◻ June 8
The Lawford was a U.S.-built destroyer escort given to the British. She was bombed by German aircraft and sank.

S.S. Harpagus ◻ August 19
A mine split the Harpagus in two. Crewmen later salvaged the stern of this British freighter, added a new forward section, and rechristened her the Halfpagus.

Villers-Bocage

H.M.S. Cato ◻ July 6

U.S.S. Meredith ◻ June 9
The Meredith struck a mine on June 8, but she stayed afloat. German bombers, menacing potential rescuers, sank the Meredith the next day. Thirty-five members of the crew were lost.

St. Lô

S.S. Empire Rosebery ◻ August 24
A German mine tore through the British tanker Empire Rosebery and touched off gasoline fumes. The blast hurled the lifeboats into the sea. The ship, ripped in half, went down with 13 men.

U.S.S. Susan B. Anthony ◻ June 7
Built as a cargo and passenger line, the Susan B. Anthony became a troopship fondly called Susie. On June 7, she lay in two pieces, sundered by a mine. Every one of the more than 2,000 men aboard was saved as she sank.

U.S.S. LST-523 ◻ June 19

Caen
Benouville
Lion-sur-Mer
Luc-sur-Mer
Saint-Aubin-sur-Mer
Berniéres-sur-Mer
Courseulles-sur-Mer
Arromanches-les-Bains
Bayeux
Longues-sur-Mer
Port-en-Bessin
Colleville-sur-Mer
Widerstandsnest 62
Saint-Laurent-sur-Mer
Vierville-sur-Mer
Grandcamp-les-Bains
Aure

SWORD | JUNO | GOLD | OMAHA | Pointe du Hoc

Bay of the Seine

Canadian 3rd Infantry Division | British 50th Infantry Division | U.S. 1st Infantry Division | U.S. 29th Infantry Division | U.S. 4th Infantry Division

LCI(L) Landing Craft, Infantry (Large). These were 160 feet (48.8m) long. They could land 188 men on lowered bow ramps or carry 75 tons (68t) of cargo. U.S. Coast Guard coxswains manned many LCIs, including some at British and Canadian beaches.

LCF Landing Craft, Flak. These ran up to 196 feet (59.7m) long. A converted LCT, the LCF was armed with anti-aircraft guns to shield troops from close-range air attacks. At UTAH Beach an LCF may have brought down a German aircraft.

LCM Landing Craft, Mechanized. Up to 56 feet (17.1m) long, the LCMs were the smallest landing craft capable of carrying a tank. Early in the invasion, LCMs delivered troops and demolition teams to destroy German beach defenses.

RHINO FERRY This was a wide pontoon raft, 176 feet (53.6m) long, used to carry LST cargo to shore. Members of the Navy's Construction Battalions, known as Seabees, invented and built these dependable, slow moving craft.

TOP: Soldiers manning a 20-mm battery on the bow of an LCI return fire on a German strongpoint along the bluffs during one of their craft's dashes to the beach. Although the LCI's larger cousin, the LST, made only "administrative" landings, LCIs regularly performed in the assault role, with their five 20-mm guns providing suppressive fire through the smoke and haze or engaging specific German targets. Two LCIs were destroyed on OMAHA Beach, and a third was so badly damaged that she went down after leaving the shore.

RIGHT: Soldiers examine a Czech-built 210-mm gun that took part in the destruction of the destroyer USS *Corry*. The aircraft that was to maintain a smokescreen between the Corry and the three-gun St. Marcouf Battery, between UTAH Beach and Quinéville to the north, was shot down, leaving the destroyer exposed to German fire. As she maneuvered into another smokescreen, the *Corry* struck a mine amidships at 7 A.M. and soon broke in two. Within half an hour, the heavy cruiser USS *Tuscaloosa* succeeded in firing an 8-inch shell directly through one casemented gun's embrasure, destroying it and killing her crew. Other guns were temporarily disabled at different times throughout the day only to resume firing as soon as they were repaired, but the last gun was finally silenced at 6:30 P.M. D-DAY evening. During this action, the monitor HMS *Erebus* was credited with dropping a 15-inch shell on the battery's number two gun, putting it out of action permanently.

We were in the first wave at OMAHA. We got close to the beach when it was just starting to get light. We had to jump off the LCT over to the LCM with the dynamite and everything, in a rubber raft. The water was very rough. It's a wonder nobody fell in between. They would have been finished. We got in the LCMs—there were sixteen of them—and then we started going around in a circle. All the LCMs were full. Suddenly, they all straightened out in a line heading toward the beach. The water that day was terrible. Everybody was sick.

Then all hell broke loose. The battleships opened up with every gun they had. The missile launchers let go. It was unbelievable. The beach was being blitzkrieged. I figured, if they're hitting it that much, we'll be okay.

Germans were shooting down straight at us. We started to go in and about 100 to 125 feet (30.5–38.1m) off the beach, we got stuck on a sandbar. There's the coxswain piloting the craft and the gunner's mate yells up, "I see you're up there! I see you're up there!" He yells all kinds of curses. He opened up with the machine gun and started blasting to hell. This kid went crazy. He was laughing like anything.

I said, "Oh my God, here goes nothing." I was still sick, as was everybody else. But now we had to get off. The ramp went down, and the first five guys in the front were the five Army engineers. They were all braced and had the Primacord tied around them. We each had the sacks of dynamite. As you hit the water, the water was over your head. I was really weighted down and went to the bottom like everybody else, and we had these life belts. I had to press to come up. And I'd had a carbine in my hand. It went to the bottom and stayed there.

The job for me and this other young fellow was to put these markers up on the beach. We started to go in. As we started up the beach, they opened up with everything. They had us pinned down. The rest of the team started getting out of the water, but I heard the five Army guys never got out. The others started heading up the beach. How they ever got up that beach, I don't know. By the time we tried to find where they'd gone, we must have been a hundred feet (30.5m) over this way, and I started following the other guy with the pole. I had mine, and we just got lost from those fellows. We really got pinned down by fire. You couldn't even stand up, it was so bad. My friend's pole was machine-gunned right out of his hand, so I yelled over to him. He was okay. At that time, I must have left my pole, and I couldn't find where the other fellows had gone.

We started to crawl up the beach. You stood up, you were dead. Machine-gun bullets were hitting the sand, 88-mm shells were coming over our head, mortars and everything. So we just kept crawling up the beach. I told the other fellow to take off his knapsack. We left those by some obstacles.

We kept crawling. I don't know how much time went by, but we found one of the guys who was on our crew, and he was hit in the leg. We tried to move him. He kept telling us to go on ahead while he waited for the medics. We reached the seawall and laid there for a while. I remember there was an Army man next to me. He looked up and got a bullet right through the head. He just rolled over, and the blood kept pouring out of his head.

BELOW: Infantrymen, probably from the 1st Infantry Division's 18th Regimental Combat Team (RCT), head for the beach just east of the Saint Laurent Exit through one of the four EASY RED gaps in the obstacle belt that engineers raced to bulldoze before the rising tide made further work impossible. German defenses on both sides of the draw had been broken in a series of ad hoc assaults by elements of the 16th RCT within hours of their landing on OMAHA's EASY RED beach. The 18th RCT arrived against light opposition from German holdouts, even as fighting continued to rage at EASY GREEN to its west and FOX GREEN— where the soldiers appear to be looking—to the east.

BELOW: This LCT was designed with a shallow draft so tanks could easily drive onto an invasion beach, but the water is still deep enough to ensure that these reinforcements at UTAH Beach will be soaked up to their necks before they reach shore, D+1, June 7, 1944.

OPPOSITE, INSET: Army engineers and other personnel at the western end of OMAHA's FOX RED beach assist the crew of an LCVP that struck a mined stake at the edge of FOX GREEN. Although not intended as a landing area, the sea between this point and the USS *Arkansas*—almost obscured by the mist on the far horizon in Fire Support Area Four—filled up with LCVPs of the 16th RCT's Company L immediately after this photo was taken. Some elements of 3d Battalion Companies I and L were swept almost as far east as GEORGE Beach, and marched unhindered all the way back to FOX GREEN to join the assault. All or most of the early shots by Signal Corps photographer, Corporal Louis Weintraub, including this one, were initially labeled in England as coming from UTAH Beach. Although the Army quickly corrected the error, published captions based on the original mistake continue to appear some six decades after D-DAY.

I saw a lot of things that day which I don't even want to talk about. Guys yelling for help. Guys going to their mates. I saw one fellow go out and try to rescue another, and an 88 landed. The two of them went up in the air and came down like a rubber ball.

A little time later, we went up the hill inside the white tracer markers. By that time, some of the soldiers started to get up the hill. They were beginning to knock off the Germans in the bunkers. I went up inside our unit's white markers. There we found what was left of our outfit. Originally, there was maybe 250 or 300 guys, and I only saw maybe about 20 or 30 up there. The commanding officer at the time was Commander Cooper. So we just got up there, and we sat down. The next thing I know Cooper yells, "Vernon! Coombs! Take all these wounded men down!" It must have been some of our men and some of the Army guys. They were all bandaged, and anybody who could walk. Now we had to go back through it again—back to the beach to board a hospital ship. Vernon took the front; I took the back. We had them all put their hands on their shoulders, and we went down in the white tape marks. As we

marched them back down, 88 mms were still landing on the beach. We had to get them out to the LCIs pulling in. We marched them up the ramp, but they made us stay with them.

I found out later, there was about seven or eight of them from our outfit who got through to the obstacles. One chief petty officer and the five Army men from our boat never got out of the water.

We didn't have any backup. Imagine all the tanks that were coming in, floating in the water; I didn't see one tank make it. They sank with the men in them. So we didn't have any tanks on the beach firing up at the hill, protecting us. It was a real rough day. Thank God there were no German planes up that day. All I could see were American planes going over, and they looked beautiful.

It was a very bleak, stormy day. My most vivid memory of that day is staying low. I never knew there was so much firepower like that. You can't imagine bullets hitting the sand, 88s going over your head. Explosions. Everywhere is the smell of death. You heard moaning, guys screaming, the smell of gunpowder in the air. ▪

—Richard Coombs

BELOW: These medics disembarking on UTAH Beach are attached to an Engineer Special Brigade. They and the 4th Infantry Division's 22d Infantry Regiment landed at high tide north of the original assault beach in order to expedite the expansion of the beachhead.

He was on his back, and his hand and arms were wiggling like a beetle that's been turned on its back. He didn't want to turn it [his gun] loose, but he wasn't capable of using it. He'd been wiped out in the face, from his nose to his chin, and his teeth were exposed.

—John Talton

The hail of enemy machine-gun fire was only one of the obstacles facing the assault force, according to John Talton.

We got in ahead of the tanks and the combat infantry team on OMAHA. We landed first. I was the first man to reach the rock pile on EASY RED Beach alive on D-DAY, by chance and by accident.

We approached the beach, grounded, and immediately dropped the rail. I was standing between two fellows on the starboard side. One was practically decapitated, and the other was hit in the back. They just slid down in the boat. Next shell got the officer, the boat crew officer, and the boat crew chief. We got one more shell that wounded one of the Army men in the back. Our officer, who had just been hit in the forehead, said, "Grab a package and let's get the hell out of here." So we ran off the end of the ramp, and then we stood in fifteen feet (4.6m) of water, with all of our combat gear, including hobnail boots, all-thermal underwear, a suit of Army ODs [olive-drab military fatigues], and a field jacket, and then that wax-impregnated canvas that was supposed to be gas-proof, helmet, gas mask, canteen, and one carbine, and ninety rounds of ammunition.

I stood on the bottom and pushed my buddy to the top. I was five years older than him and didn't panic because I was raised on the coast and was a good swimmer. I managed to get out enough gear to move, and only had to swim or paddle about fifteen feet

JOHN TALTON

(4.6m) to where I could wade. I was still trying to drag a satchel of explosives but didn't have any igniters or Primacord.

The first time I tried firing my M1, I discovered that sand had rolled up into the barrel. I crawled back down to the beach and found a wounded crew chief and took away his Tommy gun. He was on his back, and his hand and arms were wiggling like a beetle that's been turned on its back. I have a very vivid picture of this. He fought me. He didn't want to turn it loose, but he wasn't capable of using it. He'd been wiped out in the face, from his nose to his chin, and his teeth were exposed.

I fired the gun about six rounds before it jammed. When a DUKW arrived, I beat on the side and asked for a weapon. They threw me a gun and two bandoliers of ammunition. I continued the fight as an infantryman, because I had no Primacord and the tide was at our feet.

One of the Army guys was working a mine detector when we saw Germans jump out of a manhole and run up a hill through the minefield. This guy followed right behind, marking the path with white tape. To my knowledge, that was the first opening on EASY RED Beach. The men started following him immediately, without orders. These men seemed to be self-motivated to me. They were like me. They followed without command, but they had one direction—forward. ■

—John Talton, Seaman Second Class, NCDU (US)

UTAH Beach

As the landing craft drew nearer to the shore, the smell of diesel fumes and vomit became mixed with that of cordite and smoke. Wave after wave arrived with clockwork precision—and promptly piled up on the beach. Ramps from the third wave of boats dropped into the surf to the sound of sporadic gunfire and explosions, and soldiers saw Army-Navy teams of demolition experts moving from obstacle to obstacle to place explosive charges.

Special Sherman tanks fitted to travel through water sat motionless but apparently undamaged, as officers peered intently at maps. The landings at UTAH had, indeed, occurred precisely on schedule, but nothing looked right. Where was the lighthouse that was supposed to be on their right? Where was the complex of blockhouses barring access to Exit 3's causeway across the marsh?

Brigadier General Theodore Roosevelt, Jr., assistant commander of the 4th Infantry Division, came ashore with the initial assault wave and didn't like what he saw. "The

moment I arrived at the beach," said Roosevelt, "I knew something was wrong, for there was a house by the seawall where none should have been." Soldiers recalled the general walking stiffly with his cane among the dunes and stray rounds as if examining the area for a real estate deal. Discovery of a windmill known to be near Exit 2 confirmed Roosevelt's suspicions: the early loss of two control boats to German mines, the smoke obscuring coastal landmarks, and the strong current had all conspired to push the neat formations of landing craft off course. The invasion had "slipped" two thousand yards (1,829m) to the south.

Thirty thousand men and 3,500 vehicles were slated to cross UTAH Beach by nightfall, and a decision had to be made quickly on whether they should proceed to the planned target area or follow behind the assault waves. The 4th Infantry Division had originally wanted to land at that very spot, but the Navy pointed out that the waters were so shallow that the

BELOW: Elements of the 4th Infantry Division's 8th RCT move to the crest of UTAH Beach's low dunes, while other soldiers remain dug-in along the seawall. UTAH received steady, but not particularly heavy or accurate, German artillery fire during the morning of June 6. It was virtually impossible to dig safe fox-holes in the soft sand that extended inland at least 150 yards (137m), with dunes stretching out to as much as 1,000 yards (914.4m) in some places. Consequently, the seawall became the favored spot for foxholes and slit trench-es: its sturdy face provided at least one side that was safe from cave-ins.

ABOVE: LCMs, at right, and LCIs, at center and right, join a parade of LCTs and LCVPs ferrying men and vehicles to UTAH Beach.

early waves of assault troops would have to cross more than a thousand yards (914.4m) at low tide compared to roughly four hundred (365.8m) farther north. The tactical eyes of the Germans saw the same wide, vulnerable beach and had noted as well that a landing this far south would offer little room for maneuver because it was so close to the estuary. Rather than waste time and scarce resources, the Germans concentrated their defensive efforts farther to the north at the more likely invasion site, and the 4th Division was greeted by little more than some long-range shelling.

General Roosevelt called a quick meeting of his battalion commanders to sort things out. Their planned objectives were two thousand yards (1,829m) up the beach, but the men and equipment were fast piling up, and German artillery was apparently ranging in on the barrage balloons that floated like beacons over the larger landing craft. More fundamentally, the Beach Obstacle Demolition Teams and Naval Combat Demolition Units had all landed with the division at the "wrong" place and, without waiting for orders, had begun their work. By the time Roosevelt figured out exactly where his men had landed, the demolition experts were already fully engaged in removing obsta-

cles, and, thanks to the lighter-than-expected enemy resistance, they were doing their job at an extremely brisk pace. The specially trained teams would not be available for a subsequent—and much tougher—second landing.

Soldiers were already beginning to move through Exit 2 toward a linkup with the paratroopers, and there was only one decision to make. "I'm going ahead with the troops," said Roosevelt to the chief engineer. "You get word to the Navy to bring them in. We're going to start the war from here."

While the men at OMAHA were struggling through a firestorm of bullets and shells, soldiers at UTAH met light resistance. Second Lieutenant Walter Bodlander's job was to interrogate German prisoners. (A Jewish native of Germany who spoke perfect German, Bodlander had escaped the Nazis and enlisted in the U.S. Army to try to defeat them.) Although he found that they had little to say, he did encounter a famous American general.

We landed on UTAH Beach about half an hour after H-HOUR, and there was just a little bit of machine-gun fire and a few mortar shells falling on the beach. It was practically the easiest thing in the world; there was no major fighting at all in the first half-hour or so. We immediately captured a few Germans who were stunned from the bombing. They were in one of the bombed-out buildings. I stayed on the beach maybe a half-hour, trying to interrogate them, but they had nothing to say. They were as confused as we were. Continuing off the beach and up the dune, we came to where there were supposed to be trees—oak on the right and pine on the left. But there were no signs of anything familiar.

One of our communication jeeps was hit directly. Inside was a very good friend of mine, a communications officer whom I had befriended. Several people were killed. He was badly wounded and about to die. Nobody was there to help, so I gave him my morphine and killed him.

—Walter Bodlander

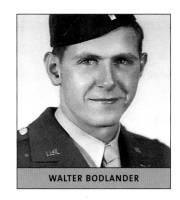

WALTER BODLANDER

LEFT: Casualties of the German shelling on UTAH Beach.

4TH INFANTRY DIVISION

The U.S. 4th Infantry Division landed on UTAH Beach amid light resistance, and immediately linked up with the airborne divisions that had landed beyond the beaches. It then attacked north up the Cotentin Peninsula, reaching Cherbourg's main defense ring on June 21, 1944. On June 25, it fought its way into the fortress-city and began three weeks of hedgerow fighting on July 6. The 4th Infantry Division played a central role in Operation COBRA by punching a hole in the German line on June 25 and by repelling German counterattacks around Avranches. On August 25, the 4th entered Paris with the French forces.

BELOW: An amphibious
Sherman tank hidden
within a fully erected flotation screen. The collapsible
steel frame and canvas
bloomer were anchored to
a boat-shaped base, fitted
completely around the
tank's hull. The screen and
frame were lifted by sending compressed air into
thirty-six vertical tubes
sewn to the inside of the
canvas screen, with por-
tions of the frame snapping
tight when full height was
achieved. Upon reaching
shore, the air was released,
vertical struts were
unsnapped, and the whole
rig collapsed down to the
boat-shaped base. A tall,
auxiliary steering platform,
made of wood, would be
jettisoned as quickly as
the fighting allowed,
but the time-consuming
removal of the flotation
structure would have to
wait for nightfall.

At a crossroads, we consulted a map, when suddenly artillery fire opened on us. We learned
never to stop at a crossroads, because that's
where the Germans liked to train their guns.

There on the beach was General Roosevelt,
the son of Teddy Roosevelt. He was a wonderful man. He must have been in his seventies.
He was unarmed, carrying only his cane. He
landed in the first wave. During the first four
or five days, I came to know him well. He
came up to us on the front lines in Normandy
to inform us about what was happening on
the beach. He told us not to worry, because
the first ships were landing and more troops
were coming. Then he disappeared and went
back down to the beach, where he told them
we were moving inland and had already
captured Sainte Mère-Eglise. Then he came
back to us.

Roosevelt was very courageous. I remember him asking how much ammunition we
had. The first week, ammunition was very
tight. I had a machine gun on the jeep and
about five hundred rounds, but I was told to
give up two hundred rounds because others
farther up needed it immediately. General
Roosevelt told us not to worry. Even though
we were low on ammunition, he assured us
more ships were coming the next day when
the weather improved. ▪

—Walter Bodlander

Amphibious Shermans

One of the principal lessons from the British
debacle at Dieppe had been that the infantry
would need the immediate support of tanks
and field guns if they were to smash through
even modest defenses. To respond to this need,
the British developed a variety of modifications
to armored vehicles, often called *funnies*, to
speed the seizure of invasion beaches. U.S.
forces rejected many as unnecessary, relying
instead on the all-purpose Sherman bulldozer
tank. However, they wholeheartedly accepted
the idea of specially designed Sherman tanks
with a duplex drive (DD) to operate either
tracks or twin propellers that enabled them
to "swim" ashore, independently of landing
craft. Training exercises soon demonstrated
that a DD tank suffered from one fundamental
drawback. Its accordionlike canvas flotation
device, or *bloomer,* which rose high above the
turret and kept out the water with the help
of a bilge pump, could be swamped or stoved
in during heavy seas. The propensity to plum-
met like a stone on such occasions was so
alarming that crewmen were issued a submarine escape apparatus—a dubious morale
booster of little practical value, since sinkings
usually occurred with no warning and the
bulky, strap-on systems impeded quick exits
from the drivers' hatches.

At UTAH Beach, the officer commanding the
last surviving control boat, Navy Lieutenant
(jg) John B. Ricker, realized that the DD tanks
would never make it through the high, wind-
tossed Channel seas, and ordered his LCTs to
carry them past the drop-off point some five
thousand yards (4,572m) offshore. Upon reaching calmer waters, roughly eighteen hundred
yards (1,646m) out, the DDs rumbled down the
ramps, careened forward into the ocean, and
headed straight for the beach after righting
themselves. With the exception of four tanks
that went down when their LCT struck a mine,
the entire 70th Tank Battalion successfully
waded to shore. But while the twenty-eight
Sherman DDs at UTAH found themselves relatively unemployed at first because of the
scarcity of German defenders, ten miles (16km)

Didn't they get the change of orders? They're trying to swim in their DDs over there! Why in God's name don't they bring in their tanks like we're doing over here?

—Wayne Robinson in *Barbara*

to the east at OMAHA, nearly half of the sixty-four DDs never made it to the beach, and the rest found themselves embroiled in a desperate battle for survival.

The LCTs carrying two tank battalions to OMAHA were also ordered to bypass their launch point almost three nautical miles from the beach, and, directed to bring their charges to within a thousand yards (914.4m). Inexplicably, the battalion on the left, or eastern, flank was released at the originally planned six thousand yards (5,486m), with disastrous consequences. Of the 471st Tank Battalion's thirty-two DDs, all went down in the high seas except for three that were

deposited at the obstacle line by an LCT with a jammed ramp and two that miraculously reached land under their own power. Together with the DDs of the 473d Battalion on the right (most of which reached the beach) and two companies of Shermans, brought directly to shore by landing craft, they provided the only direct fire support against the machine-gun nests and fieldpieces decimating the ranks of the two infantry regiments assaulting OMAHA. In addition to the DDs resting on the Channel floor, at least forty-one of the two battalions' conventional, DD, and bulldozer tanks were destroyed or disabled by mid-afternoon.

Surf-landed Sherman

ABOVE: E Company soldiers of the 1st Infantry Division's 16th RCT huddle behind hedgehog obstacles and a pair of Company A, 741st Tank Battalion M-4 Shermans fitted with wading trunks (left and center). The trunks enabled the Shermans' exhausts and air intakes to operate even if the hulls were submerged, and photographer Robert Capa reported that the tank at left was knocked out. Two of the 741st's five surviving DD tanks from its B and C Companies are at right, and their close proximity may indicate that they are part of the lucky trio of Shermans brought all the way to shore by their LCT skipper. The lead DD with a life preserver hanging over its side is beginning to lower its

Bloody OMAHA

The same coastal tide that pushed the UTAH Beach force south of its target—and largely out of harm's way—played havoc with the landings at OMAHA. Unlike the nearly empty beach rapidly exploited by the 4th Infantry Division, the assault regiments here confronted fearsome bluffs that encased the pebbled shore almost like a wall. Worse yet, the 16th and 116th Regimental Combat Teams (RCTs) of the 1st and 29th Infantry Divisions, respectively, had prepared to confront a much different enemy from the one that now occupied the area. Instead of a single reinforced battalion— roughly eight hundred men—of a static coastal division made up principally of Russian and Polish conscripts, the myriad fortifications built

into the bluffs and guarding the few heavily mined draws leading inland were now manned by a full regiment of the German 352d Infantry Division, a "mobile" formation whose cadre were all veterans of the vicious battles on the Eastern Front. Just as Allied military intelligence and the French Resistance had missed the fact that the nearby guns of Pointe du Hoc were not where they were thought to be, the 352d had remained undetected, even though it had been taken out of the German Seventh Army reserves and moved to the coast several months earlier.

None of the major fortifications inherited by the 352d were destroyed during the pre-invasion naval and air bombardments. All were fully manned and ready along the seven thousand yards (6,401m) of OMAHA Beach, and heavy weapons opened up on the assault

Surf-landed Sherman   DD Sherman lowering canvas   DD Sherman

waves when they closed to about a thousand yards (914.4m) from the surf line. High seas had already swamped at least ten small LCVPs, containing three hundred men, as well as nearly every DUKW amphibious truck carrying the field artillery for the drive inland. More artillery was lost when an LCT struck a mine and sank. Now the landing craft, many of which had been pushed off course to the east, were being raked by an unseen enemy from bluffs only dimly visible beyond a morning mist mixed with smoke and dust.

The American landing force started to pull apart under fire. Only at the extreme right flank of the target, where the westerly winds were blowing away the smoke, could landmarks be consistently observed. The assault forces here, a company each from the Rangers and the 116th RCT, were the only troops to land opposite their assigned objectives. Tragically, the nearest friendly troops waded into the surf nearly five hundred yards (457.2m) to their left, and by the time the 473d's tanks came ashore, the Rangers had suffered approximately 50 percent casualties and the 116th's company had ceased to exist. The Virginia National Guardsmen of A Company, 2d Battalion, lost roughly 190 of their 197 men in less than ten minutes to intense small-arms fire; 20 of the dead and 15 of the wounded came from the small, rural community of Bedford.

At UTAH, the landing force had drifted much farther down the shoreline but had hit the beach intact and en masse. Here, the special teams aboard the command boats could do little to coordinate the final runs from the line of departure. The displacements to the left occurred in a haphazard manner, with the flotation device, and both still have their wooden auxiliary steering platform towering above the canvas. This portion of OMAHA's EASY RED Beach is being heavily raked by machine-gun fire from a bunker to the right, outside the frame of Robert Capa's photograph, but, thanks to the tanks and the persistence of the infantry, this was the first section of OMAHA Beach to be seized. Some infantry in the distant mist can already be seen as having moved past the shale at the high-tide line. Out of this image and to the right is a third Company A tank with wading trunks, and high over the shore is the faint outline of the murderous, 150-foot (46m) bluffs.

intermingling of units becoming most extreme on the eastern flank. Each assault company had been briefed only on the specific objectives they were to seize, so landing on a strange piece of beach immediately threw the operation off stride. Extremely heavy defensive fire isolated the various Allied groups from one another, making improvised missions extremely difficult. And the tendency of soldiers to use beach obstacles for cover meant that a unit reaching the seawall above the high-water mark might well have soldiers spread as far back as 200 or 250 yards (183 or 228.6m) into the obstacle belt and taking refuge behind any number of derelict vehicles in between.

The chaos on OMAHA Beach grew as follow-up waves poured more and more men and machines into the smoking cauldron. Few demolition teams arrived at their assigned spots in the western, or 29th Division, sector, and large numbers landing in the 1st Division sector with the 16th RCT were killed outright. Heartbreaking losses of equipment plagued the operation as the tide rolled in at four feet

(1.2m) per minute—or eighty yards (73.2m) per hour. Army and Navy demolitions experts succeeded in blowing five large gaps through the obstacles by 7 A.M. and made progress at three more spots, only to find that they could scrounge only enough marker poles and buoys to delineate just one lane. Within an hour, several large LCIs lay burning in the surf, and at 8:30 the beachmaster ordered all landings of large assault craft to cease because the lower stratas of deadly obstacles were now rendered invisible by a blanket of water.

Soldiers creeping in with the tide and the flotsam of dead bodies were being packed into an ever-shrinking band of surf. Lengthy segments of beach contained no troops whatsoever, while other portions saw carpets of soldiers huddled against the seawall. In the 29th Division's sector, the seawall marked the high tide of invasion, since not one soldier or tank had been able to move beyond it an hour and a half after landing. Few tankers, in fact, were still operating their machines on the beach, but those that were—particularly B and C

Companies of the 473d—seemed to be leading charmed lives as they zeroed in on machine-gun nests and strongpoints. But there were simply not enough of them. Having lost so many vehicles before even reaching shore, they fell far short of the critical mass needed to break the defenses. Tanks were being picked off—one here, one there—but suddenly they found themselves receiving a level of fire support that no one on either side had expected.

Men of the Virginia National Guard, such as Sergeant Felix Branham of the 29th Division's 116th Infantry Regiment, were among the very first to hit OMAHA Beach.

My boat team was the first team to reach our assembly area. We were maybe two hundred yards (183m) to the left of A Company, and they just piled onto that beach. We moved out. A Company was from Bedford, Virginia. Most of them never got out of the water. Their landing craft either sunk or they got off into deep water and drowned.

It was raining, the wind was blowing, and the boat was rocking. It was awful. Many fellows became seasick; fortunately, I didn't. The water came over the side as we rode over the bumpy waves. You could see OMAHA Beach when we dropped anchor, although, at the time, we didn't know its name. It looked so much like Slapton Sands. One of the guys got up the nerve to look over the side. He said, Not another dry run.

Shells were flying overhead and bursting. Flares were going off. Turmoil. It was awful. I don't know any other way to describe it. I hit the beach at 6:30, H-HOUR. We hit a sandbar. I got into the water up to my knee, and the tide was rising a foot (30cm) every ten minutes. When our boat team landed, one of our men was killed. He was going to be twenty-one on June 21. We had kidded him back at the barracks, saying he'd never live to see it because he'd get killed when he hit the beach. Sure enough, he was the first one killed from my team. I had just told him to move up. He had said, Okay, and was shot, splattering against my face. We knew we had to get off

When I came to, part of my leg was blown away. I looked over to one of the other fellows. His leg was pulled back over his shoulder and he was unconscious.

—Felix Branham

that beach. You stayed, you died. I never spent as long as an hour and a half there.

The bad part about being in a National Guard unit was seeing guys die who I had grown up with, gone to school with. But when you saw them die, you knew there was nothing you could do to help them. It was now a matter of survival—get off the beach. We lost four men at OMAHA Beach.

We had good leaders and officers. We had outstanding noncommissioned officers. Every man could be an officer. And he had to do it on D-DAY. A private might become a commanding officer. If everything was lost, and he had to take over with just a few men, he would do that. ▪

—Felix Branham

One man experienced the assault on OMAHA Beach from an unusual vantage point—a small river barge. Seaman Albert Rogers of the Royal Navy felt his diminutive craft dwarfed by the monstrous ships surrounding him.

I worked on LBVMs—landing barge vehicles, medium—the smallest landing craft to leave England to go across the Channel to Normandy under their own power. These were the barges used on the Thames, and they affixed a ramp to the stern. Originally, these were meant for vehicles, but the ramp inside the barge was so steep that the trucks could not get out of the barges. Then they tried with infantry. And they found that it was still too steep for them to rush out to hit the beach at the right time. They ultimately decided to use them for supplies. Our particular barge had four hundred cans of petrol.

Every maneuver we went on, we thought it was the real thing, but it wasn't until the actual 5th of June when all the big ships were lined up. We had our little barges, and of course they were all laughing at us because we were so small and little in the water. They yelled, "Why don't you row?" We left on the 5th to land a day later—which would have been the 5th if they had launched the invasion as planned. Since we had no wireless, we weren't recalled. So we carried on because our speed was four knots. Traveling through the

night we heard things—ships here, ships there—but we couldn't see them because there were no lights. And then when dawn broke, we saw all these ships everywhere. It was frightening because we were so small. As they passed us, we got the wash just like a cork in a bath. One of the chaps got washed over the side. I managed to jump and grab him, because he couldn't swim. We got him back on board and carried on.

All we had was a compass reading; we didn't know where we were. [Then it was time for us to go in.] That was at 9:20 A.M. on the 6th of June. And, of course, when we got there we saw a load of LCTs, LCVPs, and LCIs on the beach. There was a lot of dead here

ABOVE AND RIGHT: Soldiers trudge past the last group of obstacles toward the shale marking the hide-tide line in a chilling filmstrip by an Army cinematographer. In the final frame, enlarged, the rear most of four men is cut down by German bullets while another has stumbled or perhaps been shot. Although these troops are often reputed to be from the 29th Infantry Division's 116th RCT, the only area of OMAHA Beach that had stakes as the last obstacle belt was in the 1st Infantry Division area running east from the Colleville draw.

RIGHT: Soldiers aboard an LCI headed for UTAH Beach are lost in their own private thoughts as they prepare to land on French soil. The silhouette of an M1 Garand rifle can be clearly seen in the waterproof Pliofilm bag of the soldier in the background. Oddly, although the troops are wearing standard olive-drab gas detectors on their left arms, there are no gas mask bags on their chests. The fiber storage tube hanging around the neck of the man in the foreground contains either a rifle grenade that can be affixed to his Garand or an individual 60-mm mortar round to supplement the stock of his company's heavy-weapons platoon.

1ST INFANTRY DIVISION

The U.S. 1st Infantry Division assaulted OMAHA Beach in the face of fierce opposition by the German 352d Infantry Division and reached the St. Lô–Bayeux highway on June 10, 1944. For the next five weeks, the division inched its way south through the tangled *bocage* country as it fought to expand the Allied lodgment in Normandy. On July 26, the 1st Infantry Division streamed through the hole that had been punched in the German lines during Operation COBRA, and its seizure of the Sée River crossings five days later allowed the U.S. Third Army's breakout across France to proceed at breathtaking speed.

and there. With our particular landing craft, we had to go in stern first because that's where the ramp was. And, of course, we had to go in at what they call half-tide and beach. Since we had four hundred cans of petrol on our boat, and as small as we were, we hit that beach and we stayed there, kept well away from [the fight]. Every now and again you had incoming shells drop over, and mortars. We were stuck where we were and couldn't run for cover. We had to stay within running distance of our craft, so when it was unloaded, we could get away as fast as we could.

After unloading the petrol, we went back to the ships and loaded up with other supplies. They told us to go farther down the beach. We didn't know it was OMAHA Beach then. I can't describe properly all the arms, legs, bodies, halves of bodies there, and they were still clearing them up then. I had seen bodies before in the Navy and had accepted that. But they weren't as close as they were there on the beaches. We saw the floating bodies, and people who were just dragging them out. There were so many bodies laying around. They talk about the three-minute mile. I'm afraid there were a lot of us there who did that in two minutes. And we were carrying equipment. ▪

—Albert Rogers, First Class Stoker, Royal Navy (UK)

🎤 *Men and supplies continually arrived as waves of landing craft made their way to the beaches. Many of those coming in the second wave, including Squad Leader Walter Ehlers, were from the 1st Infantry Division.*

The 18th Infantry Regiment was supposed to be the second wave, so we were loaded onto LCIs. These could hold nearly an entire company and they had ramps on both sides of the ship that came down. Some went off one side; some jumped off the other side. They moved up on the beach.

At about six o'clock in the morning, all heck broke loose. All kinds of firing began while airplanes flew over. There were probably about eight hundred airplanes in the air at one time. It was like a cloud cover of airplanes over us. Then all these ships fired on the shore, and we're out in these boats while the first wave was landing. The commander of my LCI said they needed more troops immediately for the beachhead. The first boats returned after dropping off the troops. They picked us up off the LCI. I call us the intermittent wave because we came in earlier than the second wave.

When we got out there in the water, we had to circle around 'til we got a few boats gathered together with the extra troops that they were sending in. As we arrived, bullets were buzzing around our heads, shells landing in the water. Approaching the beach was a terrible sight—bodies in the water; men

BELOW: The principal design feature of most landing barge vehicles, medium (LBVMs), and their major variants was an open hold and a starboard-side conning tower near the nine-foot (2.7m) stern access ramp. With a maximum speed of, at best, only three to five knots, even LCVPs could sail rings around these former workhorses of the Thames River and the London docks. The smallest LBs had no stern ramp, and all cargo had to be either winched into their forty-six-foot (14m) holds or carried aboard by hand. The largest LBs had holds of up to sixty feet (18.3m) in length and could carry three small trucks.

bailing water out of their sinking boats as fast as they could. Some sank anyway.

We landed on a sandbar rather than the beach. The ramp went down, and we jumped out of the boat. The first thing we know we're in water clear up to our necks. The little guys had it over their heads, but we just had to help them, and finally got up onto the beach itself.

Laying out there in the surf were more bodies. Defense obstacles with mines were supposed to keep the boats from going in there. Some of the boats hit them, and they were blown up. People were hiding around those and others laid on the beach, not moving. It was a gruesome sight. Then you'd see people hovering around the rocks as we came closer inland to the beach. Some of them didn't have their guns because they'd lost them in the water, things like that.

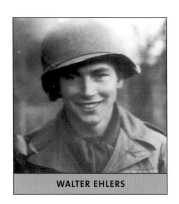

WALTER EHLERS

OPPOSITE, TOP: A machine gun crew moves west past some of the first wounded collected under the sheltering chalk cliffs at OMAHA's FOX RED Beach. The Army photographer noted that the crew belonged to the 16th RCT's 3d Battalion, which indicates that they are soldiers of L Company. The 2d Battalion's I Company also overshot their intended landing beach and passed this same outcrop on their way to the fighting at the Colleville draw.

OPPOSITE, BOTTOM: A mix of weaponless Army and Coast Guard personnel who had been forced into the water after their landing craft sank were collected in this sheltered spot, and either sent back to their ship or down the beach to their units. Some have not bothered to remove the double-tube life belts that were considerably less tight and uncomfortable after being deflated. Inflated belts lay discarded along the shore and at their feet. An aid station was set up here, and even treated 116th RCT troops that had drifted far east of their intended landing near the Les Moulins draw. Before late morning, when this area was largely abandoned because of the incoming tide, the station was visited by no fewer than three Army photographers, who may have been seeking respite from the heavy fighting further west.

I got up on the beach there and I asked the beachmaster where to head. He told me to just go up the path. If we went off the path, we'd go into a minefield. The mines had already been cleared by the men, because they didn't have any minesweepers there yet. We walked by guys laying left and right of the path, with legs blown off and other wounds. So we went on through. There were several rows of wire, and we got up to the last row of wire. It hadn't been blown yet. Some Bangalore torpedo men were there from the first wave. They had been pinned down and were unable to blow the wire. We saw that they had a Bangalore torpedo, and we asked them if they could use it to blow the last wire. They agreed, but as soon as they moved, they were shot at. I promised to keep the Germans pinned down while they moved. We laid out a fire, they put the Bangalore torpedo under the wire. The first guy got killed, so the second guy set it off and blew it. Then my squad and I went through. Next thing we're chasing Germans and captured a pillbox from the rear. We used satchel charges, but they don't blow apart from those. Even big Navy guns couldn't blow them apart. But we got it from the rear.

Amazingly, my whole squad and I went across the beach, and we didn't have any casualties. I don't know how we did that. We didn't have any casualties until about the 10th of June, when the first man in my squad was killed in action.

Since most of the men in Company L were replacements who hadn't seen combat, I told them that you had to fight as a unit. You had to say, Yes, somebody's probably going to get hurt; you just hope it isn't you. Nor can you stop because somebody else does. You got to keep going if you've got a mission to get done. I never had any of them desert me, so I was pretty lucky, I guess.

In my squad I had a combination of older and younger guys. I didn't have any problem with that until Normandy. One of the older guys was a replacement. He was sitting on a rock, and I said, "You better get off that rock. There are snipers and they're shooting at people!" He says, "I'll take care of that." I said, "No,

you won't. Get off that rock!" And he says, "I'm old enough to be your dad. You don't tell me what to do!" So I told him, "Get off that rock or get killed, because that's what's going to happen to you." They fired on him but didn't hit him. He finally got the message and got off the rock.

I would have hated to be Eisenhower in this thing and have to send all these guys on the beach like he had to. Taking a squad across is enough responsibility. Everybody wants to live, and you don't want to see anybody get killed. But that happens. It's part of the battle plan, I guess. Somebody's going to get it, unless you've got a complete victory without any casualties. They supported me; I supported them. I ran my squad a little bit different than the book said to do. They always told you to send out the scouts first, then the squad leader follows them, and the rest of the squad follows the squad leader. But I went out and led the squad and didn't use scouts. I always went out ahead myself because I knew where I was going, what I was doing, by the time I got into Normandy. So I was strictly a leader then. I was leading my squad, and they followed. They did everything that had to be done in order to get the objective completed. ■
—Walter Ehlers

Lieutenant Colonel William Gara of the 1st Infantry Division's engineers describes how he and his men felt when they realized that things weren't going well at the landing site.

We boarded the boats and were out at sea when we received word that the invasion had been postponed until the next day, the 6th, when there would be a break in the weather. These small boats were traveling at five knots, so it took two and half hours to go eleven miles (17.7km). Heavy seas and twenty-mile per hour (32kph) winds from the northwest created awful conditions for the seasick men. We heard a lot of firing from our battleships. Everything now was very tense. We noticed that the boats were drifting with the wind away from our target area.

During that two-and-a-half-hour trip, between the small boats being lowered into the sea until we could reach our rendezvous and move forward, there was a great deal of apprehension. We heard a lot of firing. We wondered whether or not the boats were going to get to their proposed landing sites, and it wasn't until maybe three hundred yards (274.3m) from shore that we could see that things were not going well. We could see that the underwater obstacle paths and gaps had not been opened, so we recognized that we were very likely going to be blown up. We knew what those three rows of underwater obstacles were like and could hear the enemy firing at us. We thought that perhaps by now the firing from our battleships and the cruisers and the rocket ships and the Air Force had done the job. We discovered that it wasn't so. The enemy had just hunkered down and waited for it to cease, since all of the firing must stop when the friendly troops began arriving. They came out of their hole and were waiting to give us a hard time.

Plans were for small boats to get as close to shore as possible and then drop the ramps, so that the troops didn't come in with water up to their shoulders. After all, the men were carrying equipment: gas masks, forty-pound (18.2kg) satchel charges, a rifle, extra ammunition, rations, etc. They were loaded down. The objective was to try to get those small boats as close to shore as possible once they passed by the underwater obstacles. Of course, it didn't happen. The landing craft were totally under the control of the Navy personnel. We had no say. They'd lower the ramp, and you'd just start running and swimming and wading to shore. We were swept one thousand to twelve hundred yards (914.4–1,097m) away from where we were supposed to land.

We were to have thirty-two DD tanks arrive in our sector alone, which was four miles (6.4km) wide. Our primary mission was knocking out the enemy pillboxes within the 1st Infantry Division sector. DD tanks were going to provide the initial artillery for us to fire directly at the pillboxes, the entrenchments, and, of course, enemy troops. Only

RIGHT: German machine-gun bullets kick spray high into the air as they bracket 16th or 116th RCT troops landing in the second wave at OMAHA Beach about H+1, or 7:30 A.M. More men follow them down the ramp of an LCI that carried two hundred or more soldiers, in addition to its crew, across the Channel.

OPPOSITE: Company E of the 16th RCT and demolitions teams made up of Army and Navy personnel take refuge from German bullets among a devil's garden of ramps, mined stakes, and hedgehogs east of the Saint Laurent draw. This was one of the few places along OMAHA Beach where the three obstacle types were thickly, yet randomly, intermingled. Some soldiers pushed forward in the face of German fire while those that didn't were forced inexorably toward the shore amid the flotsam of wooden obstacle fragments, discarded life belts, Pliofilm wrappings, and corpses.

four were able to get through the heavy seas; the others were swamped. Within moments of landing, those four were knocked out. Now, without artillery fire, no gaps were opened up and marked in the underwater beach obstacles. Two were opened but not marked, so we didn't know where they were. As a result, the small boats bumbled their way into shore. No gun emplacements or pillboxes were knocked out. The heavy fire from the battleships all went beyond the shore area because they couldn't get a good reading on where the

enemy was firing from. Air bombardment went inland, again due to overcast conditions. There was not a single trench or shell hole created for the troops to run into when they arrived. Practically the entire area of OMAHA Beach was unscarred.

The first four hours were a fiasco, scrambling tooth and nail to get ashore and work your way up. Men were hung up at the landing points. It was really very miserable. I was supposed to land straight at a beautiful building right in the center of OMAHA Beach. We landed twelve hundred yards (1,097m) to the east and had to work our way back to the area where the fighting was. So for the first three or four hours it was merely a matter of holding on and scrambling with infantry fire to get at least a toehold on OMAHA Beach.

At this point, my credit goes to the U.S. Navy. There were destroyers about seven to eight miles (11.3–12.9km) offshore that were waved in. They brought them in, so that these destroyers were about seven hundred yards (640m) from shore. They lowered their five-inch guns and they began shooting at these pillboxes, and they were our only supply of artillery for the first four hours of the battle of OMAHA Beach. Then, slowly but surely, we worked our way up and got a good toehold.

By two hours before nightfall, we were supposed to have established a beachhead three and a half miles (5.6km) deep. In reality, by nightfall we had reached about one and a half miles (2.4km) inland. Infantry had established defensive positions, dug in, and captured some prisoners. The 1st Combat Engineer Battalion had the assignment of clearing one road from the high-water mark to a transient area, so that vehicles, tanks, trucks—any type of track or wheeled vehicle—could get up this road, which was about a mile (1.6km) long and 110 feet (33.5m) high, to free our objective.

My 1st Combat Engineer Battalion had Exit E-1 to open on OMAHA Beach, removing all obstacles from the path and up to that transit area, so that the vehicles could move on and remove their waterproofing materials and prepare for the battle. There were four engineer battalions involved on OMAHA Beach. The 1st Infantry Division had Exit E-1.

The 29th Infantry Division had a road of their own, and there were two independent combat engineer units assigned to open similar roads. There were four roads to be opened by nightfall on D-DAY to get all the vehicles up into different positions.

The infantry was terribly worried about antipersonnel mines. The Germans had developed one made out of wood, making it difficult to detect with mine detectors. So they had to be literally blown up. Using Bangalore torpedoes, we created gaps for infantry troops who were pinned down and afraid to run up through these antipersonnel mines.

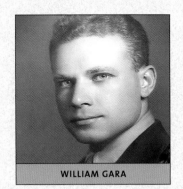

WILLIAM GARA

BELOW: LCVP landing craft stream past soldiers of the 16th RCT's E Company and a member of an Engineer Special Brigade (with crescent on helmet). On the near horizon at left, another LCVP can be seen leading back to the assault transport USS *Henrico*. This photo was shot from behind the tank pictured on page 134 that has a large "10" painted on the rear of its waterproof exhaust trunk.

We would open up gaps and mark them, so that they could scamper on up. This started at approximately H+2 hours. So instead of 6:30 A.M., it wasn't until close to 9:00 that we were able to open up gaps and get infantry troops ahead of us. Then we could proceed with clearing a fifteen-foot (4.6m) deep antitank ditch, removing the obstacles, removing mines, and opening the road, because now the beach was getting cluttered with vehicles that were coming ashore. They were on a schedule and unable to move off the beach because of the bottleneck.

We really couldn't get organized to work on the road until about 11 A.M. By that time, I was able to move twelve hundred yards (1,097m) back. We were able to radio in one of the reserve companies, C Company, to help us. The officers finally made contact with their people. We commandeered a bulldozer that happened to be there without a driver. We filled in that tank ditch. We removed the

mines and by nightfall, we had Exit E-1 [Saint Laurent]. Actually, by seventeen hundred hours—5 P.M.—I had radioed and said, "You can start sending vehicles up Exit Road E-1 to the transit area." By nightfall, Exit E-1 was the only road open on OMAHA Beach. The others were still bogged down. For that particular accomplishment, the 1st Engineer Battalion was awarded its third Presidential Unit Citation.

The artillery units attached to the 1st Division were unable to get in. They were coming in on DUKWs. They were swamped like the DD tanks. We discovered, on capturing German prisoners, another great surprise. Unfortunately, this was not a very good reflection on our intelligence gathering. They didn't tell us that the German 352d Infantry Division had been brought from the Russian Front to the Normandy beaches. ■

—William Gara

The tank is burning. It was just like rats jumping off a burning ship. Once you hit the ground, regardless of what kind of shape you're in, you tried to crawl, run, keep down, and get into a hole somewhere. I've seen a man with both legs cut off at the knee running on his stumps trying to save himself.

—Sidney Radley Walters

Karl Wolf of the 1st Infantry Division discovered that the Navy had inadvertently dropped him and his men at the wrong spot.

We loaded thirty-four men into these small landing craft. The waves were tremendous. An awful lot of people, including myself, became seasick. I remember getting sick and having to throw up in a plastic bag that someone gave me. Then someone handed me Dramamine tablets, saying these would help my seasickness. I did not have any experience with them, so I took three, which was a mistake. Later, after we actually landed—on the wrong beach—I was leading a group of men. I had already assembled the men I could find from my ship and we went down the beach. There was machine-gun fire going across. We stopped for awhile to let the fire stop. I woke up to find someone shaking my leg. Then I realized I had fallen asleep because of the Dramamine. It was rather humorous afterwards, but not at the time.

The landing craft dropped off the first ones, and they got cut down by German fire. The German machine guns were firing from the high ground to the right of us, and they were just cutting across those coming off the craft. Tetrahedrons were like railroad ties, twisted into an X shape, to capsize any landing craft that came in at high tide and hit them. I stopped to the left of one tetrahedron and to the right of me was a sergeant and a private. Water was probably about three to four feet (0.9–1.2m) deep ahead of the tetrahedron, and you could see the machine-gun fire kicking up the water in front of it. The next thing I noticed was the two people who were down on my right, floating away dead. I decided that that wasn't a very healthy place to be, and moved on. The adrenaline was up, and you tried to reach your objective and get on with your job.

When you got to the beach, everybody was laying on the beach. Nobody had gotten in the area where I landed, which was to the right of our 1st Division area. No one had gotten off the beach there, and there was sort of an incline and a little cubbyhole at the top part of the beach that prevented direct fire from the Germans from hitting anybody lying on the beach. That's why you'll see these pictures, and there are an awful lot of people who are out in the open but in reality, they were in a protected position. When we got up to the beach, I looked around but didn't see any other Big Red Ones on the shoulders of the men around me. I was trying to visualize where these fortifications were that I had studied on the map, but they weren't there. Then I realized I was in the wrong area. By mistake the Navy had put us about three thousand yards (2,743m) to the right.

I gathered up the men I could find from our landing craft. After about a mile (1.6km) or so, the firing let up a little bit. I led the men down to the left to get back to the 1st Division area. You ran across everything along the beach. There were half bodies and people wounded that you couldn't do anything about, and we would pull them out of the water, so they might possibly make it. Artillery would go overhead or shells would drop, so you'd hit the ground pretty fast. We ran, crawled, and crouched, but finally made it down to our battalion headquarters area. ■

—Karl Wolf, 3d Battalion, 16th Infantry Regiment, 1st Infantry Division (US)

ABOVE: Members of C Company, 2d Ranger Battalion, assault the German fortifications at Pointe et Raz de la Percée. The white horizontal bar on the back of the soldier firing the .30-caliber machine gun at upper right identifies him as a sergeant. The vertical bar on the helmet of the man behind him and below him indicates that he is an officer, probably a lieutenant. After taking the position, the men of C Company were to move west in support of the battalion's other elements at Pointe du Hoc, but were thwarted by German resistance. They and the 5th Ranger Battalion finally reached the besieged Rangers on D+2.

RIGHT: A German soldier, trapped by the sand in a collapsed trench, becomes an easy prisoner for 8th RCT troops at UTAH Beach.

OPPOSITE: Perilously close to shore, the destroyer USS *Emmons* fires on German positions along and behind OMAHA Beach in this painting by Navy Lieutenant Dwight Shepler, who witnessed the event. On the horizon, left of the rising black smoke, is the eleventh-century tower of the church of Colleville-sur-Mer. Although the Navy had orders to avoid damaging the church, the *Emmons* was forced to knock it down when it became apparent that the Germans were using it for observation. The destroyer fired some 767 5-inch rounds on D-DAY.

The Destroyers

About 8 A.M., various ships along the destroyer gun line, roughly six thousand yards (5,486m) offshore, started to close the beach on their own initiative, to search out "targets of opportunity." The movement became official an hour later when the commander of the escort group, Captain Harry Sanders on the USS *Frankford,* ordered all destroyers to belly up as close as possible to the land battle. The captain apparently believed in practicing what he preached, and moved his ship to shoal water barely eight hundred yards (731.5m) off the high-tide line, opposite the 1st Division.

The *Frankford* sailed slowly to the east end of the assault beach, firing all the way, then put her engines in reverse and traversed the same waters backward. The ship was not in radio contact with the troops, but hit upon a unique method of fire control using its rangefinder optics. Gunnery Officer Owen F. Keeler related that as they pulled close to the beach they noticed a tank with a broken track at the water's edge fire at something on the bluff. "We immediately followed up with a five-inch salvo," said Keeler. "The tank gunner flipped open his hatch, looked around at us, waved, dropped back into the tank, and fired at another target. For the next few minutes, he was our fire control party." At the other end of OMAHA, where the Virginians had been massacred, the destroyer *Carmick*'s gunners spotted a group of tanks in trouble and, from nine hundred yards (832m) out, blasted the point on which they seemed to be firing. The process was repeated for a group of infantrymen

GERMAN 352D INFANTRY DIVISION

Composed principally of units that had survived the grueling Eastern Front battles outside Moscow and Kursk, the 352d Infantry Division fought with deadly effectiveness against American forces landing at OMAHA Beach. The German division conducted a series of costly defensive battles throughout June and July 1944, its strength maintained by absorbing men and equipment from three other severely mauled divisions. Struck hard during the American breakthrough of July 25 to 29 (Operation COBRA), its survivors were placed under the command of the 2d Panzer Division until the 352d's reconstitution as a *Volksgrenadier* division in the fall.

She [the USS *Frankford*] was headed straight toward me. Even though she wasn't listing or smoking, my first thought was that she had either struck a mine or taken a torpedo and was damaged badly enough that she was being beached. . . . She started to turn right and, before she completed the turn to be parallel to the beach, all her guns opened fire.

—James E. Knight,
299th Combat Engineer Battalion

shooting at a spot on the bluff, and the crew got the satisfaction of seeing the soldiers move out from behind their cover and advance when the *Carmick* ceased firing.

At different times throughout the day, destroyers *Doyle*, *Harding*, *Baldwin*, *Thompson*, *Emmons*, and *Satterlee* all closed on the beach, and used either their optics or the few functioning shore fire control parties (FSCPs) to direct fire. The *McCook* was working over targets enfilading OMAHA from the west when its sailors saw what appeared to be Germans at one position waving a white flag and attempt-

ing to contact the destroyer using flashing lights and a naval semaphore. Unsuccessful efforts to communicate in either German or English continued for an hour before the *McCook* finally gave up. The ship's signalman blinked that they were going to resume fire, and the Germans on the bluff immediately signaled back, "Cease fire!" The *McCook* accepted their surrender, signaled for them to move down to the beach, and, although her gunners continued to fire on another coastal gun, kept an eye on the Germans until they were taken into custody by the Rangers.

From Toehold to Foothold

The destroyers were going a long way toward filling the gap left by the loss of so many tanks, but only the infantry could seize the draws cutting through the wall of bluff along the beach to enable the 1st and 29th Divisions' RCTs to move inland. Small groups of men, often led by sergeants or officers they had never laid eyes on before, began working their way up lightly defended or partially shielded spots along the bluffs. By mid-morning, multiple penetrations had been made along the heights, two by elements of the 116th RCT in the west and two more by the 16th RCT in the east, including the draw on the extreme left flank that was not as well fortified as the other exits from the beach. Confused fighting raged for two hours in the heights above the Saint Laurent draw, as a pair of platoon-strength "companies" fought their way into a maze of German pillboxes and trenches. The weight of the attack steadily

grew, as battalions threaded their way up the bluffs behind them and destroyers provided direct fire against pillboxes in the draw and in the fortified zone above.

The end of organized resistance at the vital exit leading to Saint Laurent before noon markedly lessened the traffic jam on OMAHA, but this was not so apparent to senior commanders at sea, who were receiving sketchy, breathless reports from shore and could see only tangles of vehicles and milling assault craft through their binoculars. Lieutenant General Omar Bradley on the cruiser *Augusta* feared that if the troops ashore did not make more headway, the large force scheduled to begin landing in the early afternoon might have to be diverted to UTAH Beach. The Navy officer in charge of the OMAHA assault, Rear Admiral John L. Hall, reminded the assembled senior Army officers aboard his command ship, the *Ancon,* that opposed amphibious landings are always messy affairs that look "hopelessly confused," and that the battalion and company commanders were certainly "straightening things out." At 1:30 P.M., Bradley received the message: "Troops formerly pinned down on beaches EASY RED, EASY GREEN, and FOX RED are advancing up heights behind the beach."

Both the 1st and 29th Divisions had landed additional regimental combat teams, which were now fighting their way inland. Although the day's inland objectives would not be taken, and the new formations had been bloodied along the shore by German fortifications that had not been subdued, they nevertheless provided enough punch to push the beachhead well beyond the coast road, except for short stretches in front of both divisions. The key towns of Vierville and Saint Laurent, with their roads leading into the French interior, were firmly in American hands, and the German units at Colleville were surrounded. The Atlantic Wall had been pierced, and a stream of fresh U.S. battalions, some well supported by armor, came pouring from the Saint Laurent draw. Meanwhile, with the exception of a German battalion quickly bottled up in Colleville, the defenders were receiving virtually no reinforcements.

Thank God for good planning and self-sacrifice.

GINO MERLI

German reports throughout the morning, of American dead littering the beach; of burned-out tanks and destroyed landing craft; and of the masses of soldiers huddling under the seawall, all seemed to clearly indicate that the landing at OMAHA Beach had failed. German commanders on the scene assured 352d Division headquarters that the invasion had been repulsed, and the good news, that "the situation in the area of the 352d Division is now restored," traveled up the chain of command to the Seventh Army and OB West in Paris. Even as more waves of men and equipment poured ashore, German counterattacks were confidently directed not at the still-vulnerable toehold at OMAHA, but against the Rangers at Pointe du Hoc to the west and the British landing at GOLD Beach to the east. It was almost nightfall before senior German commanders realized that, far from being repulsed, the Allied invasion forces had arrived in strength and were pressing inland.

🎙️ *Troops arriving later in the day were witnesses to the carnage of the invasion. Bodies, whole and dismembered, were strewn along the beaches—a sobering reminder of those who had seen their last sunrise. Machine gunner Gino Merli, 1st Infantry Division, recalls his reaction to the Normandy invasion.*

On D-DAY, the 16th Regiment was the assault unit. They led the troops, with us right there behind them for replacement purposes.

When we landed, the first sight we encountered was the dead GIs laying on the beach. As we moved forward about sixty yards (54.9m), we hit a tank trench made by the enemy. It was something like ten feet (3m) across and about twelve feet (3.7m) deep. We had to use ladders to get up from one side to the other in order to continue going up the hill. When we reached that point, we ran into small antipersonnel mines the enemy had placed on the land. If you stepped to the right, you hit a mine. If you stepped to the left, you hit a mine. You stepped forward, you wouldn't hit nothing. They had them staggered, and if you knew how they were staggered, you had the case won. We finally arrived on top of the hill about two-thirty, three o'clock in the afternoon. Our sergeant gave a big sigh when we got to the top of the mountain. He said, "This is it, baby. We're not going back." We dug in

LEFT: A pair of troop-laden LCIs search in vain for a clear lane to the 29th Infantry Division's sector on OMAHA Beach. The smoke at the center of the photo rises from grass fires at the base of the bluff, while that on the right defines the contours of the Les Moulins draw and the three-story stone villa that had been integrated into the German defenses. The overcrowding of men and equipment in the 29th's sector had reached critical proportions by H+2, because no men or vehicles had been able to move past the seawall, and it was almost as bad in the 1st Division's area. The situation forced Navy beachmasters to suspend the landings of any additional vehicles.

LCTs with tanks and artillery milled about while LCIs—which were allowed to land foot soldiers— stood off the beach or tried to pick their way through obstacle belts. The impasse was broken only when some of the fifty milling LCTs and LCIs, on their own initiative, began to charge the shore in an effort to crash through the obstacles under the cover of destroyers that had also moved inshore. Other craft were pulled back from the beach and reformed, to be sent in as gaps were created.

Two kinds of people are staying on this beach—the dead and those about to die. Now let's get the hell out of here.
—Colonel George A. Taylor, 16th Infantry Regiment

RIGHT: Taken by a reconnaissance Mosquito flying low over a band of ramp and stake obstacles on the late afternoon of May 19, 1944, this photo of the Saint Laurent draw shows that work is either done or almost done on the hedgehog placement. This was the only portion of OMAHA Beach never to receive a band of Belgian gate obstacles. The pyramidal structure to the right of the house is a bunker protecting an antitank ditch, and marks the lowest portion of strongpoint WN65, which stretches back up the hill and occupies the opposite side of the draw, coded E-1 by Allied planners. The boxy structure to the left of the house is the ruins of another house.

OPPOSITE: The provisional headquarters element for the 5th and 6th Engineer Special Brigades established their command post in front of a destroyed German bunker roughly halfway up the towering southwest face of the Saint Laurent draw. This is part of strongpoint WN65 and is sited to engage not targets at sea, but along the mouth of the draw and further east along the beach. The tapered concrete apron at right protects its embrasure from the direct fire of naval guns, and a tarp covers a gash inflicted by such a weapon. That shell's strike, however, did not destroy the fortification, which took a heavy toll on the 741st Tank Battalion. It was eventually put out of action by the high-volume fire from two M-15 A1 motor gun carriages of the 467th Anti-Aircraft Artillery Battalion, which penetrated the shield of its 50-mm antitank gun. Once it and other strongpoint positions on both sides of the draw were destroyed, the route inland to Saint Laurent, directed by these men, became the focal point of nearly all OMAHA Beach reinforcements on D-DAY.

our machine guns to prevent any counterattacks that evening, but we didn't have any, thank God. The next day, we just moved six or seven miles (9.7–11.3km) inland, and took the first small town in France and freed that small town, a small town by the name of Caumont, population about three-hundred-something, but that was the first town taken. ▪

—Gino Merli, H Company,
16th Regiment, 1st Infantry Division (US)

 Major Thomas Lancer of the 1st Infantry Division recounts a sadly ironic story about one of his MPs.

In Dorset County was an old manor house where one of the inside rooms was used as the war room. We had MP guards outside, inside the war room, and at the door to the room, on twenty-four hours a day. So every night I used to go in and check the photographs, because every day a Mosquito plane flew along parallel with the coast of Normandy taking low-level pictures. Every day those pictures would be developed and compared with the pictures taken the day before, to see what changes had been made in the defense. So I went in and looked at them every night. When I went in, my MP came to attention. I was only in there about ten or fifteen minutes, and I found the MP asleep. Sleeping on guard is a very serious offense. I kicked the leg of the table and he jumped to attention. I said, "Report to me in the morning." All night I was wondering what I could do with him. I couldn't give him KP for thirty days for sleeping on guard. He had been a good soldier, never been in trouble. He reported to me the next morning, and I reminded him that all our lives are in that room—remember that. He said, "Yes, sir."

As we were getting ready to board the ship, he went by me. He was boarding another landing craft and was carrying a bazooka on his shoulder. Bazookas are not normally issued to MPs, but we had a lot of weapons that weren't issued to MPs. As he walked by me, he did the rifle salute with the bazooka and said, "I'm going to get a tank for the Major," meaning me. He was the first one off his landing craft and he was killed. So he became a dead hero. But if I'd tried and court-martialed him, he'd be out of the Army and alive.

When I landed, one of my lieutenants was lying on a litter. There were German mortar shells hitting the beach all around us. Direct fire had been pushed back. They couldn't hit us with machine-gun fire, but they were hitting us with mortar fire. As soon as I saw him, I knew he'd be killed waiting to be evacuated from the beach. So I got four of my men, two in front and two in rear, on the litter, and carried him up and put him in a German bunker. We evacuated him the next day. He received his second Silver Star.

The landing at Normandy was the toughest of our three landings—North Africa, Sicily, and Normandy. Although the carnage at Normandy was depressing, I always thought it could have been worse. ▪

Thomas Lancer, Major,
Military Police,
1st Infantry Division (US)

THOMAS LANCER

The Channel was loaded with shipping of all description: landing craft, infantry; landing craft, tanks; large ocean liners; anything that would float. The 16th Infantry [Regiment] was assigned, along with the 116th Infantry [Regiment] of the 29th Infantry Division, to go ashore at dawn. This is where the attack would take place on OMAHA, on the beach just behind us. It was a debacle. A man-made hell. Confusion. You didn't know where the people were. Nobody around that you knew. Artillery shells coming down like rain. Machine-gun bullets, anything you can think of, being fired at you. You tried to find the safest place you could. Now, the first infantry was the 16th going ashore in those initial waves. They lost a tremendous amount of men. Not all were killed [by gunfire or mortar fire]. Many drowned. We had a life vest called a Mae West. It went around your middle. If you weren't careful and inflated it, it'd tip you upside down and drown you. You were just as bad off being upside down as you were being shot or killed. You went ashore with any-where from 75 to 100 pounds (34–45.4kg). And at that time I think I weighed 132 pounds (60kg). Soldiers were heavily laden.

My infantry regiment didn't land until approximately six o'clock in the evening. History books say five, but my company commander, who landed at that time, said it was six or six-thirty, to the best of his knowl-edge. Captain Robert Bridges commanded D Company, and his executive officer was Lieutenant Yume. The lieutenant had reported that all of the company was ashore, just prior to German artillery hitting and decapitating him, as well as knocking the captain into a bunker with a terrible wound, ending his military service. That's what you run into. Constant movement. You hope to keep the enemy off you by attacking, because an offense is better than a defense, just like in football. First battalion, 26th [Infantry Regiment], was given the mission to sideslip

OPPOSITE, TOP: The price of victory. A soldier receives blood plasma from Army medics after his landing craft is sunk off OMAHA Beach.

OPPOSITE, BOTTOM: Members of the 607th Quartermaster Graves Registration Company sort and identify the bodies of Americans killed near one of the draws. A knocked-out German pillbox is visible partway up the bluffs.

TOP: Survivors of a Coast Guard vessel that struck a mine and sank grasp the line thrown from an LCVP. Other stricken men were unconscious when rescued, held safely afloat by their kapok life jackets. The sinking was reputed to have occurred off UTAH Beach.

BOTTOM: An LCVP carrying troops of the 18th RCT's 2d Battalion reaches the shore on the eastern end of EASY RED on the afternoon of D-DAY. This was the only portion of OMAHA Beach—other than the heavily defended draws—where the steep bluffs gave way to a more gradual climb to the coastal plain. Lines of infantry can be seen moving both south and southwest, but vehicles, such as this DUKW and half-tracks towing 57-mm antitank guns, had to drive west along the shore to use the Saint Laurent exit.

BELOW: Huge swaths of UTAH beach had been fully cleared of obstacles—principally by bulldozers, after mines had been removed—before the arrival of these troops on the afternoon of June 6.

RIGHT: Shellfire harassed operations on UTAH Beach throughout D-DAY morning. German artillery spotters had no direct observation of the landing area, but used the invasion force's barrage balloons for targeting until they were temporarily hauled down. By mid-afternoon, air and ground action had eliminated most of the troublesome guns, and the balloons were sent aloft again to help prevent air attacks.

INSET: Soldiers of the 320th Barrage Balloon Battalion (VLA) (Colored) maneuver a balloon on UTAH Beach. VLA (very low altitude) balloons could be easily held in place by sandbags if there was no high wind. Note that the soldiers have lined the slit trench at right with sandbags to prevent cave-ins.

in beside the second battalion, the 16th, and they did so.

When close to landing, there wasn't much, if any, talking. I suspect that most people were saying the last prayer that they might ever say. You were not only going to be shot at, but there were mines laid on those beaches that could decapitate you, take your legs off, and do all kinds of bodily injury to a man. You could drown. You had to allow the instinct that you have been trained with to kick in. You were too busy trying to find out what was happening, who was next to you, where you were going to take the next step, and how you were going to see that next hill ahead and how to reach it. You didn't have time to worry about yourself. It was just literally ingrained in you to keep going. As long as another guy was ahead of you, you were not going to stop either.

You either go forward until you dig that next foxhole, or you go back wounded. You never think about the one that might kill you. At least I never did. I never heard a round, I never heard a shell, I never heard a piece of

TOP: German soldiers and Atlantic Wall laborers surrender to U.S. troops, inland from OMAHA Beach.

BOTTOM: A soldier lies dead beside an OMAHA Beach ramp obstacle after taking shrapnel in his right leg and most likely receiving other unseen wounds. Someone has placed crossed rifles by his feet, and a mine has been unstrapped from the stake obstacle arranged in conjunction with the ramp.

OPPOSITE: Mortar crews of the 87th Chemical Battalion fire 4.2-inch rounds into German positions as U.S. forces move north along UTAH Beach, destroying the isolated German positions one by one.

artillery hit around me that had my name on it. I never thought I was ever going to die. The last time I saw Lieutenant Yume was in England. He said to me, "Lee, I'm not going to survive this war." I told him that's just that liquor talking. I said, "You'll be all right like the rest of us. You'll live to have kids and you'll see all kinds of people, you'll be married to the girl that you're going with in England." Then he was killed. Other people had that premonition. There were some who knew that their time was up. But I never did feel that way. I always thought that I would survive, and I did.

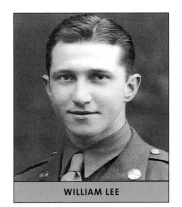

WILLIAM LEE

If a guy tells you he never was scared in the war he's lying to you, or he wasn't there. You're scared to death, literally. Your buddies are all around you; they're suffering the same turmoil and stress in this terrible undertaking. So you just stay there and do the best you can. There's only one way you're coming out—either dead or alive. You fight like hell,

as the guy says, and you hope that help is on the way. It's kind of like the western where you see the cavalry is only two miles down the road, and they're hollering, the bugles are blowing and they're coming to help. That's the way you are in war. You're surrounded, but somebody's going to make it to your aid and assistance. That is literally what happened. You suffer casualties, but you keep going. It's nothing for a company to have 50 percent strength. They started with 300 men, which is pretty much what a company is, but if they've got 150 men when the battle's over, they're pretty well off. We fought many actions with 40 men. One company was down to 10, and still beat the Germans. How? I don't know—some fortitude, some good American luck, and the grace of God. ■

—William Lee, Private First Class,
D Company, 26th Infantry Regiment,
1st Infantry Division (US)

Not a single order from a higher formation was received by me. . . .
[At 10:30 A.M.] I was given my first operational instructions: . . . Stop the
move of my tanks against the Allied airborne troops, and turn west and aid
the forces protecting Caen.
—German Major General Edgar Feuchtinger, 21st Panzer Division

Chapter Five

A DANGEROUS TRIO

The Germans never considered the American sector to be the principal threatened area in Normandy. The beach itself and the country inland from OMAHA Beach were easily defended because of the nature of the close-in terrain. In addition, the wide, double water barriers beyond UTAH made it a deathtrap for any Allied force foolish enough to land there. Credible mobile forces, like the 352d Infantry Division and the 91st Air Landing Division, had to be allotted to buttress the static coastal divisions in this area, but the Germans believed that an incursion into western Normandy could be contained and rebuffed long before the Allies built up enough forces to exploit a lodgment. The beaches opposite Caen were another matter entirely.

Between the headlands overlooking the Seine Estuary at Le Havre and the steep bluffs and cliffs of OMAHA and Pointe du Hoc lay long stretches of sandy beach rising gently to only forty or fifty feet (12.2 or 15.2m) above sea level. A narrow coast road connects more than a dozen villages and small towns, many of which dot the shore with seaside cottages spreading up and down the beach. Three of these towns contained harbors so small that German demolition experts failed to pay them much attention, yet they were capable of modest development to support Allied troops coming ashore. A fourth town, Arromanches, had no useful harbor but was situated at the head of two well-placed roads: one running southwest to Bayeux, where the British planned to establish their headquarters, and the other running southeast to Caen. It was here, at Arromanches, that the Allies planned to construct MULBERRY "B."

Below the Cotentin Peninsula and OMAHA Beach, the thick *bocage* country—a crazy quilt of woods, sunken roads, and hedge-encased fields—extended south for roughly sixty miles (96.5km). The Normandy area around Caen, by contrast, marked the western end of a broad plateau extending across the face of France and beyond the Seine to the Belgian frontier. The areas running northwest to southwest of Caen were also particularly well suited for the construction of airfields. A well-developed, but now little-used, air base already existed just outside of Caen to the west at Carpiquet. Another German field eleven miles (17.7km) to the northwest at Crepon was abandoned and plowed with crisscrossed ditches to prevent its early use by Allied fighters and transports following an invasion. The airfield was a scant two and a half miles (4km) from a wide, inviting beach that would soon be known to the world by the code name GOLD.

Both the Germans and the Allies understood that this ground was tailor-made for mobile warfare. It was the surest route to Paris, key to the defense of France, and, ultimately, the best approach to the great German industrial center in the Ruhr. Allied plans called for the British trio of beaches—GOLD, JUNO, and SWORD—to bear the main weight of the inva-

sion. Of paramount importance were the rapid consolidation of the beachheads and the quick thrusts inland by tanks and infantry to seize Bayeux, Caen, and land for airfield development as far south as Falaise. All of this was to be accomplished on D-DAY or very soon thereafter.

Once the British were established south and southeast of Caen, the German Seventh Army's ability to maintain a defense of the *bocage* country to the west would be greatly reduced. Plans called for the British "to protect the eastern flank of the U.S. First Army" while the First Army set about capturing Cherbourg. The British Second Army was then to pivot on its left (Caen) and offer a strong front against enemy movement from the east.

The British expected the German reaction to be swift and violent. Even if the chimera of an Allied landing in the Pas-de-Calais held most Panzer and mobile divisions in check, the three that were located within easy striking distance of Caen—the 21st Panzer, the 12th SS Panzer *Hitlerjugend* (Hitler Youth), and the Panzer-Lehr—might well be able to reach the front between D+1 and D+3, and possibly sooner. To parry the German counterattack that was sure to come, the British planned to land a full armored brigade on each beach at about noon on D-DAY, with advance elements of the vaunted "Desert Rats," the 7th Armored Division, coming ashore by nightfall. Unknown to the British, however, the 21st Panzer had already moved in force directly to the Caen area, with some artillery elements actually north of the city. Its Panzer regiment and two *Panzergrenadier* (armored infantry) regiments were arrayed south of Caen, along with the support units and the balance of its artillery.

BRITISH 7TH ARMORED DIVISION

All elements of the British 7th Armored Division were ashore in Normandy by June 12, 1944. In a series of actions beginning at Villers-Bocage on June 13, the veterans of the North African desert experienced setbacks during offensive operations amid the close-in terrain and heavy German resistance. On July 19, during Operation GOODWOOD, it defeated elements of the 1st Panzer Division along Bourguébus Ridge. Aunay-sur-Odon was captured on August 5 as the division put pressure on stretched German forces, then it struck out far beyond the Seine, dislocating German efforts to hold the Somme River sector.

Observing the sheer numbers of the flotilla in the English Channel, Geoffrey Parrett, an officer in the 1st Commando Brigade's 3d Battalion, felt supremely confident about the invasion's outcome.

I thought, My God, the Germans don't stand a chance against us. It was impressive. On the boat we were told where we were going. They issued the maps to the officers, so we were really in the picture going over before we landed. I always was confident it was going to work out okay because of the vast number of ships I saw as well as the planning I knew they'd done and showing us the photographs and models. I thought, Nothing could be planned so well. Jerry doesn't stand a chance.

We were not the first ones in. There were bodies on the beach. Some were badly hurt. Suddenly you realized that it was not only the Germans who would become casualties, but our boys as well. We moved up on the beach. It was still swampy as we moved to the road parallel with the water. Then we formed up to march inland. As I crossed the beach, I was disturbed by the bodies and thought, I must not lose my identity disks [dog tags] because I

don't want to be like that and someone not know I've gone.

Moving inland, we were being mortared and artillery fire was coming down. There were lots of minefields, so we had to pretty well stay on the road. We were bunching up terribly, one behind the other, making progress very slow. At times, we'd come to a dead halt, and we'd be sitting there for awhile, you know, while they cleared things up front. As we went along that morning, we saw gliders scattered all over the fields. Some broken up and smashed. Some in good condition. I just couldn't believe the hundreds of them all over. We also found silk parachutes just strewn around.

I remember thinking, I'm in a foreign country. I would look at the advertisements painted on the sides of buildings, which were foreign to me. They were in French, of course. Then along came some German prisoners being escorted to the beach. I remember thinking to myself, I didn't know their uniforms were like that. I had been brought up on a diet of *All Quiet on the Western Front* and books of that sort. They always mentioned the German field-gray uniforms. Looking at the prisoners' uniforms, I thought,

BELOW: An MP from either the 7th or 8th Canadian Beach Group and a soldier with a fixed-spike bayonet guard the first Germans taken alive on JUNO Beach. The Germans, as well as the Canadian casualties being collected behind them, await transportation to England. Note that the nearby German 50-mm gun emplacement is what a naval officer might describe as "down by the bow." The bunker evidently lacked a wide concrete apron and was undermined by a near miss during the pre-invasion bombardment. The Beach Groups in the British sector were analogous to U.S.-sector Engineer Special Brigades. Barely visible on the MP's shoulder is a white patch with red anchor, signifying his membership in one of the Beach Groups, most of whose soldiers wore standard-issue British helmets with a wide white band painted above the brim.

They're not gray, they're green. They were also rather shoddy, which surprised me, because I used to think of them being such a smart-looking army. But they appeared scruffy to me.

When we reached the Bénouville [Pegasus] Bridge, we weren't being shot at. We ran across on the double. Then we were detoured to go south, and guarded the Airborne Brigade Headquarters temporarily.

We got there and started our first digging, which is the most horrible thing about Normandy. You dug all the time. Those hedgerows were so tough to dig up because they're on a high mound with a ditch on either side. So when you dug, you were digging into those roots. I think we in the British Army were rather lazy people, and we never wanted to go down too far. The Germans, on the contrary, had beautiful trenches. We captured them at different times. There would be structures of wood inside and blankets put around it like wallpaper. They were so industrious. Ours was always just a sort of a hole in the ground, but we always made sure that we put on roofs. My mate and I always used

to throw six shovel-throws extra of dirt on every day.

I think we all had anxieties by the end of the day [D-DAY] about an enemy counter-attack, but it had not been bad for me at all. When I got to the end of the day, I realized I hadn't fired my rifle once. ∎

—Geoffrey Parrett

GOLD Beach

H-HOUR in the British sector ranged between 7:25 A.M.—nearly one hour after American troops had waded ashore to the west—to as late as 7:45. The area had some minor patches of shoal water and soft spots of clay surface at low tide, but the delayed, sequenced landing schedule was principally driven by the need to avoid a dangerous reef that jutted into the approach lanes to JUNO, the center invasion beach, and by the necessity that the assault on the three British beaches be mutually supporting. The five extra feet (1.5m) of water rushing over the rocks as the tide came in provided enough clearance for DD tanks and medium-size landing craft to pass safely. But the incoming tide also meant that there would be no time to clear some of the obstacle belts at JUNO Beach and only about twenty minutes' time at the flanking GOLD and SWORD beaches. Because of this special problem, the British beaches were allotted underwater demolition teams to supplement the Royal Engineers.

Like OMAHA, which saw the 16th and 116th Regimental Combat Teams landed side by side, GOLD Beach was assaulted by two equivalent formations of the British 50th Infantry Division, the 69th and 231st Brigade Groups. Yet there was one important difference—a full brigade of tanks was slated to land in the initial waves.

Sherman DDs were brought directly to shore because of the turbulent seas, and all but one were quickly destroyed by German guns. Additional waterproofed Shermans brought in for support suffered the same fate, as did many of the Centaur tanks mounting 95-mm howitzers, bulldozer tanks, and mine-clearing flail tanks. The tide and obstacles also conspired to

sink a number of LCTs and forced many water-proofed tanks to land either late or away from their assigned areas, resulting in some infantry fighting without support. The weight of the unexpected British 8th Armored Brigade assault was such, however, that the many surviving machines ground up the defenses and were soon moving inland, bypassing the villages without either firing a shot or receiving anything other than sporadic German small-arms fire.

The elements of the German 716th Division defending GOLD were principally Russian and Polish conscripts. Some units and strongpoints fought hard until they suddenly surrendered,

BELOW AND RIGHT: A Royal Navy gunner on LCI 164 keeps a watchful eye for hostile activity as lines of soldiers leave their LCIs and head to shore. The sailor mans a 20-mm Oerlikon mounted in a "tub" perched on the bow of the LCI.

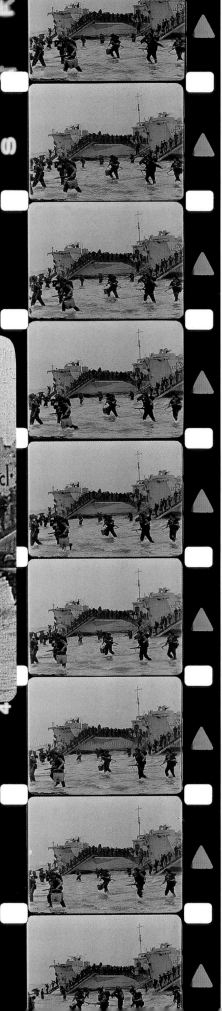

but a common memory of many British troops who landed was the rearward flight of small, green-clad groups as the *Ost* (Eastern) troops broke down under the pressure. The fortified coastal village of Le Hamel, however, took eight hours to subdue in heavy fighting. Resistance also stiffened inland, and the British were briefly thrown off the heights beyond the beach. But the Germans possessed few anti-tank weapons—who ever heard of an armored assault from the sea? Even if they had, nothing

About two minutes later a tank was hit by shell fire. The turret blew off from the caterpillars, leaving just the wheels tearing along the beach.

—George Foster, Royal Marines

could protect them from the screaming shells that rained down on them from British cruisers and destroyers offshore.

The heights southeast of Ver-sur-Mer were retaken, and British battalions with colorful names—the 7th Royal Dragoon Guards, the 6th Green Howards, the 5th East Yorkshire, and the 1st Dorset—fanned out to push the 50th Division's perimeter as deep as possible into France. A German counterattack near Bayeux by the 352d Division's reserves was brutally savaged by Allied fighter aircraft before it could even reach its jump-off point, and then was simply brushed aside by a mass of thirty-five tanks from the freshly landed 56th Brigade Group. Coastal batteries and the important radar station at Arromanches, west of the beachhead, were attacked in stages during the late afternoon and through the late evening. The area was secured before nightfall, thus clearing the way for work to begin on MULBERRY "B." By the close of D-DAY, the

50th Division held a defensible lodgment six miles (9.7km) wide and an average of six miles (9.7km) deep.

Arriving amid the confusion of artillery shells pounding and soldiers dying were the men of the Essex Artillery, including Lieutenant Tony Richardson.

The sea was rough. The boys wanted to stop and pick up the men in the water. I had an ex–London police officer driving my LCT. I told him, We're not slowing up. We're going to hit this beach hard, and I'm going to go ashore dry. And we did.

There was a certain amount of shelling coming back toward us. It was landing in the minefield just across from us, so it wasn't really a harassing fire. It didn't affect us at all. We were far too busy doing our own thing and firing and sport and getting information from the OPs [observation posts]. They were telling us what the targets were and where we were to shoot and what we were to do in order to get the infantry covering fire and get them on.

You're told what you're going to have to do, and there's a plan. But those plans have to be adjusted because things don't happen quite as you expect. I knew the best thing I could do was to get the guns into action when we landed on the beach and that was it and get going. My other troop in the battery was also in action. The other two batteries weren't in action. They were trying to get through. And they were stuck. So they weren't being useful. So we reckoned that we were doing our bit. We were there and all the OPs wanted us. So that's why we fired a lot of ammunition.

It was St. Crispin's Day. Any man who wasn't there would be ashamed. We were glad to have been chosen. We weren't going to let anybody down. And we never did. ■

—Tony Richardson, Lieutenant, Essex Artillery, 50th Division (UK)

Following the infantry were support vehicles and tanks. Captain Sidney Radley Walters of the 27th Canadian Armored Regiment arrived only to find himself in the middle of a traffic jam.

The skipper of our landing craft put us halfway up the beach. He was sure it was the Navy's responsibility to get troops ashore. When we arrived, there was a traffic jam of vehicles all trying to move through the two or three holes in the seawall. Only one at a time could go through. As we went through, there was a church in Bernières-sur-Mer. That church steeple was our guide. There were then about three or four roads running past the church that took you out into the open. Traffic was all lined up at the corner, as my divisional commander and the commanding officer of our brigade attempted to play military police there. Fortunately, there were no German aircraft. We were extremely vulnerable. ■

—Sidney Radley Walters, Captain, 9th Brigade, 3d Infantry Battalion, 27th Armored Regiment (CAN)

SWORD Beach

The British 3d Infantry Division's D-Day target was a holiday beachfront—little more than a mile (1.6km) wide—between strongpoints at Lion-sur-Mer and the village resort of La Breche. Hemmed in by shoal waters encroaching on the west and by the Orne River sandflats that stretched more than a mile into the English Channel at low tide on the right, Sword Beach offered only enough room for a one-brigade attack. The resulting tricky navigational problem confronting the final run to shore was solved by positioning a midget submarine seven thousand yards (6,401m) off the coast, so that it could surface on D-Day morning to emit sonar, radio, and visual signals to guide in the assault craft. Still, the narrow frontage required that the 3d Division's one armored and three infantry brigades, plus a large commando element, would have to pile in relentlessly, one behind the other, and fight vigorously to get off a beach that shrank to as little as ten feet (3m) wide between the high-water mark and seawall by noon on June 6.

TONY RICHARDSON

BELOW: British troops examine "Goliath" tanks left behind by the Germans. In spite of the poor showing of the miniature armored vehicles at Anzio five months earlier, the Germans planned to use them against Allied landings in France. Filled with 150 pounds (68kg) of high explosives, the Goliaths were to be steered by use of a remote-control device, then detonated among concentrations of tanks or concealed infantry.

All in all, SWORD was not a good place to conduct a forced landing in the teeth of a determined enemy, but its one advantage solidly trumped all drawbacks: SWORD was located only seven short miles (11.3km) from the most coveted prize of the invasion—Caen. Together with the 3d Canadian Division landing to the northwest, more than ten miles (16km) from the city, the British 3d Division was to dash inland, storm the city's German garrison, and push inland as far as possible from the beachhead by nightfall.

Naval gunfire here, as at the other British beaches, began almost as early as the bombardment in the American sector, but had carried on far longer due to the delayed landing times. At first, there was little response from the German batteries. The initial wave of LCAs to reach the obstacle line also benefited from the fact that they were small vessels, comparable in size to American LCVPs, and that most obstacles were still visible and spaced widely enough that the coxswains could frequently navigate through them. To the tune of "Roll out the Barrel," broadcast from the loudspeaker of a rescue craft, twenty boats jerked to a stop as their bows struck bottom, deposited their infantry in the surf, and backed out with nary a loss. Playing on the English translation of the name of the French village La Breche, "the Breach," a cheeky officer with the 2d East Yorkshire Regiment, Major C.K. "Banger" King, was moved to regale his men with a famous line from Shakespeare's *Henry V*: "Once more unto the breach!"

The landings of the "Yorks" and the 1st South Lancashire Regiment of the 8th Brigade Group were to have been preceded by forty Sherman DDs of the 18th Royal Hussars, but, instead, passed them by as the tankers struggled to get their ungainly vehicles to dry land. Launched much closer to the shore than the 471st Tank Battalion at OMAHA, only two of the British tanks foundered. By the time the DDs reached SWORD, the Germans had largely recovered from the prolonged pounding by the Royal Navy and were now targeting what looked to them to be slow-moving "toaster ovens" until the canvas skirts were dropped to reveal Sherman tanks. Six DDs were knocked

BELOW: Medics work feverishly among the dead and wounded beside a spigot mortar–armed AVRE of the 1st Royal Marine Armored Support Regiment while, in the background, fellow soldiers of the Hampshire Regiment's 1st Battalion take cover behind other engineer vehicles and a pair of M-10 tank destroyers of the 102d Anti-Tank Regiment. The murderous fire pinning down these troops came from a German strongpoint built around the Le Hamel sanitorium, which included a 75-mm bunker. While other elements of the British 50th Infantry Division were able to plunge deep inland on D-Day, these men were only able to subdue the strongpoint at around 5 P.M., after fighting their way close enough for an AVRE armed with a 290-mm spigot mortar—a notoriously short-ranged weapon—to systematically blast apart the bunker's fortifications.

out while still in the surf as were four more along the beach, but that still left twenty-eight operational vehicles to climb the seawall with the help of bridge-laying *funnies*.

Yet more tanks and self-propelled guns of the Royal Marine Armored Support Regiment came ashore to lend their weight to the attack, but SWORD and its sea approaches were steadily becoming a considerably more dangerous place, as LCIs and LCTs struck mined obstacles and vehicles fell prey to German artillery.

The partially recovered Merville Battery and mobile guns well inland were now targeting the beach, even as it narrowed with the incoming tide. Many soldiers thought it was a miracle that the massive traffic jam extending from the seawall to well into the waves did not experience far more casualties from the incoming shells. Luckily, the German fire was largely conducted "unobserved," since the defenders had few radios and their land lines had been

severed during the bombardment. Fire noticeably slackened when the unneeded barrage balloons, sent up to deter air attacks, were cut loose. Just as it had been at UTAH Beach, it was realized that enemy gunners were using the easily seen balloons to mark the range and location of the landing sites.

Arriving on the beaches that day were men, and more men, arriving in the tens of thousands. Small wonder, then, that the beachmaster did a double take upon seeing Iris Bower and her friend Molly Giles from Princess Mary's RAF Nursing Service.

Eventually we saw the beaches. We could see red dust and fighters taking off and being shot at. A destroyer was near us firing her guns. It was pitch dark when we landed. We couldn't see things properly, but we could hear terrific movement and noise going

CANADIAN 3D INFANTRY DIVISION

Avenging the 1942 disaster at Dieppe, the Canadian 3d Infantry Division stormed ashore at JUNO on a rising tide that hid deadly beach obstacles. The division's initial surge inland fell short of Carpiquet Airfield outside Caen. A month of grueling combat followed, and Carpiquet fell on July 8, 1944, after a four-day battle with the fanatical Hitler Youth of the 12th SS Panzer Division. The Canadian division was one of the principal formations to close in on the German Seventh and Fifth Panzer Armies from the north in mid-August, then struck northeast to prevent remnants of these forces from escaping across the Seine River.

down. I could just about see the ramp, and
then suddenly they said, "Alright, off you go!"
and we rushed down the ramp and I felt
something under my feet and I had landed on
JUNO Beach in the pitch darkness. I remember, when I was standing there before going
down the ramp, I had no emotion at all. No
fear or anything. I think it was because so
much was happening. Molly and I were given
an armed escort and guided down the LCT.

We were told not to hang about on the
beach. We could see people moving in the
dark, and suddenly I heard a voice almost in
my ear saying, "Where are you off to?" It was
the beachmaster. I found my voice and I said,
"Number 50 Mobile Field Hospital making
our way to the assembly area." He came right
up to me. I was in my battle dress and tin hat
and I had a pack on my back. He looked right
at my face and all he said was "Good God!"
Then he told us he'd take us down there. So

Molly and I and our armed escort followed
him. We didn't know what he meant by
"down there." Then he came to the steps and
to me it looked as though it might be an
underground shelter, but it was actually a
gun emplacement. He told us to wait there
for a jeep. There were troops inside. One soldier, on seeing us, shouted, "Watch out, Adolf.
You've had it now!" We stayed with these
wonderful young men for about twenty minutes and then the jeep came.

We got into the jeep, but we didn't go
many yards before the driver told us to get
out and take cover. This happened about two
or three times before he said we'd be better
on foot. I remember crouching by a little
bush. It wasn't a very big bush. Molly and the
escort were somewhere crouching nearby. I
could see these red balls of tracer fire coming
toward me. They were called flaming onions.
I thought they were coming straight at me,

ABOVE: The Canadian 3d
Division's reserve forma-
tion, the Regiment de la
Chaudière, disembarks
from LCAs during the mid-
afternoon of D-DAY. A variety of knocked-out tanks
lay exposed on JUNO
Beach as the tide recedes
from the high-water mark
reached at 12:45 P.M.

ABOVE: The 2d Battalion, East Yorkshire Regiment, pushes east toward a pair of German strongpoints near the southwest corner of Ouistreham, supported by a DD tank of the 13/18 Hussars. The Sherman's gun is trained on a possible target, and it wears a now-deflated canvas flotation screen around its hull. Even though two Hussar DDs were lost at sea and ten more were lost on the beach, the battalion still remained a potent force, with twenty-eight operational tanks.

but I was told afterwards that they weren't all that close. But it didn't help me at the time. I felt, Well, this is it. I'm going to be killed before I see to one casualty. There was a bit of a lull, so we made tracks toward the road, where we got a lift in a lorry. ∎

—Iris Bower

🎙️ *Danger lurked under each step the soldiers took. A nasty assortment of mines lay buried under the picturesque French countryside. Clearing those mines for the Canadian troops was another duty for RAF ground crewman John Murphy.*

To clear the mines, my friend and I would set into motion on our hands and knees. He would take the north and I would take the south. In other words, we were bottom to bottom and moved in a circle to clear that place. We started doing that and we cleared a few antitank mines and put them very carefully aside. But what we didn't know at that time was that antipersonnel mines were planted underneath the antitank mines. So my friend Jack put his toe into the hole of a mine that we had taken out. We heard the click and knew that that was trouble. All we could do was lay flat. It was a jumping mine, otherwise known as Bouncing Betties. These mines

had a tip on them like a three-pronged green flower. They were on a stem just like a flower and being green meant it blended in well with the fields. If you touched the top, it downed and depressed the charge. If you were lying flat, you might miss the charge or minimize it. But you didn't want it to explode when you were on your feet. There was no getting away from the explosion. This one jumped about four feet (1.2m) and exploded with ball bearings. As it exploded, Jack panicked a bit and started to rise. Ball bearings hit his back and head. They tore off his clothes and equipment. He survived, but he had quite a few wounds. ∎

—John Murphy

Pushing Inland

The British 8th Brigade did not wait for the beach strongpoints to be subdued. By mid-morning the brigade had surged inland with the few available Shermans and Churchills that had extricated themselves from the chaos on the beach, and was tackling additional German fortifications just beyond the inland villages of Hermanville and Colleville. Meanwhile, the British commando battalions landed and peeled off to perform their assigned missions, and yet another formation, the 185th Brigade Group, slated to spearhead the drive to Caen, pushed out on foot when it became apparent that its tank support had become similarly stuck. The "Tommies" deployed in a wide battle formation and marched steadily south for roughly two hours before the lead Shermans caught up with them. German antitank guns on Périers Ridge delayed the advance and destroyed nine tanks before being overwhelmed. Much to the surprise of the British, they discovered that the unit belonged to the 21st Panzer, a division that they were not supposed to confront until they had driven south of Caen.

As other British forces set up defensive positions on the ridge, the attack continued down the road to Caen. Three miles (4.8km) from the city's outskirts, British armor smacked into the forward tank elements of the 21st

Panzer Division rushing north along the same road to assault the invasion beach. The Staffordshire Yeomanry and an attached anti-tank gun unit bested the 21st by knocking out ten Mark IV Panzers before the two forces broke off the engagement. The British continued south along the general line of the road and the forward elements of the 21st struck out north across the fields toward the beachhead. Approaching darkness and stiffening resistance only two miles (3.2km) from Caen convinced the British that their stretched-out force was far too weak to take on the enemy that might be gathering unseen along their front. Reluctantly, they pulled back to the town of Bieville for the night, not knowing that the high-water mark of their advance was the closest that any British unit would come to D-Day's key objective—the capture of Caen—for more than a month.

LEFT: Canadian soldiers battle Germans attempting to retreat through St. Lambert on bicycles and troop carriers. Some of the most effective "British" troops in the Normandy campaign proved to be the aggressive Canadians.

BRITISH 50TH INFANTRY DIVISION

The British 50th Infantry Division landed on Gold Beach and quickly pushed inland. It captured Bayeux on D+1, but found continued progress hampered by Normandy's hedgerow country and the appearance of German reinforcements. Determined attacks by elite formations such as Panzer-Lehr and the 12th SS Panzer Division were beaten back in savage fighting, and the 50th's slow progress mirrored that of the U.S. Army to the west. The division eventually ground its way past Caen and took part in the reduction of the Falaise-Argentan pocket in mid-August.

JUNO and "Those Damned Rocks"

That the Canadian Army would be an integral part of D-Day was never in doubt. After the tragedy at Dieppe, where the Canadians lost an appalling 75 percent of their raiding force—some 3,363 men killed or captured—national honor demanded it. Yet the decision to place the 3d Canadian Division at the center of the British onslaught must have given some planners pause. Juno was arguably the spot most likely to generate serious casualties.

German defenses along this summer vacation spot were generally on par with those of the flanking Gold and Sword Beaches. Strongpoints were mutually supporting and centered on pillboxes not facing out into the Channel, but sited to fire up and down the beach. Their seaward sides and extended portions of their fronts and rears were protected behind wide, gradually sloping banks of reinforced concrete, earth, and sand that not only were proof against anything short of a direct hit by a battleship's heavy guns, but were essentially invisible from the water. Beachfront cottages and houses in the towns of Courseulles, Bernières-sur-Mer, and St. Aubin-sur-Mer were strengthened for defense with generous amounts of concrete; minefields and barbed wire were both thick and cleverly placed. Yet none of these defensive measures were so impregnable that a determined, well-supported invader could not systematically breach them over a period of hours.

All planning for Juno, however, had to be shaped around the key terrain feature of the British invasion beaches—the Calvados Reef, which extended across the eastern half of the landing zone and abruptly ended at a mile (1.6km) wide channel in front of Courseulles. No assault during the June 5–7 window could be conducted before there was sufficient water to safely float DD tanks and LCIs over this barrier. A landing here could not be effected before 7:45 A.M. on June 6, and this dragged back the schedule all along the British front, severely complicating obstacle clearance.

LEFT: Second-wave troops of the 9th Canadian Brigade coming ashore near Bernières-sur-Mer on Juno Beach. The tide has almost reached its full height in this late-morning photo, making it difficult for vehicles to approach the bridge span running from the beach up to the seawall without flooding their engines. Another wave of landing craft will soon arrive, and the narrow strip of beach will become completely jammed with tanks and trucks until the tide begins to recede in the early afternoon. The thirty-foot (9.1m) span had been dropped into place by an AVRE of the 5th Assault Regiment, Royal Engineers, during the initial assault.

RIGHT: An LCA carrying Canadian soldiers in the first wave at JUNO Beach has just dropped its ramp, and the left-hand door is being opened to allow the men to emerge. The helmeted figure just above the three-quarter-inch (2cm) armor shield at right is the helmsman, and the individual crouching behind him in a life vest at upper right is another member of the crew, balancing on the craft's thin starboard deck. Subsequent frames show the troops piling out through the door while the other side remains closed to provide a semblance of protection to those still inside, and the hand of the crewman at upper right can be seen waving men forward.

OPPOSITE: Canadian troops trudge past a large bunker on JUNO Beach. Although the painted decoy image of a large coastal gun may look laughable, in the heat of battle—with smoke and haze obscuring its details—the decoy could well draw fire away from real German positions or confuse the attacking Allies.

With GOLD and SWORD's landing times coming twenty minutes earlier, demolition teams could make at least some headway against the devil's garden of mine-tipped stakes and hedgehogs, but, at JUNO, there was no way around the fact that the necessary delay would send the first waves of the 8th Canadian Brigade Group directly into obstacles. The 2d Canadian Brigade Group's landing craft, approaching the western half of the beach opposite Courseulles, were to be given a ten-minute head start, so that their demolition teams would have at least some semblance of a chance at blowing and marking gaps.

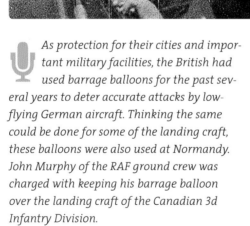

As protection for their cities and important military facilities, the British had used barrage balloons for the past several years to deter accurate attacks by low-flying German aircraft. Thinking the same could be done for some of the landing craft, these balloons were also used at Normandy. John Murphy of the RAF ground crew was charged with keeping his barrage balloon over the landing craft of the Canadian 3d Infantry Division.

We hoped the bombing would be sufficient for us to land without too many casualties, which proved very much [to be true]. The ship that was shelling our particular beach, JUNO Beach, was HMS *Belfast*. That was the city of my birth, and I felt rather proud that it was doing its stuff. As soon as we boarded the landing craft, the balloon was flying. It could be brought in at nighttime when it wasn't required. Ours was a small balloon. It was ten feet (3m) in length and about four feet (1.2m) in diameter. There was always a hazard with hydrogen as a storm came up. Many a balloon was burst with lightning. They just collapsed and dropped to the ground. The cable could rub round [saw back and forth], which was a hazard in itself, especially since it was explosive. So many casualties happened with that. The storm that was threatening on D-DAY didn't help much when trying to judge the height and the position of the balloon on top of that LCT. We used the top deck to fly the balloon.

The sky looked bleak. The winds were blowing. We were anxious about saving our balloon, and we brought it in to less than five hundred feet (152.4m), so we wouldn't lose it. Otherwise, we couldn't give cover to the Canadians landing on the beach. We brought it in to three hundred feet (91.4m). Nevertheless, it was swaying viciously from side to side, and we were hoping the cable wouldn't snap before we had done our shooting. Meanwhile, there was an awful lot of seasickness, and I wasn't exempt from that. I thought if an enemy aircraft flew over, they would probably recognize it, but I couldn't do much about it. I couldn't try to avoid it because I was so seasick.

As we witnessed the shelling from the warships, we knew that we were getting very close. As soon as we saw the shore, we were blowing the alert, Get ready. That meant [keeping] our ammunition high up so as not to get into the water, and our backpacks, Sten gun, and one hand grenade clipped on the side. Then the order came to drop the front of the LCT. The tanks went off at first, the infantry followed, and we followed them. We were told that the tide was flowing to the extent that it wouldn't reach over our knee, but that didn't happen. We went off the ship and found that it had come up to the lower waist. There was the hazard of carrying the balloon and your ammunition and keeping it dry while watching for floating

We could hear the guys inside [the pillbox] yelling. We didn't know what they were yelling, and I told the sergeant maybe they wanted to surrender. . . . He said, "F--k 'em," and yelled at the guy with the flamethrower to turn on the heat, and you should have heard those Germans in the pillbox screaming. God it was awful.

—Barry Broadfoot,
in *Six War Years: 1939–1945*

The Great Race: The Allied and German Buildup in Normandy

Who would win the race to dominate the invasion area? Would the Germans, deceived by Operation FORTITUDE, commit only a half-dozen or so fresh divisions to the defense of Normandy in the week after D-DAY? Or would they quickly recognize that, far from being an Allied feint to draw their forces from the Pas-de-Calais, Normandy was indeed the site of the long-awaited invasion of "Fortress Europe"? For Field Marshal Bernard Law Montgomery and the other Allied leaders, this latter possibility was the nightmare scenario.

Three weeks before the invasion, at St. Paul's School in London, Montgomery conducted a final briefing for King George VI, Prime Minister Churchill, and the most senior Allied generals in Britain. Montgomery warned that although elements of six German divisions would face eight Allied divisions on D-DAY, a decisive reaction by the Germans could result in the ten and a half Allied divisions expected ashore on D+1 to be confronted by nine enemy divisions—four of them Panzer formations launched at the British near Caen. By D+8, eighteen or fewer Allied divisions could be fighting for their lives against twenty-four German, including ten Panzer divisions.

Even if the Germans continued to be deceived by FORTITUDE, and the massed attacks by more than a thousand tanks and self-propelled guns failed to materialize, the Panzer divisions held in readiness near the targeted beaches were expected to launch a coordinated assault as early as D+3. Yet even this never happened. Confident that they would easily sweep the British and Canadians into the sea, German commanders threw their Panzer divisions one by one into the battle, and each was repulsed in turn. The number of German divisions in Normandy briefly surpassed those of the Allies by sixteen to fifteen on D+7, June 13, but all had suffered serious losses and several had been beaten down to little more than battalion strength.

Superb defensive terrain—and a resolve that crossed into fanaticism in some units—held the steadily growing Allied armies at bay for more than a month, but German forces received few reinforcements and almost no equipment during the battle of attrition. By the end of July, some fourteen British-Canadian divisions and twenty American divisions had landed in France. Ironically, the number of U.S. soldiers disembarked across the invasion beaches passed the one-million mark on July 4, 1944. The stage was set for the breakout from Normandy.

BELOW: A line of Shermans from the 2d Canadian Armored Brigade moves carefully between the surf and a very crowded JUNO Beach on its way to an exit inland. The tide is receding in this photo taken on D-DAY afternoon.

The balloons were spread to create cover, but also not to be close enough to entangle with one another because of the weather conditions that were prevailing at the time. It would never have done for two balloons to entangle and lose [both]. One balloon was allotted to every six landing craft, infantry, or tank with just enough space to let them fly freely. If any were shot down, there weren't any replacements at that time. Meantime, we didn't lose ours. We carried on with it and advanced with the Canadian 3d Division.

We were called a combined operation squad, to fit in with the Navy and the Army. We had a special badge to denote that. The badge had the wings of the RAF, the rifle and bayonet in the middle for the Army, and the anchor representing the Navy. We were truly combined with all three on D-Day. ■

—John Murphy

The Assault

Rough seas forced the British Army and Royal Navy commanders to delay the landings by ten minutes on both sides of JUNO beach in hopes of making a coordinated attack, but the carefully crafted timetable had been knocked completely awry with Royal Engineers arriving uselessly a further twenty minutes late. Obstacles were fully submerged and landing craft could do little more than simply plow straight ahead toward the shore with expected results. Fully 90 of the 306 landing craft taking part at JUNO were either sunk or damaged, yet, at the end of the day, Canadian casualties were much the same as those at GOLD and SWORD beaches. Each had lost about 1,000 men, and the Canadian 3d Division's final tally amounted to less than 1,000 men, including 335 killed.

While some German strongpoints held out well into the afternoon and inflicted very heavy casualties on the Queen's Own Rifles and the North Shore Regiment, lower than expected rates of fire from other formidable but lightly manned positions allowed the highly motivated Canadians to consolidate quickly. Effective use of the *funnies* was credited with keeping casualties down, and JUNO, the one D-Day beach that truly required the use of DD tanks capable of steering between obstacles, was also the only site at which a significant portion of the tanks actually landed ahead of the infantry to start the reduction of the beach emplacements.

By mid-morning the Canadian-Scottish Regiment and the Royal Winnipeg Rifles were pushing inland, and armored units followed as soon as they were able to break free of the inevitable congestion along the high-tide line. The Canadian 3d Division linked up with SWORD near La Rivière on their right by nightfall. It had seized more territory than any other division, expanding its beachhead to twelve miles (19.3km) wide by six miles (9.7km) deep, but it would be July before the soldiers of the Canadian 3d Division finally overran their D-Day objective, Carpiquet Airfield, west of Caen.

Those landing on the beaches included journalists such as Charles Lynch of Canada, serving as the correspondent for Reuters News Service. His equipment for landing varied from that carried by the soldiers.

We went on board the ships. I had my typewriter and a wicker basket full of carrier pigeons that I was told to bring ashore. They had been trained to find their way back to their home loft in Southampton. My ship was the command ship for the 9th Canadian Brigade, the reserve brigade. The 7th and 8th were the assault brigades. The 9th was to go in an hour afterwards.

The ship was an old Irish sea ferry. It had a lounge and a piano. I played the piano and we sang songs 'til the dawn broke and the shore of Normandy was in sight. I retrieved my pigeons and my typewriter before climbing down the nets into the ALC [landing craft]. It was H-HOUR+1.

The only feeling I recall having when landing at Normandy was indignation. I stepped off the landing craft, and the water was four feet (1.2m) deep instead of two feet (0.6m), as we had been told. On my head I had a typewriter and a basket of pigeons. I wanted to roar at the guy who opened the ramp too

ABOVE: British casualties wounded during the first landings in France are helped ashore at an English port on D-Day afternoon. They were brought back across the Channel on an American LST(H) acting as a hospital ship.

went over and he said, Come in. I went in and he served me some strawberries and cream while showing me his photograph album of himself as a French war veteran of the Madagascar campaign in 1895. Here I am on D-Day, two hours into the assault, looking at this album. I excused myself. He invited me back if I needed a place to sleep.

I wandered around but couldn't find my colleagues. I saw as much as I could, talked to everybody I could find, and when night fell I returned to the farmhouse. The old man put me up. I slept between sheets. We had an attack that night when the *Luftwaffe* made a few passes, and there was some gunfire. I must have passed the most peaceful night of anybody in the Normandy beachhead.

From then on, it took me about three days to really get my bearings. We thought the assault was going to be by far the toughest thing. It wasn't. There were much heavier battles for the Canadians after the assault and the actual landing on the beach. You began to get excited and to get a feeling that there's no place that you'd rather be. ▪

—Charles Lynch,
Reuters Correspondent (CAN)

soon that this wasn't on the schedule. Some did even worse and got dumped out to their death. Some drowned. Some tanks sank because they drove off the end, and it was twenty feet (6m) deep instead of being ten (3m).

The Canadian beach was a flat beach. Not thinly defended, but not nearly as vulnerable as OMAHA. So the battle on the beach was over very quickly. By the time we arrived, there were bodies lying around. Not a lot, but enough. The great fear when we arrived at H-HOUR+1 was mines. Already the white tapes were in position for the troops, and they were running up the lanes without fear of being blown up, so I ran up the beach, too, and that was great. The battle was a mile inland by that time. Here I was. My new uniform and I had no idea about the military. But I knew a lot about journalism.

I wandered around and started walking toward the sound of the battle, figuring that was the way to go with my pigeons. I passed a French farmhouse and there was a French farmer on the stoop. He summoned me. I

The Commandos

A unique feature of the British invasion plan was their extensive use of commando battalions to perform special missions independent of the assault divisions. This battle-hardened force had been conducting operations large and small since before the fall of France and was a model for the recently formed U.S. Army Rangers, which stormed the cliffs at Pointe du Hoc. The 41st, 47th, and 48th Royal Marine Commandos (RMCs) formed the 4th Special Service Brigade and were landed, one each, on the three invasion beaches. The 3d, 4th, and 6th Commandos (Army units), plus the 45th Royal Marines and two companies of Free French *fusiliers-marins,* all came in at SWORD and made up the 1st Special Service Brigade.

During the mid-morning hours of D-DAY, a number of follow-on units suffered badly along portions of the obstacle belt that had not been cleared before the incoming tide washed over them. The 47th RMC, landing on the extreme right flank of the British lodgment, shared their misfortune. The commandos were tasked to move cross-country for five miles (8km), avoiding all enemy contact until reaching Port-en-Bessin, then seize the town at the eastern boundary of OMAHA Beach in a lightning strike. The submerged obstacle belt off GOLD ensured that this operation would not go off as planned. Three of the 47th RMC's five LCIs struck mines and sank, killing forty-three commandos and resulting in the loss of much vital equipment. The survivors swam ashore, re-formed, and re-equipped as best they could inland of the Le Hamel strongpoint, and marched west through German territory. Hours behind schedule, they were unable to reach their target before nightfall, but they did capture Port-en-Bessin the next day.

Change a few details, like place-names and the number of landing craft struck, and you largely have a description of the 48th RMC's operation to link the JUNO beachhead with SWORD at the town of Langrune-sur-Mer. Moving west out of SWORD to meet them, the 41st RMC, greatly weakened by casualties suffered on the shore, had just begun to break their way into Lion-sur-Mer when both commando groups were ordered to halt their

converging attacks and organize for defense. Throughout the slender length of SWORD Beach penetration, units were told to prepare for an onslaught of Panzers. Along the coast, the two depleted 4th Brigade battalions were separated by a gap of almost three miles (4.8km). Although very lightly armed, they possessed a pair of weapons that had proved unbeatable during massed tank attacks along the shores of Sicily and Italy—radios for contacting the ships offshore and the guns of the Royal Navy.

On the other side of SWORD, the 1st Special Service Brigade's 4th Commando and the Free French fusiliers-marins methodically reduced the Riva Bella strongpoint and other defenses in Ouistreham. The brigade's commander, Brigadier Lord Lovat (known affectionately as "Skinny"), had promised to relieve the paratroopers at the Bénouville bridges by noon, but he was delayed by the sinking of three landing craft as well as enemy forces along the four-mile (6.4km) route to the bridge. The 6th Commando strode up to the hard-pressed men at the bridges alongside a group of Hussar tanks as their bagpipest played "Blue Bonnets over the Border," and Lovat sincerely apologized for their late arrival. Behind the 6th came the 45th RMC, which passed through the bridgehead and swung north with a squadron of Hussar Shermans in the first of several attempts to secure the Merville Battery area.

BELOW: A shot over the bow of the LCI(S) bringing the command group of Lord Lovat's 1st Special Service Brigade to SWORD Beach opposite La Brèche. LCI(S)s, frequently used by commandos, carried half the men—roughly one hundred—of an LCI(L) and were capable of quickly disembarking troops over four bow ramps, while their larger cousins only had two. At right, out of range of the photo, a bridge-laying AVRE had dropped its span over the edge of the seawall only moments before. The plethora of vehicles on the rapidly shrinking shoreline belong to Squadron B of the 13/18 Hussars; the 22d Dragoons; and the 5th Assault Regiment, Royal Engineers.

LEFT AND BELOW:
Soldiers, possibly comman-
dos, come ashore on a
British beachhead on D-
DAY afternoon.

🎙 As Geoffrey Parrett and his fellow commandos moved inland, they encountered one of the devastating hazards of
war—friendly fire.

Once we started moving forward, it got better. We were in a different place every night,
and we began to sleep in barns and farm-
yards and things like that. It was so much
better than the slit trenches.

Our entire brigade went out, one behind
the other, in the blackest night of the year.
You couldn't see a hand in front of you. The
intelligence officer reconnoitered ahead with
the maps and laid a white tape for us to follow. We did this all night. The fellow in front
of me had a white enamel mug on his pack. I
could just see that, and I desperately kept looking at it. I thought, I
don't want to lose
him, because you
couldn't even see the
tape on the ground it
was so black.

It was just about
five o'clock in the
morning and starting
to get light when we
reached our comman-
do's objective. There
was a fairly nice
house on the right as
we were going up. All
of a sudden there was
a scream, and this German officer came running out. Our forward men had shot him. We
passed him. I remember looking at him,
thinking he had an awful five o'clock shadow
because he had probably just gotten out of
bed. He was probably the duty officer, and
was wearing high black boots.

My troop commander ordered my
sergeant's squad to clear that house. So we
walked up to this house. We were in the front
garden and my sergeant said, "Okay, Parrett.
You and Richards stay here and watch out on
to the flanks." And there's a little crop of trees
behind it. Meanwhile, they went into the
house. The other fellows in the squad went
into the bedroom, and there were five

Germans still fast asleep in bed. In the next room there was a German sergeant—six people total. Our sergeant sent them downstairs and they came out of the front door to where Richards and I were. We were beginning to organize them when automatic fire suddenly came cracking all around us. I was petrified and threw myself on the ground. I found myself looking down the breach of my rifle and wondering what I was going to do. Just then the sergeant came out the front door and threw himself down beside me. He realized what was happening and yelled, "Cease fire, you fools! You killed one of my men." It was Number 45 Royal Marine Commando coming up behind us. They had seen the caps of the Germans and thought we were all Germans, so they had just let rip at us. Poor Richards received a whole magazine of Tommy-gun fire. Meanwhile, the Germans were disappearing into those trees; the whole lot of them escaped. It was really the most shaken I've been in all my life. To see Richards— I'd dug in with him, and I felt very sad.

You really relied on one another. There never did seem to be enough men to go around for anything. One thing that struck me was the loneliness of it. Before I went, I used to feel that everybody was there together. You had sixty-eight men in a troop and all sixty-eight of you were there together, so we could do anything. But in actuality, you saw two people there and two people fifteen yards over there and that was all. You thought, We're here practically alone. The front line could be a very lonely and deserted place sometimes.

My troop commander used to say, Only the good ones go, and we all gradually get good and then we go. I always remembered him saying that because it was the real decent ones who seemed to become casualties.

I felt very lonely at times. Richards had gone, and there was another fellow in the troop who was very well educated. I liked him, and he really looked after me and helped me. A couple of days later he ran across a gap in the hedge and was killed. I pray for them still—all of them. ▪

—Geoffrey Parrett

BELOW: Smoke rises from a Sherman flail tank that has been hit by an antitank round during the initial landings on SWORD Beach. A carpet-laying Churchill and an unidentified AVRE are at left.

As inroads were being made on the Allied beaches, the men of the British 6th Airborne Division were thankful for the reinforcements. Nearly twelve hours had passed since their gliders had touched down on French soil. Corporal Wally Parr heard the sweet call of a bugle heralding the arrival of Lord Lovat and his men.

All of a sudden, listen. We heard a bugle, another one there, then another bugle, and Major [John] Howard said, "That's it chaps. The commandos are nearly here, they're coming." We let rip with everything. Fired at anything or everybody we could. About half an hour later, we heard a bugle sound in Bénouville, followed shortly by the sound of bagpipes. I shot out of the gun pit and went to the end of the bridge and looked over toward the T-junction, and marching down the road was Lord Lovat and his commandos. He was wearing a white roll-neck pullover, a pack on his back, and marching to his right and two paces in front of him was a bloke playing the bagpipes. They came out and for

some reason I dashed across the bridge to meet them. I don't know why, it was just an impulse. Lovat held his hand up. I saluted and said, "We're very pleased to see you, sir."

He replied, "Well done, well done." He asked where our company command post was located. I said it was on the other side of the bridge. As I turned back, the proprietor of the café came out holding two bottles of champagne and three glasses. He was shouting, laughing, and crying all at the same time. Lord Lovat just looked at him, spoke to him in French, and all I understood him to say was "Non, non." Charlie Gardner dashed over and joined me. We stood there and drank champagne outside the café. That was it.

The story ends on Pegasus Bridge at eleven o'clock that night when I handed over the six-pounder [antitank gun] to a sergeant who was part of our reinforcements. His complaint was he was infantry, not artillery. I reminded him that I was infantry, then showed him how to work it and left him to get on with it. ◼

—Wally Parr

OPPOSITE, TOP AND BOTTOM: Soldiers of the 4th Special Service Brigade command group come ashore at the eastern end of JUNO Beach near St. Aubin. In the image at top, commandos can be seen manhandling the headquarters' motorbikes at center and at the top of the neighboring LCI's ramp. In the bottom photo, a commando with a bicycle heads for the drink after his footing fails on a broken rung.

BELOW: Lord Lovat's personal bagpiper, Bill Mullin, starts down the ramp that will take him to SWORD Beach and immortality as the piper who marched into the paratrooper perimeter at the Bénouville Bridge playing "Blue Bonnets over the Border." The soldier between the line of commandos running to the beach and Mullin's left shoulder is reputed to be Lord Lovat.

mines, which were all around. In fact, our very first casualty was a Canadian soldier who drowned. He had gone into a very deep portion of the sea, and his equipment took him under.

The beaches were heavily mined. This was where the old training and searching for the mines began to take effect. We cleared a space for ourselves on the beach, despite the sniping and the machine-gun fire. We were glad the German Air Force wasn't in sight. We had anticipated that there would be plenty of raiding by the German Air Force and it was a few hours later before we encountered the first of the German aircraft: a *Messerschmidt* had breached the defenses of the hundreds of Allied planes flying all day long.

We anchored the balloon on the Canadian front line. Then we had to dig a foxhole and try and make contact with our beachmaster, who was about a mile (1.6km) up the beach for the next advance forward. I've never dug a foxhole so fast in all my life. I jumped into it.

ABOVE: A "Cromwell" with wading trunks emerges from an LST on GOLD Beach. Cromwell tanks armed with 75-mm guns were the mainstay of British armored divisions during the Normandy campaign.

LEFT: The appearance of the Sherman "Firefly," mounting a high-velocity 17-pounder gun, came as a nasty surprise to German Panzer formations.

to ask the king for his pass. He was the one who was not to be approached. He didn't have a double. Winston Churchill rather grumpily showed me his pass. For General Eisenhower, I said, "Excuse me, sir. Could I see your pass?" He was talking to his friend, put his arm around me, and retrieved the wallet out of his pocket. He said, "Here you are, son. Help yourself." I had to go through his wallet looking at all the photographs of his wife Mamie and their children until eventually I got the pass and handed it back to him. He thanked me. He was like a favorite uncle. Monty was more like the headmaster. Not unfriendly. He was thought highly of by the troops because they knew that in his way he was a winner. People had faith in him. The ordinary men trusted Monty.

You had to be extremely careful about who you let in. There were no rows of barbed wire to keep people out. Monty relied on the loyalty of the men—the guards and the sentries—to keep him safe. One day, soon after we'd established ourselves in the park of Créullet, a sentry sent for me. I went there and found the sentry with his gun and fixed bayonet. I asked what was the problem. He said the man refused to show his pass. There towering above us was a man about six-feet-six (238cm) in height, standing there like a monument, refusing to show his pass. He said he was General de Gaulle. I said, "I'm sorry, sir, but no one gets in here without a pass." He was furious. Again, I said I was sorry, but he still needed to show his pass. Eventually he did show his pass. The sentry heaved a sigh of relief, and the general walked in. He reported me and the sentry to Montgomery for impertinence. Monty told him to stop bellyaching, because his men had a job to do.

Monty was a lonely man. He wanted solitude but complained of loneliness. He was very fond of animals. We had a menagerie that traveled with us wherever we went. In his caravan were two dogs, one called Hitler, the other Rommel, a horse, a cow called Mabel—the only female allowed in the camp. He had a cage of tropical birds and a tank of tropical fish. Perhaps he felt animals were more reliable than human beings. ■

—Norman Kirby

OPPOSITE: A never-ending stream of trucks belonging to the Canadian 3d Division rolls past an LST waiting for high tide to float it free from Juno Beach.

ABOVE: Commandos move inland from one of the British sector beaches.

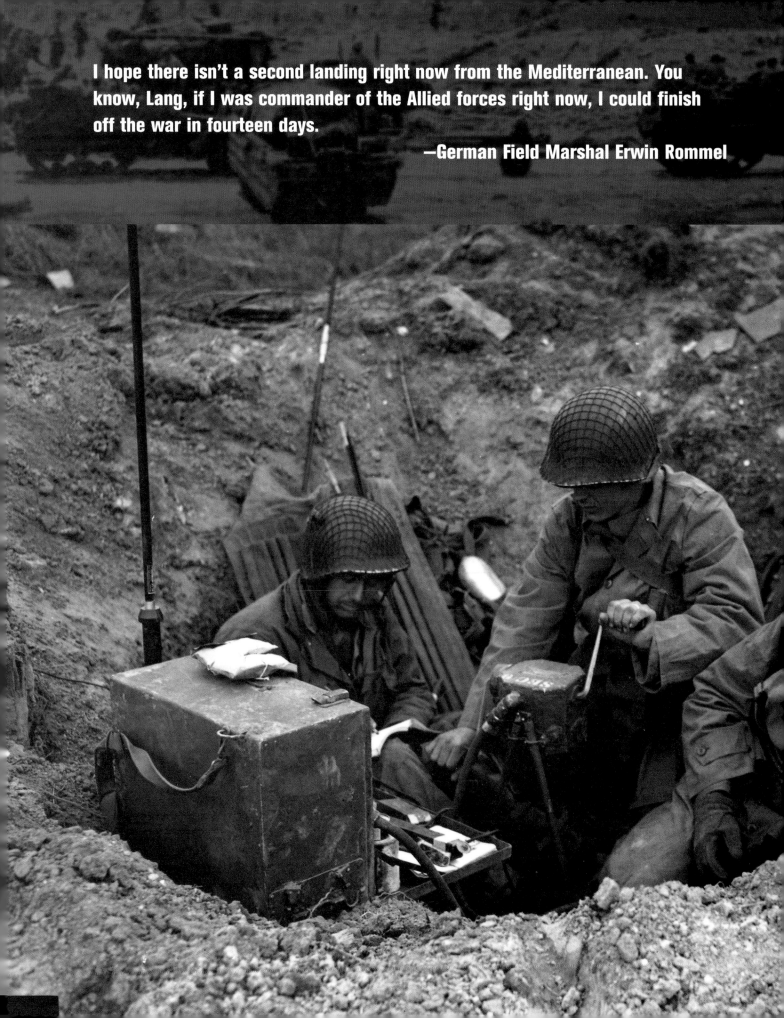

I hope there isn't a second landing right now from the Mediterranean. You know, Lang, if I was commander of the Allied forces right now, I could finish off the war in fourteen days.

—German Field Marshal Erwin Rommel

Chapter Six

COUNTERATTACKS AND CONSOLIDATION

Communications within Normandy were so thoroughly disrupted that His Majesty's forces were already fighting their way inland from GOLD and SWORD beaches before the German Seventh Army learned at 8:45 A.M. of the British landings. Remarkably, absolutely nothing was known of the completely unanticipated use of UTAH Beach for a large-scale operation until 11 A.M., some four and a half hours after the Americans came ashore. Other information reaching German commanders was seriously flawed and led to a wasteful commitment of scarce reserves. For example, Germany's realization that Pointe du Hoc had been attacked prompted the 352d Division's reserve battalion in the OMAHA Beach sector to send a platoon to strengthen the garrison—which had already fallen. Then, throughout the day, ever-increasing forces arrived on the scene until nearly the full battalion was battling the Rangers at the Pointe—forces that could have been much more profitably deployed against the few vulnerable penetrations in the bluffs to the east.

But as far as the 352d Division's commander was concerned, his two regiments at OMAHA Beach had the situation well in hand. As late

The writing [is] already on the wall for our proud 6th Regiment. . . . Enormous explosions can be heard in the north and the northeast, which must be coming from the enemy's naval heavy artillery. We can also hear the noise of battle from that direction.

**—German 1st Lieutenant Martin Pöppel,
6th *Fallschirmjäger* Regiment, Carentan**

PAGES 190–191: A Shore Fire Control Party inland from UTAH Beach communicates with warships of Bombarding Force A. The soldier at center is cranking the generator for the bulky SCR-284 radio at left, while the soldier at right uses a walkie-talkie to receive fire coordinates from ground units fighting the Germans nearby. Unlike the British, who commonly moved such equipment on carts, this and similar-sized radio sets were carried on the backs of American soldiers. One of the large rubber bags used to carry radio equipment through the surf is at the upper left.

as 1:35 in the afternoon, Rommel's Army Group B headquarters received a message passed up the chain of command from LXXXIV Corps, responsible for the defense of all of Normandy, that "the situation in the area of the 352d Division is now restored," and the corps staff perceived the threat from the British beaches to be much more serious. Consequently, the 352d Division's third regiment and attached units, called *Kampfgruppe* Meyer, was tasked with assaulting the western flank of the British lodgment.

Their's was an impossible task. Since 3 A.M., when it was first put on alert because of the parachute landings on the Cotentin, *Kampfgruppe* Meyer had been marched, countermarched, divided up, regrouped, and countermarched again as it received a series of different missions from the LXXXIV Corps staff at St. Lô, which was desperately trying to come to grips with the contradictory reports flooding into its headquarters. The unit, which had begun D-Day threateningly close to OMAHA Beach, had ultimately gravitated well to the west, near the American airdrops, then was ordered in mid-morning to turn around and move laterally across the OMAHA sector to strike the British forces threatening Bayeux.

Throughout the rest of the day *Kampfgruppe* Meyer painfully worked its way east, its progress marked by tall columns of oily, black smoke as vehicle after vehicle fell victim to Allied fighter-bombers, or "Jabos," searching for prey along the Normandy roads. Thrown piecemeal against the invaders in evening assaults, one German battalion and some self-propelled guns briefly retook Colleville from the U.S. 1st Infantry Division, pushing inland from OMAHA Beach, before being surrounded. About

5:30 P.M., the balance of the *Kampfgruppe* formed up for a two-battalion attack against the British 69th Brigade Group from SWORD, but was simply overwhelmed by the size and violence of the British advance. The ninety men of *Kampfgruppe* Meyer who survived D-DAY were absorbed by one of the 352d Infantry Division's other severely mauled regiments.

The paratroopers had been fighting in the French countryside for hours prior to the landings. Later that morning they headed toward the beaches and hoped to link up with landing forces coming from the other direction. Others had the task of holding certain key points, ensuring that they were not taken by the enemy. Sergeant O.B. Hill of the 82d Airborne Division faced stiff German opposition as he and his fellow paratroopers from a variety of units moved out.

We had lost five men by ten o'clock. Our ranks numbered men from the 504, 505, 507 [Parachute Regiments], as well as some from the 101st [Airborne Division]. Those guys had been dropped probably fifteen miles (24.1km) from where they were supposed to land. But they were there with us too. All of us had experienced the same type of training. We had equal amounts of faith in the one to our right as in the one to our left, no matter what unit he was from. So we felt like we were a pretty good group. We had no heavy weapons, nothing but our rifles and grenades. We had no officers, and after we crossed the road and all of us were together, we wondered what was around us. We couldn't really tell from where we were because of the two-story buildings in front along the road. We decided that if we got one of those buildings, we could see what was around us.

So Ray Humboldt and I shot the back door off one of the houses, went upstairs, and there were two big windows overlooking the road. Coming down the road were three German tanks. One of them stopped right in front of our house. The turret opened, and this German stood up in the tank and looked around to see what was going on. So I handed Ray a Gammon grenade, and he dropped it inside the tank, right in front of this German. After it went off, the tank was like an eggshell and out of action. The other two tanks started looking around to see what had blown up the third tank. They didn't know that we were up there. But we took off. At that point I just knew those tanks were going to come back, and we had no chance to wipe them out. I had a few moments to think, and I remembered my hometown square. There was a plaque of all the names of the World War I dead, and I wondered if my name would be listed for World War II. At times like this, it doesn't pay to have time to think, because you become depressed.

By noon of the sixth, we learned from a couple of Frenchmen that we were in Beuzeville-la-Bastille, and Chef-du-Pont was straight ahead to our right across some causeways. So we started moving in that direction and every time we would move from one hedgerow to the other, we were fired at from both ends by the Germans. We were surrounded on two sides by the river. And we couldn't go out that way because they were across the river and could see us. The other two sections had roads. There was a house at the corner of that crossroad. We reached the last hedgerow, and that's as far as we could go, and we stayed there five days. The Germans had us in that house and were firing on us. In the middle of the afternoon, we realized that they had some of our men as prisoners, so we stopped firing for a while. After about an hour and a half, they started shelling us with mortar shells, so we started firing back. Evidently they had moved the prisoners out of there by that time and taken them down the road elsewhere. Ray and I dug foxholes along the hedgerows, some of them facing one way and others the opposite way.

BELOW: A farmhouse burns as U.S. troops fight to clear German troops from the UTAH Beach area.

ABOVE: A 79th Infantry Division soldier uses an M7 launcher to fire a fragmentation grenade from behind an earthen embankment during the drive north toward Cherbourg. The opposite sides of hedgerow-enclosed fields were usually well beyond the range of even the best throwing arm, and lofted grenades were more easily deflected by thickly tangled branches and vines than those shot from grenade launchers or than rockets fired from bazooka launchers. Although each infantry company had a section of three 60-mm mortars capable of firing tight concentrations of rounds at selected targets behind hedgerows, the rugged terrain and difficult communications resulted in M7 launchers and almost-as-plentiful M1A1 bazookas serving as the "mobile artillery" of individual rifle squads and platoons.

We were determined not to give up. We referred to that field as "hell's half acre." By the fifth day we were down to our last couple of clips. The sound of friendly weapons approaching was a welcome sound. When a platoon of men from the 90th Division drove the Germans out with a bazooka, we stood and cheered. They thought we would get shot, but we were so happy we didn't care!

The feeling that all of us had there in that field was just pure frustration because there weren't enough of us to overrun the Germans on this crossroad, and we didn't have the right kind of equipment. If we could have had access to the equipment bundles and gotten some bigger guns, a couple of machine guns and a mortar or two and maybe a BAR, we could've really done some good. We did all right with what we had, but we could've done a lot better. ▥

—O.B. Hill

Bill True of the 101st Airborne Division was greatly relieved to find troops marching in from the beaches as he was attempting to find more men from his F Company, 506th Parachute Infantry Regiment.

From the time of landing, the thought was we needed to get toward the beaches and take care of as many of our objectives as possible, so that the infantry coming up the beaches could be successful. By the time we got closer to the beach and daylight was starting to come, we could hear the big naval guns. That was a mighty welcome sound to hear the Navy coming in, knowing that those guys were landing. By daylight there were infantry troops coming up from the beach. I hollered over at the guy heading the column and said, "Hey Mack, what outfit is that?" as a friendly way to greet some other Americans. He hollered back and told me what it was, and as they got closer, I realized he was a full colonel. I had called him "Mack." I felt a little sheepish, but he didn't take offense.

On the afternoon of D-Day, Joe Flick in my squad volunteered us to go out on a reconnaissance patrol. There were six of us. It was intended strictly as reconnaissance—we were to go out and make a big circle around an area and see if there were any Germans. If we ran into any Germans, [we were to] come straight back. I can remember Joe was the last one, and a guy from another platoon was at the head of the patrol. I was next to the last.

While walking along this hedgerow, I glanced out into the field and a German soldier was just aiming his pistol at one of the guys up the line. That was the first time I had a really clear picture of what I was shooting at. There was the enemy. Later, thinking about it, I was impressed with how good my training had been because it was the most automatic thing to bring my rifle to my shoulder—taking the safety off as I brought it up—and squeezing off the trigger as calmly as on a firing range. But I missed him. By the time I squeezed off another round, my rifle jammed. Then by the time I got that straightened out—which probably was only about three or four seconds—he was down because the guys in front had cut him down in a hurry. There were two other soldiers with him that I had seen just a little ways behind him. Of course, they disappeared in the deep grass. So we figured, Okay, this is the reconnaissance—let's go back and tell 'em that there are Germans out here. On the way out we had seen a field that had a lot of American ammunition—30-caliber machine-gun ammunition. We said, "Gee, we might need that sometime—we'd better stop and get that." So the guys went on into the field to get this ammunition, and I said, "I'll stay here on the road and look back here where those guys were to keep an eye out." I didn't know if those Germans might have been the advance part of a bigger unit.

At any rate, the guys were down in the field picking up the ammunition and a little black dog came trotting down the road. I figured little black dogs don't run around out there unless they're with somebody. Sure enough, there were three German soldiers coming along the hedgerow. And they were

close enough that I couldn't holler at the guys without the Germans hearing me too. I figured the best thing is fire a couple of shots at the Germans to alert my guys. Of course, the Germans disappeared the second I pulled off a round. Joe Flick, my buddy—he was always kind of a flamboyant sort of a guy—he said, "Where are they? Where are they?" as he's peeking out of the hedge. I whispered, "They went down that way." I loved the M1 rifle, but Joe liked the Thompson submachine gun. He jumped up on the road and was spraying that sub-Thompson in the general direction. He looked like John Wayne holding off a banzai attack. We didn't see any more of those Germans and returned from the patrol.

We did get involved in a fairly heavy firefight. I don't remember the details of it, except that I do remember one of our sergeants in company headquarters—a real bold guy who was one of the first guys to make sergeant

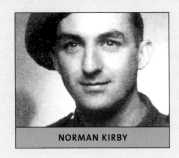

NORMAN KIRBY

Following the troops were the high-ranking officers. Sergeant Norman Kirby helped with preparations for Montgomery's (Monty's) arrival, as well as establishing headquarters for him. From this position, Kirby enjoyed the opportunity of meeting some of the twentieth century's most fascinating characters.

I think Monty arrived on D+1. Whenever he arrived anywhere, the morale went up. It's strange, because he was a small man with a rather thin, piping voice. He liked to work in solitude. There were three caravans for Monty. One of them was a map lorry. One was his house where he lived with his wardrobe, his bed, and his washbasin. The third one was a caravan he had liberated from the Italians in the desert.

Montgomery's officers found the park of the Château de Créullet for his headquarters. We settled there for awhile. Monty didn't live in the château. He lived the whole time in his caravan parked in the garden. On this French farm, the main body of the headquarters was in this big field. Monty was in a separate field with his very small elite group of officers. I had to report daily to Monty's caravan. When I entered that field, it was like going to see the headmaster or the prime minister. Even though I was walking through grass, it felt as if I was walking on somebody's best carpet. All the cows had to be removed. The hedge had to be taken down to create a little runway for Monty's aircraft. The farm gate had to be taken away, so that the tanks could go in. All the windows looking on to our field had to be blacked out. The owner wasn't allowed to use his front door; he had to use the back door. They had to put up with a lot from us.

I was on duty at a number of conferences where Monty was in charge. We had Winston Churchill, the king, General Eisenhower, General de Gaulle, and a number of big names who came to visit Monty once the beachhead was established. I wasn't allowed

back in Toccoa, Georgia, nearly two years before he died. A real good soldier, but I can still remember thinking at the time that he was exposing himself unnecessarily. I actually saw him killed. He was the first person I saw and knew who was killed. It was a traumatic and sobering experience. There was also a feeling of "at least it wasn't me," which sounds selfish, but it was basic survival. In the heat of a battle, you don't mourn a fallen comrade. Later, you have the time for it to sink in. Incidentally, he was one of five of our men in company headquarters to die. Years later is when you really feel it and really mourn buddies who died. Johnny Sepko was a little guy, and one of the youngest guys in the company. To stand at his grave in Normandy and know that I've lived a full life and had children and grandchildren, but he'll always be a boy who died there. It gets you and really punches you one. To visit a place like OMAHA Cemetery and know personally some of the fellows who are there affects you in a way nothing else does.

We figured we only had to do this for three days, then we'd get out of there and get back to England to get ready for another mission. Everything we had—the rations, the clothing, everything—was aimed at a three-day "crash mission" by the paratroops, and then out you go. But we ended up staying a month and a half. They needed us longer than they expected. ∎

—Bill True

Fallschirmjäger vs. Paratrooper

Allied invasion planners had become aware of the German 91st Air Landing Division's move onto the Cotentin Peninsula only at the end of May, just weeks before D-DAY. Drop zones for the U.S. 82d Airborne Division were shifted east to ensure that the Americans would not be coming down practically on top of the Germans, but it was still clear that the 82d

would be landing astride the assembly area of one of the division's reinforced grenadier regiments, with another nearby to the north. A dozen miles (19.3km) to the southeast, the 91st's third formation, the 6th *Fallschirmjäger* (Paratrooper) Regiment, and a battalion from one of the division's grenadier regiments guarded the town of Carentan at the inland junction of the UTAH and OMAHA sectors. The newly created 6th *Fallschirmjäger* was one of the best-trained infantry units in the German Army of 1944. An exceptionally large, all-volunteer regiment consisting of fifteen companies, the average age of its 3,457 men was just seventeen and a half.

The 91st Division's largely uncoordinated local attacks might have made some progress against the understrength and scattered elements of the 82d Airborne, but the Germans were just as hampered by the terrain as the Americans were. Their presence in force west of the Merderet River, however, was more than enough to throw off the U.S. VII Corp's timetable for its planned drive across the peninsula from UTAH Beach, then north to strike at Cherbourg. Plans had called for the port to be taken by D+8, June 14, but three days after the invasion, the paratroopers and supporting armor were still consolidating the single bridgehead across the Merderet in the face of determined resistance from the 91st Division.

The most serious D-DAY counterattack in the UTAH sector was launched after dark by the 6th *Fallschirmjäger*. The German paratroopers were to have followed on the heels of *Kampfgruppe* Meyer, adding depth and impetus to the armor-infantry strike. But with the *Kampfgruppe* jerked back to the east, the *Fallschirmjägers* became the sole assaulting force. Bypassing the 101st Airborne Division, two battalions of German paratroopers met little resistance as they thrust north through the growing dusk to attack Sainte Mère-Église and continued northeast toward the beach, with the regiment's attached grenadier battalion and a third parachute battalion in reserve.

About 9 P.M., an event occurred that would ultimately prove disastrous for the 6th *Fallschirmjäger*'s 1st Battalion, which was closest

OPPOSITE, TOP: German *Fallschirmjägers* maneuver a 37-mm antitank gun into position. A pre–World War II weapon, the 37-mm had long since been rendered obsolete by rapid advances in the armor protection of Allied tanks, and was not even useful against the frontally thin-skinned Sherman. However, the success of the Germans' highly effective handheld *Panzerfaust* rocket-propelled grenade—a "hollow" or "shaped" charge rocket that literally burned its way through thick armor—led to the development of an even larger, 6.25-inch grenade. The new weapon was affixed to the barrel of the 37-mm gun and fired in much the same way as the far smaller American rifle grenade, but with much more deadly results.

OPPOSITE, BOTTOM: Licks of flame appear through the smoke rising from a German bunker silenced by U.S. soldiers. The position was destroyed, but not without cost, as a medic treats a U.S. soldier gravely wounded in the assault. Although some German coastal strongpoints were easily overrun during the drive north toward Cherbourg, others had to be eliminated in sharp, set-piece actions that largely escaped the attention of the press.

Mulberries, Gooseberries, Whales, and Blockships: The Artificial Harbors of D-Day

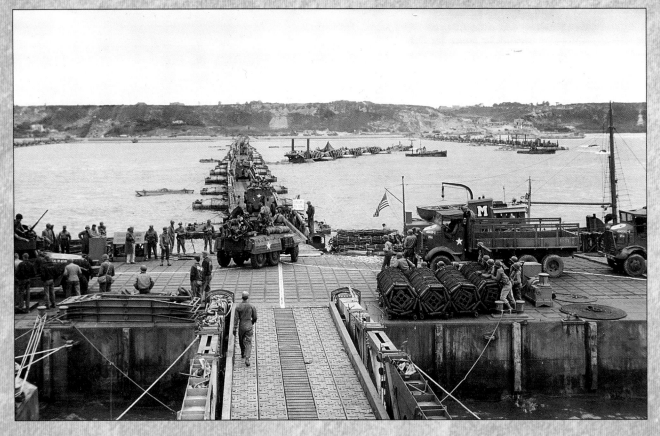

During the Normandy Invasion, a pair of protective breakwaters and piers were erected to permit the rapid unloading of vehicles and supplies. The sheer size of the Allied invasion force, and the quantity of vehicles, munitions, and provisions for this force in sustained conflict were considerable, and Allied invasion planners expected that it would be at least several weeks before a major port could be captured. Proposals for simple causeways and pontoon-type piers were impractical because of the exceptional spring tides—as high as twenty-four feet (7.3 m)—and expected storms for that

time of year. In addition, any scheme for piers and breakwaters had to be mobile, so that the components could be towed from England to the beachheads, easily assembled in a short time, and able to withstand heavy weather.

Each Mulberry harbor had breakwaters consisting of sunken merchant ships and huge concrete caissons, dubbed Phoenix units. After being towed to their proper position, the ships and concrete caissons were flooded and sunk. Floating piers several hundred yards long—called Whales—were then installed for ships to come alongside to unload, with trucks carrying their cargo

ABOVE: This busy floating intersection near Saint Laurent may not have traffic lights, but it does have a traffic cop in khaki.

OPPOSITE, TOP: A protective line of Phoenix caissons shields Mulberry B's harbor at Arromanches, while ships awaiting their turn to unload are purposely moored to buoys in such a way as to further dampen wave action. The raging Channel seas calm to barely a whisper long before they reach the floating piers.

OPPOSITE, BOTTOM: Storm-twisted piers and causeways mark the end of Mulberry A.

ashore. These floating Whales had fixed "legs," to permit them to rise and fall with the tides. MULBERRY A was installed at Saint Laurent to support the American beachhead and MULBERRY B at Arromanches for the British landings.

Another sixty unneeded ships were sunk to provide shallow-water shelters to protect the smaller landing craft from rough seas while they were unloading larger ships, and when they were at rest. The old British battleship *Centurion*, the French ship *Courbet*, the British cruiser *Durban*, the Dutch cruiser *Sumatra*, and a number of merchant ships were sunk as the blockships for these harbors. The ships were given the code name CORNCOBS, and a complete harbor was labeled GOOSEBERRY.

Some of the components of the MULBERRY and GOOSEBERRY projects began their tow from British ports six days before the invasion. By June 18, the daily cargo moving across MULBERRY A and the OMAHA and UTAH beaches was averaging about 14,500 tons. That night, the Normandy beachhead was struck by a major storm that lasted until June 22. The winds and high seas destroyed MULBERRY A off OMAHA Beach and damaged the British MULBERRY. Scores of ships and hundreds of landing craft were sunk or damaged, and an American division that was forced to wait out the storm aboard ship eventually came ashore sick and exhausted. Loss of the MULBERRY harbors temporarily disrupted the flow of supplies. The wrecked American MULBERRY was abandoned. The British one was repaired with components from MULBERRY A, and matériel continued to come across the beaches at increasing rates.

—NP

BELOW: A U.S. 90-mm anti-aircraft battery is pressed into service as conventional artillery near Vierville on D+4, June 10, 1944. Similar in size and capability to the famous German 88-mm, the towed 90-mm was frequently used for "direct fire" against ground targets, but, other than during Germany's December counteroffensive in the Ardennes, it saw few opportunities for use in an antitank role. At right are stacked two-round crates for 90-mm rounds. Discarded protective canisters for individual rounds are heaped in the foreground, and spent brass shell casings lie where they were heaved, behind the weapon's pit at left. Another gun is visible beyond the shoulder of the man at right.

Meanwhile, for several critical hours before receiving orders to sweep away the small British contingent at the Orne River bridges, the three regiments of the 21st Panzer Division had been cooling their heels by their warmed-up tanks and half-tracks. The British glider troops and a company cut off in nearby Bénouville had been confronting only light, local German forces, and although they had received reinforcements in the form of an understrength airborne battalion, the British would not likely be able to withstand the swift night assault of a *Panzergrenadier* regiment at full blood, let alone an entire division. The 21st Panzer Division's commander had still received no instructions, but knew he had to act. The 21st's march order was finally issued just before dawn, and by 9 A.M. most of the division was grinding inexorably northeast toward the apparently doomed paratroopers—away from the British landing beaches on the opposite side of the Orne River.

At 1 P.M., the first of two British commando battalions arrived at Bénouville and the Orne River bridges with a single company of tanks and another coming up the road. The 21st Panzer Division, which the British believed

would not reach the battlefield until the next day, was a fifteen-minute drive from the eastern span; was in contact with the German 711th and 716th Infantry Division elements feebly attacking the bridgehead on both sides of the river-canal system; and was beginning to form up for a massed attack. Then, suddenly, orders were received to halt all preparations to storm the bridges. The division was to launch itself at the British beaches on the *other side* of the Orne.

General Friedrich Dollmann, commander of the German Seventh Army, directed the change of plans at 10:30 that morning. The Panzer division received its instructions about noon, and notified the regimental commanders an hour later after hastily developing a new plan of action. The result was near chaos, as major elements of the division were ordered to backtrack along their approach route instead of punching through the thin British screening force ahead of them—the direct route to SWORD, little more than three miles (4.8km) beyond Bénouville. "The regrouping of the division took hours," said regimental commander Major Hans von Luck. "Most of the units from the east side of Caen and the Orne had to

ashore. These floating Whales had fixed "legs," to permit them to rise and fall with the tides. MULBERRY A was installed at Saint Laurent to support the American beachhead and MULBERRY B at Arromanches for the British landings.

Another sixty unneeded ships were sunk to provide shallow-water shelters to protect the smaller landing craft from rough seas while they were unloading larger ships, and when they were at rest. The old British battleship *Centurion*, the French ship *Courbet*, the British cruiser *Durban*, the Dutch cruiser *Sumatra*, and a number of merchant ships were sunk as the blockships for these harbors. The ships were given the code name CORNCOBS, and a complete harbor was labeled GOOSEBERRY.

Some of the components of the MULBERRY and GOOSEBERRY projects began their tow from British ports six days before the invasion. By June 18, the daily cargo moving across MULBERRY A and the OMAHA and UTAH beaches was averaging about 14,500 tons. That night, the Normandy beachhead was struck by a major storm that lasted until June 22. The winds and high seas destroyed MULBERRY A off OMAHA Beach and damaged the British MULBERRY. Scores of ships and hundreds of landing craft were sunk or damaged, and an American division that was forced to wait out the storm aboard ship eventually came ashore sick and exhausted. Loss of the MULBERRY harbors temporarily disrupted the flow of supplies. The wrecked American MULBERRY was abandoned. The British one was repaired with components from MULBERRY A, and matériel continued to come across the beaches at increasing rates.

—NP

TERENCE OTWAY

BELOW: C-47s towing Horsa gliders overfly a 2d Naval Beach Battalion command post just north of the initial landing site on UTAH Beach.

to the coast. Glider landings bringing additional men and equipment to each of the Allied airborne divisions were scheduled to take place before nightfall on June 6. Nearly 150 gliders came down in the immediate vicinity of the 1st Battalion, as more than 320 transport aircraft disgorged tons of supplies by parachute. The glider troops unfortunate enough to come down closest to the Germans immediately came under direct assault from the *Fallschirmjägers* and an attached artillery battery.

As the 1st Battalion fell upon the disorganized glider troops, advance elements of the U.S. 4th Infantry Division from UTAH Beach were already groping their way through the darkness south of the *Fallschirmjägers,* threatening to cut them off from the grenadiers and their escape route south. Naval gunfire destroyed the supporting German artillery and fell indiscriminately on the enemy, as American infantry probed the positions of the now defensive-minded Germans.

At first light on D+1, yet another mass parachute and glider landing occurred, and the 6th

Fallschirmjäger's lead battalions were finally ordered to pull back. The battalion on the left accomplished this with little difficulty. The 1st Battalion, however, was cut off. With no hope of skirting around the 101st Airborne again, it split into two groups to fight its way south after destroying or disabling five American tanks during a 4th Division attack.

The *Fallschirmjägers* struck out toward the La Barquette Lock and a lightly held pair of Douve River bridges near Le Port captured by the 101st Airborne on D-DAY. After intense but brief fighting, in which the outnumbered Americans inflicted heavy casualties on their airborne opponents, some 225 young Germans surrendered at the bridges and 350 at the lock. Throughout the day the number of prisoners was further swelled by the survivors of platoon-size units that tried to infiltrate through the thin outpost screen along the river marshes. Mercilessly assailed by small groups of American paratroopers, only 25 soldiers of the highly trained 1st Battalion made it back to Carentan from their first action.

Colonel Terence Otway and his British 9th Parachute Battalion had taken the Merville Battery and then advanced down the road to their next objective.

Round about between half past five and six, we moved off toward Onverville. I moved deliberately between the corn, since it was high. Whether it made sense or not I don't know, but it occurred to me that if we moved through the corn the Germans might be misled, only seeing the tops of our heads. It must have worked, because they didn't seem to know that we were there. As we went through, the U.S. Air Force got a straight string of bloody great bombs about fifty to one hundred yards (45.7–91.4m) from us. I don't think anybody had bothered to tell them that we were there. It was pretty frightening.

We went on to Onverville, where we took up a position. Nothing happened. I was walking around the village green the rest of that day. The Germans did attack us over the next day or two, but we repulsed them.

We were down to eighty men. The Germans outnumbered us, and I was literally on the point of surrendering. I think we had three rounds of ammunition left per man. One of my officers, a chap called Greenway who afterwards became Lord Greenway, a captain then, came up to me. Without ceremony at all, he didn't say "Colonel" or anything else, but he came up and said, "Look, stop mucking about. Take a brace on yourself and get out there and do it." Really, literally, like that. He saved my life. I needed somebody to do that.

Meanwhile, we had been joined by men of the Black Watch [Royal Highland Regiment of Canada] and the engineers. We even had glider pilots in the front line who had landed and joined the groups. Couple of RAF men there. I think I got up to a total of about 450 men altogether. Eventually we went to this place called the Château St. Com. I was ordered to take that. Anybody who held that bit of ground commanded the whole thing, including the bridge, everything. And that was what I was told to hold "at all costs," which in the parachute regiment means "until the

last man." It was tough, but it was something you could handle. You planned for it. I deliberately made it so the Germans only had one way of attacking me. ▪

—Terence Otway

ABOVE: Soldiers from the 4th Infantry Division splash through a shallow portion of the flooded area behind UTAH Beach. The riflemen have removed their M1 Garands from the waterproof Pliofilm covers, but the principal weapon of the man leading this group is a bazooka, and he has left his rifle covered. The leader has left his rifle and sling in the bag, using an ordinary piece of rope as a shoulder strap. The man with the bazooka has also retained the inflated double-tube life belt tied to his launcher during the landing, and his loader trailing behind has likewise left his four rocket canisters tied to a life belt. All these troops still wear their gas mask pouches over their chest.

March and Countermarch—East

Airdropping straw dummies at locations where they would be easily found, in combination with the widely—and unintentionally—scattered appearance of real Allied paratroopers, gave rise to a profound reticence among the various German headquarters to do almost anything other than simply place troops on high alert. Fully aware of just how few forces were available for a countermove against the Allies, they were reluctant to commit their scanty reserves until they could discern the objectives of the air assaults. With Normandy long identified as the most likely site of a pre-invasion feint by paratroopers to draw forces away from the Pas-de-Calais, German military planners gave little thought in the early morning hours of D-DAY to defending against mass *seaborne* landings.

Meanwhile, for several critical hours before receiving orders to sweep away the small British contingent at the Orne River bridges, the three regiments of the 21st Panzer Division had been cooling their heels by their warmed-up tanks and half-tracks. The British glider troops and a company cut off in nearby Bénouville had been confronting only light, local German forces, and although they had received reinforcements in the form of an understrength airborne battalion, the British would not likely be able to withstand the swift night assault of a *Panzergrenadier* regiment at full blood, let alone an entire division. The 21st Panzer Division's commander had still received no instructions, but knew he had to act. The 21st's march order was finally issued just before dawn, and by 9 A.M. most of the division was grinding inexorably northeast toward the apparently doomed paratroopers—away from the British landing beaches on the opposite side of the Orne River.

At 1 P.M., the first of two British commando battalions arrived at Bénouville and the Orne River bridges with a single company of tanks and another coming up the road. The 21st Panzer Division, which the British believed would not reach the battlefield until the next day, was a fifteen-minute drive from the eastern span; was in contact with the German 711th and 716th Infantry Division elements feebly attacking the bridgehead on both sides of the river-canal system; and was beginning to form up for a massed attack. Then, suddenly, orders were received to halt all preparations to storm the bridges. The division was to launch itself at the British beaches on the *other side* of the Orne.

General Friedrich Dollmann, commander of the German Seventh Army, directed the change of plans at 10:30 that morning. The Panzer division received its instructions about noon, and notified the regimental commanders an hour later after hastily developing a new plan of action. The result was near chaos, as major elements of the division were ordered to backtrack along their approach route instead of punching through the thin British screening force ahead of them—the direct route to SWORD, little more than three miles (4.8km) beyond Bénouville. "The regrouping of the division took hours," said regimental commander Major Hans von Luck. "Most of the units from the east side of Caen and the Orne had to

squeeze through the eye of a needle at Caen and over the only bridges available in this sector [while] under virtually constant bombardment from the Navy and fighter-bombers."

🎤 *Survivors of the Naval Combat Demolition Units moved inland as the hours and the fighting on D-DAY wore on. Seaman 2d Class John Talton emerged from that day visibly shaken—and changed.*

By nightfall it looked like there were miles of carnage going on down the beach. The Germans stopped. Then we started evacuating the wounded. My buddy and I carried wounded from then until hard dark, which was late in the night. We waded up to our chins and slid these stretchers or muscled these people on the landing craft to get them off the beach, because there was no treatment there. They didn't have sufficient medics to take care of them. We did all we could for them, loaded them on, and got them out. Some of the landing craft hit mines that were mounted on the stakes going out.

Then we went up and dug in. It was dark then. We dug in beside an LCT that was broached on the beach. We took our helmets and dug out, and got in a crouched position. The first thing I heard was a gas attack. During the day we had lost our gas masks. We tore our shirttails off and dipped them in salt water and covered our faces. But it was a false alarm. Then the *Luftwaffe* started strafing the beach. With the help of another fellow from our group, we wrestled a 30-caliber off of an

LCVP, and there were belts of ammunition with it. Two of us bent over and the third used us as a tripod. We fired all of that [ammo] at the direction of the planes. When that was gone, and the planes were gone, we went back in the trench. The Germans bombed the beach that night, and they hit the LCT that we were dug in next to, and it caught on fire. We crawled out, and I took a step and fell. I thought I'd been hit, but I was only suffering from lack of circulation, and found a medic tent. By that time I had developed a strange condition. It's called the fox-

ABOVE: Bam! The lanyard is pulled by the artilleryman in the foreground. A gunner behind him squints and plugs his ear facing the howitzer, as the loader at left turns away from the deafening sound and sharp recoil of the barrel. Hundreds of the workhorse 105-mm howitzers—like this 4th Infantry Division cannon firing on Carentan—were used in Normandy, and their numbers would grow into the thousands as more U.S. divisions arrived in France.

BELOW: A sobering sight for any German prisoners marched back to OMAHA Beach: invasion craft and warships of all types seemingly reaching back to the horizon as countless vehicles push inland.

hole shakes. But I didn't know what it was. I was talking as calmly as I'm talking today, but my hands were shaking and I couldn't stop them. I asked a medic if they had a pill for that. He said, "Son, there ain't no pill for that." ◾

—John Talton

🎤 *With the NCDU's job on UTAH Beach largely done, locating a fallen comrade became the task of American Ensign Nathan Irwin.*

After the tide came in, we went up on the beach and got into a pillbox that the Germans had evacuated. We went out again about 4:00 in the afternoon because the skipper told me there was another line of defenses down the beach that were not covered, so our crew

worked on those. We set explosives and blew them up, just the way we planned to do.

My most vivid memory of D-DAY is after I returned from a meeting of other officers. I found one of my men missing. They said he had gone to the beach. He never returned. So the next morning, the chief petty officer and myself went behind the lines a couple hundred yards, where they had Graves Registration. There they had the bodies, mostly paratroopers. I went to the officer in charge and told him we had lost a man and were trying to find him. He informed us that they had no way of knowing, so we would have to look for ourselves. This chief petty officer and myself went down row after row. There must have been a few hundred, but we found his body. We had no idea what killed him. ◾

—Nathan Irwin

"Panzers—March!"

The effect of Rommel's absence from the Normandy battlefield was nowhere more clear than in the befuddled employment of the 21st Panzer Division. Although Rommel was far removed in the command chain from the division, the 21st was the only German armored force immediately available to implement his plan to strike the invasion force while it was still disorganized and half in the water. Through direct orders to corps commander General Erich Marcks or his own personal presence, Rommel would have ensured that, at the earliest possible moment, the 21st was wielded as a single mailed fist, smashing directly into SWORD Beach, which still held the British 27th Armored Brigade in its embrace of clogged exits, destroyed vehicles, and backed-up landing craft.

Instead, the division was ordered to make a classical attack from a completely different area from which it had originally been sent. This forced a delay of nearly three and a half hours, which the British 3d Division put to good use by establishing preplanned defensive concentrations along the very axis of attack that the Panzers were ordered to take. The 21st's commander, Major General Edgar Feuchtinger, a darling of Hitler's who had worked on the massive Nazi Party rallies before the war and on the secret weapons program once the war got under way, did not protest the move, and compounded the misstep by breaking up his division. A third of the formation was left behind to assault the bridges at Bénouville. Strong enough to take the position at the original time planned for the attack, the 21st now faced a much tougher job later in the day when the 6th Airborne defenders were able to call in naval gunfire at will. The *Panzergrenadiers* would fail to take the bridge and, in any event, had no forces behind them to exploit a success.

On the west side of the Orne, Marcks had driven unscathed from his St. Lô headquarters to see the attack off, and he warned the commander of the main *Kampfgruppe*: "If we don't throw the British back into the sea we shall have lost the war." The division lost numerous vehicles and tanks to marauding Allied aircraft before the attack finally got under way at 4:20 P.M., and lost still more upon smacking into the Staffordshire Yeomanry north of Caen.

The Panzers then moved around the left flank and seemed on the verge of splitting the British lodgment in two, when they started to climb the Périers Ridge stretching back to Hermanville-sur-Mer and ran into three troops of "Firefly" Shermans armed with the new high-velocity 17-pounder cannon. Before the invasion, the Staffordshire Yeomanry's commander, Lieutenant Colonel J.A. Eadie, informed his colleagues that he planned to establish a "backstop" of these tank-killing machines at just this spot in anticipation of a German counterattack. The Panzers came on exactly as Eadie had envisioned the previous

ABOVE: Thick, oily smoke from a nearby burning vehicle blackens the sky as wary *Panzertruppen* of a Panther medium tank scan the horizon for returning Allied fighters. The high-velocity 75-mm gun on the Panther was far superior to the short-barrel 75-mm gun mounted on most British and American Shermans, and the 88-mm gun of the German Tiger tank was in a class by itself until the appearance of the British Firefly Sherman with a 17-pounder antitank gun. Consequently, Sherman crews avoided one-on-one duels and concentrated on maneuvering their more nimble vehicles around to the flanks of the heavier German tanks—which were also fewer in number—to fire at the more lightly armored flank and rear portions of the hulls.

> [Colonel] Oppeln, the future of Germany may very well rest on your shoulders. If we don't throw the British back into the sea we shall have lost the war.
> —German Lieutenant General Erich Marcks, LXXXIV Corps

May while training in England. Six tanks were destroyed in quick succession, and an attempt to outflank the ridge on a further move around the left netted the Germans three more burning hulks for no British losses.

Elements of the 21st Panzer Division even further to the left eventually reached the German troops holding out in Lion-sur-Mer about 7 P.M., but plans to reinforce them by skirting a *Kampfgruppe* around the deadly British guns along the ridge were scuttled when, just after 9 P.M., an unending horde of nearly six hundred Allied transport aircraft, gliders, and escorting fighters thundered low overhead. Thoroughly spooked by the unexpected air armada and with darkness drawing near, the 21st—from *Panzertruppen* to division commander—were convinced that they were in danger of being immediately cut off, even though the mass of aircraft was clearly banking toward the east, where the 6th Airborne had established their drop zones. Orders were hastily issued to withdraw from the gap and the Panzers pulled out, followed in the darkness by an undetermined number of the coastal troops.

The correspondents who covered the war obviously needed to get the story of the invasion to places where it could be wired back to the States and Canada. To this end, war correspondent Charles Lynch had arrived on the beaches complete with carrier pigeons. Following his restful sleep in a farmhouse, he was ready to launch his story for Reuters via the pigeons.

On June 7, I'd heard that the rallying point for the Canadian media was Courseulles and I went there with my pigeons. Sure enough, they had set up a press camp in an old German headquarters. They were happy to see the pigeons because that was to be our only means of communication until the wireless sets came in. We had to write our dispatches on thin tissue paper, like toilet paper. We had combat censors with us. When you censor something that's likely to fall physically into enemy hands, you had to censor it with scissors. Cutting out these pieces made the copy look like old piano rolls with the slits in them. We then put the dispatches in capsules tied on to the pigeons, and launched them. This is my famous scene from *The Longest Day* when I launched the pigeons. They circled once around our beach then headed straight for Berlin over the German lines. I shouted after them, "Traitors! Traitors!" and said forever after that we should have eaten them. They were fat and good; our rations weren't that great. Not one pigeon got back anyway, so those dispatches never arrived. But the Canadians brought in some quite sophisticated wireless equipment on the second day. From then on we were in communication. ∎

—Charles Lynch

Marching into France provided assorted opportunities to meet with its people as well as the occupying forces of the Germans. These experiences proved memorable for the Allied participants. John Murphy of the RAF ground crew recalled his surprise upon discovering the international quality of the prisoners they had captured.

Sniper fire was coming from a château a little way inland. Those snipers were picking off drivers [from] the supply boats that were coming in with ammunition and food. The Canadian beachmaster was told about this, and he wanted to do something about it. And he did. He sent a platoon of Canadians in to clear that château, and they asked me and my friend to give covering fire at the back. We got close enough to use our Sten guns, cleared that château, and also took prisoners. What was amazing was that some of those prisoners happened to be French women who had associations with the Germans after many years; some had even married them. One of the sergeants who was being taken away to the beach to be taken to England had his French wife. She pleaded to go with him but was held back. I was given four prisoners to escort down the beach to board landing craft. Out of that four, two were Russian, one was Polish, and one was German. They did not look displeased to be in that position. When

they caught sight of the boat, I'm sure they actually smiled as they went aboard. ▪

—John Murphy

Die Another Day

Most of the *Panzertruppen* and *Panzergrenadiers* surging toward the sea on D-DAY would be dead within the next six weeks, long before the remnants of the German Army escaped from Normandy and withdrew across the Seine. Reaching the Channel on the evening of June 6 would have only hastened their demise, as well as spelling the end for the lead element of the 12th SS Panzer *Hitlerjugend*, a *Panzergrenadier* regiment with attached battalions of armor and artillery. Naval gunfire on the eastern side of the Orne, fighter aircraft, antitank guns, and the Fireflies' high-velocity 17-pounder cannons had stripped the 21st Panzer Division of fifty-four tanks since mid-afternoon. If the division's seventy surviving tanks had not pulled back, the morning light would have revealed them, the divisions' half-tracks, artillery, and forty or so self-propelled guns, all assembled in the gap for a coordinated assault on SWORD, while the 12th SS's *Kampfgruppe* formed a mobile front facing JUNO. Once the 21st Panzer Division had rolled up the eastern invasion beach, it would be the turn of the, by then, fully assembled *Hitlerjugend* to attack the Canadians.

These objectives were simply out of reach. Other than a possible feint along the west side of the Périers Ridge—where nine of its tanks had been destroyed the evening before—the 21st Panzer Division would have had few tactical options open to them. At first light, the mass of Panzers and other armor would storm into a shallow box north of the ridge and Hermanville-sur-Mer, bounded by a thick, anti-tank screen along the Caen road on the east, and the hastily fortified, British-held portion of Lion-sur-Mer on the coast—all buttressed by the 27th Armored Brigade, a formation with approximately 190 tanks. The initial goal of British ground forces—aside from destroying as many German tanks as possible—would be to keep the German armor from breaking into the British defense and, thus, confined to the dangerously compressed area between the two beachheads.

ABOVE: Sherman Fireflies, with tank-killing 17-pounder guns, lie in wait for any German Panzers attempting to strike the long, vulnerable British column barreling down the road. The 21st Panzer Division was twice bested on D-DAY by a combination of Fireflies, M-10 tank destroyers with 3-inch guns, and towed 17-pounders, like the one in the foreground.

Further west we heard the sound of battle . . . where our armored group was supposed to attack. The enemy was apparently concentrating his naval fire against this dangerous thrust . . . We made good progress . . . Then all hell broke loose. The heaviest naval guns, up to 38cm in calibre, artillery, and fighter-bombers plastered us without pause.

—German Major Hans von Luck, 125th *Panzergrenadier* Regiment

Trained on this zone and the vehicle-packed area running west to the JUNO lodgment would be the naval guns of bombardment groups "D" and "E" from SWORD and JUNO beaches. Uncontested by anti-aircraft weapons, a slowly orbiting parade of spotter aircraft would direct the largest concentration of naval gunfire per square mile during World War II. Even with some ships siphoned off for other duties, the force could call on approximately 120 destroyer guns (4- to 4.7-inch), 98 cruiser and secondary battleship guns (mostly 6-inch), as well as 19 15- and 16-inch guns.

Concentrations of naval firepower vastly smaller than this had shredded German counterattacks in the Mediterranean and continued to do so in Normandy as late as July 8, when the battleship HMS *Rodney* broke up a force of three dozen LXXXVI Corps Panzers southeast of Caen at a range of 32,000 yards (29,261m). For now, though, the men of the 21st Panzer and 12th SS Panzer Divisions would live a little longer. The battered 21st pulled back toward Caen, and the *Hitlerjugend* launched their own failed counterattacks against the lodgments after the rest of their division reached the front on Wednesday, D+1.

Part of the credit for that day's victory is due to the courageous actions taken by sailors of the Allied navies. Their help—the shelling of German positions—continued past D-DAY's initial actions, recalls Captain Sidney Radley Walters of the 27th Canadian Armored Regiment.

It took a while to straighten out everything, including reuniting tanks with their companies. Until about ten o'clock that night we moved through the villages on our way to our objective. We did not reach it, but dug in for the night. We had met some resistance, but nothing we couldn't handle. It did slow us down, though, for twenty minutes here or thirty minutes there. We had moved out early that morning.

We were helped by the battleships. The *Rodney* and the *Roberts* firing their 16-inch guns. Sometimes they would fire at 1,500 to 2,000 yards (1,372–1,829m) ahead of us toward a German position, on perhaps a farm with two or three buildings around it. You'd see the rounds coming in. Suddenly there's no house. No barns. Nothing. Everything was gone, rather like a small atomic bomb. Everybody would clap their hands and say, "Good show! Let's do it again!" ▪

—Sidney Radley Walters

The morning of June 7 found thousands of Allied soldiers awakening to an unknown future, and many believed that the worst was over. German resistance, while intense in places the day before, would only solidify and concentrate on the Allies as they moved inland. Casualties grew, and the work of the medical staffs increased as well. British nurse Iris Bower awakened in her slit trench that morning and was soon busily tending to the wounded.

At six o'clock in the morning, we were awakened. We made some tea and had some biscuits from our rations. We put on a bit of makeup. I had brought my little bag of Elizabeth Arden makeup. When packing, I had decided I'm not going to land in Normandy looking a sight. Then we went on the convoy to the assembly area. Of course, it was a slow process through bomb craters. We got to the assembly area, to discover that one of the four doctors allocated to arrive in the evening of D-Day to prepare a site for us had been killed.

Months of practice now came to the fore. The tents were put up at a terrific speed, slit trenches dug in the tents. Of course, all our equipment was put up. In the center of it all [was] a forty-foot (12.2m), blood-red cross on white canvas that hopefully would be seen from the air. Very shortly, over two hundred casualties arrived from the Army casualty clearing station. We were a mobile field, as opposed to an Army carrying station. We

ABOVE: Frightened prisoners are hustled up a tree-lined road by Tommy-gun– and carbine-wielding GIs. The number of Germans captured or killed by the Allies during the Normandy campaign ultimately topped 530,000.

was wonderful to see these Dakotas there. Molly and I took turns doing this for five days before moving on. During that time, we had seen to 1,023 casualties.

When we were moving to our next site, the convoy came to a halt. We could see white bits of material on both sides marking the place of mines. You see safe lanes for us to go through. Molly and I felt very respectable going into the bushes to answer the call of nature. But, of course, at this stage we couldn't because we'd be blown to kingdom come. We saw a little cottage a few yards down, and if the road had been cleared of mines, perhaps that cottage had. So I said to the driver, Wait for us, and he said yes. He knew what we were up to and told us not to go beyond the white tape. So down we went and to our amazement, we saw a little old man back standing by the cottage. He was the first civilian I'd seen. Molly in her schoolgirl French asked if we could use the toilet. He just looked at us with no reaction at all. Molly saw the door open and she went in. He just stared. Then I heard her say, I found one, so I rushed in. Then when we come back, the little man has a broad grin of comprehension on his face, and the next thing he's giving us kisses on both cheeks and big hugs. We went back to the convoy, and they were glad to see us in one piece. Before we reached our destination, the first ambulance was blown up; I was riding in the sixth. ◾

—Iris Bower

were only looking after them for a short time, because we were sending them back on the landing craft and the naval medical team were looking after them. We worked nonstop, seeing to field dressings, transfusions, etc. We said goodbye to them and wondered what their fate would be, because we could hear the gunfire from both sides.

In the meantime preparation was being made for an airstrip. The royal engineers were putting wire meshing down for Dakotas [C-47s] to land. They were going to be used as air ambulances. After a few hours, we were to be in charge of this, and also see to doing operations in our surgical tent for the very serious ones. I felt a wonderful sense of gratitude when they used to smile in spite of their injuries sometimes. They were glad for anything that we could do to help them, and that was a great comfort. Molly and I were told that we were to take turns escorting these casualties to this airstrip. It was a dangerous place, because there was a tank battle going on at the end of the strip and shelling overhead. I was the first to go with them, and it

The Linkups

The opposing armies in Normandy now settled into a month of attacks and counterattacks as they raced to build up their forces in Normandy. The first order of business for the Allies was to form a contiguous lodgment from the Merderet and Douve rivers in the west to the Dives River in the east, while taking the three key D-Day objectives of Carentan, Bayeux, and Caen along N13, the French highway to Cherbourg. Bayeux was taken and the Sword-Juno gap closed early on June 7, since

German troops had largely abandoned both locations during the night. Yet, close to the southwest, Britons and Canadians were already receiving a taste of the brutal fighting that would rage around Caen and beyond through the middle of August. In the American sector, the 4th and 101st Divisions closed up on the 82d Airborne Division, which had depleted nearly all of its ammunition, but the outnumbered Ranger battalion at Pointe du Hoc was thoroughly cut off and receiving violent attacks. Most seriously, large gaps separated the divisions at OMAHA Beach from the other beachheads, with both flanks facing UTAH and SWORD Beaches very hotly contested by the Germans.

Elements of the 29th Infantry Division, including attached Rangers, succeeded in fighting their way through to Pointe du Hoc on D+2, June 8, and found that the Ranger battalion at the Pointe had been whittled down to just ninety men in three days of nearly continuous fighting. Further gains that day forced the stubborn grenadiers of the 352d Division back toward the Vire Estuary, and they escaped south through Isigny on the flooded Aure River before the 29th Infantry Division could cut them off. In two days of fighting on the other side of OMAHA Beach, neither the U.S. 1st Infantry Division nor the British 30th Division were able to make permanent gains against a German mobile brigade and other elements that had lodged themselves into the area running south from Port-en-Bessin. During the night of June 8–9, the 1st stormed Ste. Anne at the base of the German position. Vicious, confused fighting erupted as the Germans fought to keep open an escape corridor across the N13 highway, and most of a German regiment was able to escape south.

OMAHA was now linked with both UTAH and JUNO, but Carentan and its stretch of the N13 were still firmly in German hands. The surviving battalions of the 6th *Fallschirmjäger* Regiment and attached grenadiers blocked the approaches to the city in the hedgerows near St. Côme-du-Mont. The weight of the chaotic, seemingly inconclusive fighting wore heavily on the paratroopers of both armies, but the Germans were finally, on June 8, levered out of

the tangled countryside and forced to retreat across flooded farmland and down an elevated railroad causeway to Carentan. One large body of retreating *Fallschirmjäger* up to their waists in marsh water, staved off attack from Allied aircraft by taking off their helmets and waving them as if they were U.S. troops.

On June 10, the exhausted 101st Airborne opened a two-pronged drive on Carentan, and the Germans, their ranks seriously depleted after nearly a week of combat, withdrew from the city after nightfall on June 11. Highway N13 was now under Allied control across the length of the invasion beaches. The stage was set for the capture of Cherbourg and St. Lô; the drive toward Avranches, then to the Brittany ports; followed by the planned advance to the Seine River in conjunction with the British. Allied leaders were dismayed that both armies were far behind schedule, but, a week after D-DAY, it was not yet apparent that they would be held to only limited advances for the next two months, even though Caen was, as expected, attracting German armor like a magnet. The word *breakout* was on no one's lips, and no particular significance was attached to the

ABOVE: An American Sherman tank rumbles past a destroyed German armored vehicle. The Sherman sports factory-made appliqué armor in front of the driver and assistant driver positions in the hull, and the scratches of a diligent censor on the metal plate in front of its starboard headlight. Unlike the first-class Panzer and SS divisions, the static German divisions manning the thin crust of the Atlantic Wall were frequently outfitted with weapons and equipment captured during Nazi Germany's initial conquests, or that had long since stopped being produced by the Reich's armaments industry. That their equipment was old, obsolescent, or downright oddball is borne out by the upturned tank, whose road-wheel configuration clearly shows that it is a *Panzerspäwagen* II Lynx or some variant of the Lynx—a vehicle that had not been produced for more than a year.

ABOVE: A squad of paratroopers from the 101st Airborne Division moves cautiously past the church in St. Marcouf northwest of UTAH Beach on D+2. The trooper keeping a watchful eye behind the patrol still wears a sheathed trench knife tied next to his right calf, and the busy censors have blotted out the "Screaming Eagle" patch of the man with a fixed bayonet at right.

intelligence from 101st Airborne patrols that the 6th *Fallschirmjäger* had reestablished their new defense line in the hedgerow country south of Carentan, and appeared to be buttressed by the arrival of a new formation, the 17th SS *Panzergrenadier* Division.

First Lieutenant Sidney Salomon of C Company, 2d Ranger Battalion, had his squad reduced to nine men. After an uneventful night, he and his men rejoined the others after being treated to Norman hospitality.

The next morning we went to meet the remnants of other Ranger companies on the blacktop road that paralleled the cliff. Two old French ladies had been out early, rounding up any cows not killed by artillery. They milked them and offered us milk or cider as we walked by with our rifles at the ready.

Some of the men were trying to conserve their ammunition, so they picked up a German weapon and started to fire that. German weapons had a distinctive sound, just as American weapons did. The people at

Pointe du Hoc heard the German weapons and figured they were Germans. We were leapfrogging and had a little fight there with our own men until somebody got smart enough and realized what was happening. There we learned a lesson: never pick up an enemy weapon. ■

—Sidney Salomon

Just as the 29th Division endured substantial casualties, so did the 1st Infantry Division, but they kept moving forward. Captain Joseph Dawson and his men were among the first to break through their part of the beach.

As we moved ahead, I led the men, and halfway up the bluff we encountered a squad of men [under the] command of Lieutenant Spalding of E company who had successfully gotten off the beach and were working the area between the top of the bluff and the beach. They had encountered some enemy soldiers entrenched halfway up the beach. I took those men from him and had some of my men take them down to the bottom of the shoreline where they would be turned over to the MPs. [Spalding's squad] joined us in support. I went ahead on up to near the crest of the bluff where there was a machine gun and a trench with defenders. They were firing with such success down along the beach. Just before you reached the crest of the bluff, it became virtually sheer for about ten feet (3m), so I was able to crawl up within ten feet of the machine gun without being seen by the enemy. I was under them and therefore they were unaware of my presence. Their guns were holding up the advance and particularly on the lower group of my men. We had some casualties at that time. I threw a couple of grenades in there, silencing the machine gun and its crew. I had alarmed the defenders, who began emptying the trenches and withdrawing as a result.

Nobody was ahead of us except the enemy. We didn't have any support on either side, except a handful of men here or a straggler there who had managed to crawl up and join us. I urged my men forward and we engaged the enemy from there all the way into Colleville, a little town about a mile (1.6km) inland, which was our objective of the day. That objective took four hours to reach, and we took it by defending ourselves and wiping out the enemy.

I had probably the strongest group of veterans of anybody, because G Company had excelled both in North Africa and in Sicily, so there was a hard core of veterans who were the leaders. They were examples for the men who had joined us as trainees and had never been in combat. That was essential to the success of it. I was honored to have the privilege of having that kind of personnel. ■

—Joseph Dawson, Captain,
G Company, 1st Infantry Division (US)

Awakening to the fire and thunder of pounding cannonade, Karl Wolf's Dramamine no longer lulled him into drowsiness. There was no sleep or rest for hours for him or his men as the 1st Division moved onward.

Between ten and eleven we got into our assigned area. By that time the rifle company people had captured some of the high ground and [had] at least lessened fire on our position. Until probably four or five in the afternoon, our landing was pretty precarious. It was touch and go in our area, on the extreme left, at least until noontime. If the Germans had released the infantry they held in reserve in the Panzer outfit, they could have pushed us back into the water. But once we started clearing the high ground and taking the emplacements, then there wasn't much chance of that. By afternoon, it was just a question of progressing inland to increase the landing area.

Other than the five minutes I slept on the beach, I really didn't get any sleep. I'd say until about two or three o'clock in the morning, I personally was in the CP, which was just in the dugout area on the side of the hill, and fell asleep sitting down or leaning against the wall. I don't recall having any food at that time. You had a ready-ration you could use, but no hot food until the next day.

We were encouraged by the buildup that was taking place. They brought in all these reinforcements from ships. You'd turn around and look out to sea, and it was just filled with supply ships coming in. They had barrage balloons to prevent the German airplanes from attacking them. You could hear a lot of fighting going on, and you'd have Germans trying to advance on your position and you'd beat them off. We'd send patrols out to try and figure out what the Germans had out there. ■

—Karl Wolf

Another member of the 1st Division was John Franz, a welding technician whose arrival on D-DAY was delayed because of a traffic jam. He was not unmindful of the sacrifices made by those who had gone before.

Our landing was to be on EASY RED Beach at OMAHA. Originally we were scheduled to land at three o'clock in the afternoon. When we got over there, they couldn't get us in there, 'cause they were backed up. We were towing a Rhino, a big barge. We were supposed to be

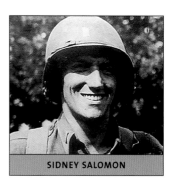

SIDNEY SALOMON

Kill Hitler: The "July 20 Plot" and Suicide of Rommel

LEFT: Hitler, in black cape, with his deputy for Nazi Party affairs, Martin Bormann, on his right and SS chief Heinrich Himmler on his left, walks to a tea party immediately after the failed attempt on his life. In the rear group, *Luftwaffe* chief Hermann Goering, baton in hand, chats with Italian dictator Benito Mussolini.

BELOW: Hitler peers through a magnifying glass at his Rastenberg headquarters. *Luftwaffe* General Karl Bodenschatz, at center, was severely injured as a result of the bomb blast.

On July 20, 1944, at a conference called by Hitler at his field headquarters, the "Wolf's Lair," in Rastenburg, a powerful bomb exploded, killing one person and mortally wounding three others. Hitler's life had been spared only because an officer had casually moved the briefcase containing the bomb and the force of the explosion was partially deflected by a heavy wooden table. Hitler emerged from the ruined headquarters with his hair singed, a sore right arm, and his hearing temporarily impaired.

The plotters included several politicians and senior active-duty and retired officers of the Army and the German intelligence service. Erwin Rommel, one of three field marshals implicated in the plot, did not take part in the assassination attempt. The man who placed the briefcase bomb was Oberst Claus

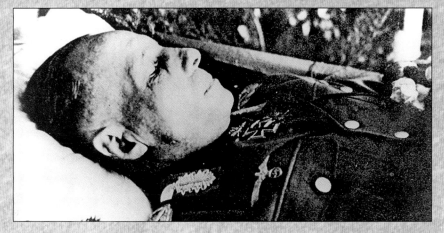

LEFT: Field Marshal Erwin Rommel lying in state after committing suicide to avoid being tried along with the other captured conspirators.

BELOW: Field Marshal Gerd von Rundstedt (far left, at lectern) gives the oration at Rommel's funeral. Between the honor guard lies the flag-draped coffin topped by Rommel's baton, dress sword, and field helmet. The officer at far right folds a pillow containing decorations earned by Rommel during the course of two world wars.

Schenk, Count von Stauffenberg, an officer who had lost his left hand and the fingers on his right hand while fighting in Tunisia.

Stauffenberg departed from Hitler's headquarters before the bomb exploded and, assuming that Hitler was dead, flew to Berlin, which the plotters had hoped to seize with Home (Replacement) Army troops. The nominal leader of the plotters, General Ludwig Beck, former chief of the German General Staff, whose opposition to Hitler went back to 1938, was to become the head of the provisional government. But when news of Hitler's survival reached Berlin, loyal Army officers began rounding up the conspirators. By midnight, Stauffenberg had been shot by a firing squad, and Beck, after bungling his suicide, was killed by a coup de grace from a sergeant's gun.

In a rampage of vengeance, some seven thousand suspected plotters were rounded up. Many turncoats, seeing the plot fail, tried to betray the cause or plead innocence. Most of them were also arrested and put to death. The conspirators, Hitler decreed, "must be hanged like cattle." The first eight tried were strung up on meat hooks in nooses of piano wire, and a movie for Hitler's viewing was made of their final agony. About two hundred accused plotters were executed. Thousands of friends and relatives were sent to concentration camps.

The attempted assassination of Hitler came three days after Rommel was wounded in an Allied air attack. The field marshal had continuously—and fruitlessly—pleaded with Hitler for flexibility in his tactics, and suspicions were soon raised that Rommel had known of the plot beforehand, which he had. But Rommel had opposed assassination, arguing for the arrest of Hitler by the Army and a trial in civilian court. Rommel's role was confirmed, and on October 14, 1944, SS troops surrounded his house. A German general confronted Rommel with a choice of suicide or a rigged trial. He accepted proffered poison, told his wife and fifteen-year-old son that Hitler was charging him with treason, and said he would be dead in fifteen minutes.

The death of the extremely popular officer was publicly attributed to war wounds obtained in Normandy, and Rommel was given a state funeral with full honors. Had he not taken the poison and demanded a public trial, Hitler had promised retribution against his wife and son following his sentencing and execution.

—NP

taken to the beach on this Rhino, but the traffic jam delayed us for hours. About nine o'clock, as it started getting dark, they opened the doors of the LST and brought the Rhino to the front of these doors. We rode the vehicles onto the barge, but no farther.

We spent the night of D-Day on the Rhino, and the Germans shelled the entire time. That night was the darkest night of the war for me because we didn't know what would happen if the men didn't hold the beach. We were just sitting out there with nowhere to go and nothing we could do. We were just out there in the open, in no-man's-land.

When daylight appeared the next morning, we brought the barge in. As we approached, I saw Omar Bradley already on the beach. Bodies were in the water, in the surf. Dead soldiers lay everywhere. We had to step over the bodies. I have never seen so many dead people in all my life as I did there on those beaches. They couldn't clear the beaches yet because men were busy just trying to make headway to get a little farther in. I really was so thankful that I wasn't one of the first waves going in because most of those fellows must have died. So many bodies were laying there. I thanked the Lord for those men who went first, so that we didn't have to experience that.

Germans continued shelling because we had not gone far. Therefore, they had to be careful in bringing more troops than they could handle. After a couple days, more headway was gained, and we moved farther inland. Although earlier expectations had been for us to be a lot farther inland, that was before running into considerable resistance.

The night of the third day, some self-propelled, 155mms or 105mms were moved to the field next to us, and they were shooting these self-propelled guns all night long. The next day, they moved out, and the following night the Germans started shelling. They were looking for these guns and shelling us. Luckily, the only thing they hit in our area was our supply truck. The next day our company commander moved us to another field to escape further enemy shelling. ▪

—John Franz, Welding Technician,
1st Division (US)

Living through the invasion left its scars—some were noticeable immediately; others appeared as the years passed and the soldiers and sailors relived it in their minds, robbing them of peaceful slumber. Sergeant Felix Branham of the 29th Division vividly remembers the events of that day and night.

We got off "Bloody OMAHA" and moved farther and then hit the hedgerows. Snipers were a terrible problem both there and on D-Day. I recall one sniper who gave us a difficult time trying to figure where he was. He shot twenty-five times and killed twenty-three men. You had to watch what you did. They would booby-trap everything. If a guy got wounded, you had to watch out if he laid there any length of time. They would climb over the hedgerows and booby-trap him, so when medics came to work on him, they would blow up. They even booby-trapped their own people.

That first night, we dug a foxhole in the center area. We had two people who dug together. One would dig while the other was on watch. I was sitting with my rifle on alert, but I was crying like a baby. I thought about all that had happened since getting off the *Charles Carroll*. I thought about how close we'd come and all we had gone through. We were so tired. ▪

—Felix Branham

Second Lieutenant Walter Bodlander was a member of the intelligence corps for the 4th Division's 8th Infantry Regiment. He took part in a rather unusual episode involving some indecisive Germans. Should they surrender and become prisoners of war: to be or not to be? That was the question.

Around the second day or the third day, the first prisoners were taken from units that had been rushed to stem the invasion. One of these was the 6th German parachute regiment. I was asked to come up to the front early one morning. The front was merely a hundred yards (91.4m) away. A member of our company said there were some Germans

wanting to surrender, and they needed me to talk to them. I went, and in front of me was an empty field and then there was a hedgerow on the far side where the Germans were sitting. I said, I don't see any white flag. But they said there was a white flag and they wanted to surrender. So we waited for a little bit, and nothing happened. Finally, I said, "I'll go out with a white handkerchief and see if somebody wants to surrender. They probably won't shoot me." I walked to the middle of the field. A German sergeant came up. I spoke to him in German, saying, "I hear that you guys want to surrender." He said, "No, I don't know what you're talking about." And I said, "My unit just told me that they saw this white flag." He replied, "Oh, we had a wounded soldier and used a white flag to get him back."

I said, "As long as we're talking about surrender, how about it? Don't you think it's a good idea?" He said, "I don't know. I really don't care about the war and would surrender, but I can't without permission." I asked him who could give him permission, and he said his lieutenant. So I tell him to go ask the lieutenant. I asked if he thought the lieutenant might agree, and he thought he would. We agreed to meet again in ten minutes. So we both returned to our units. I was very excited because I was getting my first surrender of a whole bunch of soldiers.

Major Todd, my immediate commander, was a hundred yards (91.4m) back, someplace in a command post. I telephoned him and told him I was getting a unit to surrender. He asked when, and I said I didn't know, but we

ABOVE: Paratroopers arrive at the spot where other members of their 101st Airborne Division unit were cut down by German snipers. This photo was taken near Carentan, south of UTAH Beach, on June 14, 1944. The trooper in the foreground was apparently killed by a single bullet that penetrated his helmet.

ABOVE: Young, highly trained, and fanatical, *Panzergrenadiers* in the 12th SS *Hitlerjugend* Division averaged between 16½ and 17½ years of age in the summer of 1944, and many of the members joined when they were just 15. This dangerous lad carries a MG42 machine gun with a 50-round drum.

now." I finally persuaded him not to move, and I went out again.

This time a lieutenant appeared. He said they had talked to the colonel, and now he wanted to talk to me personally. If I would come over, he guaranteed my safe passage. I said I couldn't do that without permission from my commander, so wait here.

I rushed back and telephoned Todd, who told me I was nuts. I said, "No, no. They're taking me behind the lines. They must be serious." I was thinking this was the greatest thing in the world. I was stopping World War II, by myself alone, right here on the invasion front. Major Todd said, Wait a minute, and he called Colonel [James] Van Fleet. Todd came back and said, Get out, because the 12th Regiment had already advanced a mile and a half (2.4km) while we were sitting on our ass. "Get the hell out of there! Tell them that it's out of the question."

And so I had to go back and say, Sorry, no dice. The lieutenant went back and the sergeant was lingering. I asked, "Is there anybody who wants to come with me?" The sergeant said he had to wait for the lieutenant to leave. I said we had no time. He just stayed out in the field; I promised him nobody would shoot. I continued to stay in the field. Five minutes later, four people came over and surrendered. Two of them were wounded, and one was the sergeant himself. I got four people out of this whole deal. I also got holy hell because we were held back from the attack, which started immediately.

This regiment turned out to be one of the top regiments that the Germans had available. They would never have surrendered. It was absolute madness on my part to assume that they would. ■

—Walter Bodlander

were meeting in ten minutes. He said we'd better hurry because we had been ordered to attack, so we had to move. But he said ten minutes was no problem. So I went back out. In ten minutes the sergeant showed up.

He said he had talked to the lieutenant, and they discussed it with the men, and everybody was willing to surrender. However, they must have permission from their commanding officer, a colonel. I asked how long that would take, and he said about a half-hour. He asked us to wait for half an hour, and if the colonel agreed, then the whole unit would surrender.

I asked, "Is this for real?" He said, "Absolutely." But I said I could only wait for fifteen minutes. Then we agreed to meet again. I reported to Major Todd, and five minutes later Todd came back on the phone, and he said, "Get the hell out of there. We have orders to attack and you've got to stop this nonsense. We're moving." I told him, "You can't do that. I'm getting to know these people in good faith. We're trying to arrange a surrender, so we can't attack

GERMAN 12TH SS PANZER DIVISION, HITLERJUGEND

After a pair of counterattacks on June 7 and 8, 1944, failed to reach the Canadian beachhead at JUNO, the *Hitlerjugend* (Hitler Youth) Division settled into a grim defensive battle that stalled Allied forces before Caen for more than a month. The division's heavily depleted ranks were still full of fight when they withdrew from the city on July 15, but were nearly decimated during the British offensive, Operation GOODWOOD, several days later. Remnants of the division were instrumental in preventing a Canadian breakthrough at Falaise on August 8, and it broke out of the subsequent Allied encirclement on August 21.

Sergeant Felix Branham, fresh from watching his boyhood friends from his Virginia National Guard unit cut to ribbons on OMAHA *beach, saw the German prisoners differently.*

We would use cows or other livestock to walk over minefields. Sometimes we'd make German prisoners do it. We had been told, Don't jump up and take those guys prisoner; let them come to you. Some guys didn't do their homework, and when they took a handful of prisoners and walked over to get them, the Germans dropped flat, and machine guns behind them opened up and killed the Americans.

I didn't believe in taking prisoners. I would see Germans in stretchers, and I'd kick them out of their stretchers. I said, This is the way it's got to be. They're the reason we're over here. They are the reason we don't go home. The sooner we get rid of these guys, the sooner we go home. ▪

—Felix Branham

With the German guns at Pointe du Hoc destroyed, Sergeant Leonard Lomell and the remnants of the 2d Ranger Battalion fought off repeated German counterattacks as they waited for their fellow Rangers to fight their way to them from OMAHA *Beach.*

By 8:30 that morning, we reported that our mission was accomplished, communication was cut, guns rendered inoperable, and a roadblock had been established. By destroying those guns, a serious threat to all was removed. Those were six-inch guns that could have destroyed ships, landing craft, as well as shot the American beaches to pieces. They had a twelve-mile (19.3km) range and were mobile. The Germans were taken by surprise, because when they returned, they found their guns totally inoperable. This must have caused some aggravation, because that night we were counterattacked three times.

Leading up to D-DAY night, the survivors of E and F Companies of the 2d Battalion came out to D Company's area. We managed to gather together eighty-five guys to set up a perimeter near the guns to defend the area. We established a perimeter and a quadrangle sort of thing among the hedgerows for our defensive position, to hold the land around the guns and the roadblock through the night. Later on that evening, along comes Lieutenant "Ace" Parker of A Company of the 5th Ranger Battalion. He and his men joined our little defense, giving us a total of eighty-five Rangers holding that inland position near the guns and the roadblock, about a mile (1.6km) from the actual point.

Starting at about 11 P.M. and ending at about 3 A.M., we faced three horrendous counterattacks against over three hundred Germans. Not only did they outnumber us, but they also had heavier firepower. There was no moonlight; the day was stormy and the night was dark. Both sides suffered heavy casualties. One of E Company's platoons was captured. They pulled them right out because the battle was within a hundred yards (91.4m). We of D company had to remain in our position because we were responsible for the roadblock.

Suddenly everything was quiet, and the Germans withdrew. We didn't know why. Maybe they felt it was a wasted effort. Then soon the dawn broke for D-DAY+1. D Company stayed in our positions on the roadblock until relieved the next day by Rangers from OMAHA Beach and part of the 116th Regiment of the 29th Division. By the end of the battle for Pointe du Hoc, of 225 men only 90 could continue; some were lightly wounded. Eighty-one had been killed. During that time we never went more than two hundred yards (182.8m) from those guns. We went back to the Pointe for the first aid station to get our wounds dressed. Now, for the first time, we saw the dead bodies lining the road, waiting for Graves Registration and the trucks. You could see the dust on their whiskers and hair. These were the buddies you loved like brothers. The other subsequent deaths and killings never affected me as much as those first ones. ▪

—Leonard Lomell

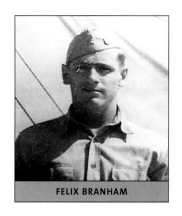

FELIX BRANHAM

The landing operation in Normandy will certainly not be the only attempted major landing by the Allies. A second attack must be expected definitely in the Pas-de-Calais and therefore the withdrawal of troops from that sector to assist in Normandy cannot be allowed.

—OKW, Berlin, to Army Group B

Chapter Seven

BREAKOUT AND THE RACE ACROSS FRANCE

Rommel had always maintained that if the invasion were not utterly defeated within the first forty-eight hours, when the Allied lodgment was most disorganized, it would only be a matter of time before the war was lost. When informed of the Normandy landings at his home in Bavaria, Rommel canceled his meeting with Hitler and sped to his headquarters outside Paris by car, understanding full well that he would have no influence on the developing battle before late evening. The Seventh Army, meanwhile, was receiving a stream of requests for aid from hard-pressed units, while both Rommel's Army Group B and von Rundstedt's OB West made increasingly urgent appeals that they be freed to hurl the powerful 12th SS Panzer *Hitlerjugend* and Panzer-Lehr at the British beaches.

The divisions did not receive their marching orders until 4 P.M., far too late for them to mass with the 21st Panzer on D-Day or even on D+1. Instead of an armored onslaught striking at the heart of the Allied landings, the Panzers were employed piecemeal, their strikes contained in a succession of savage battles often fought at very close range. As more

PAGES 220–221: A soldier from the U.S. 35th Infantry Division stands isolated and vulnerable in a sunken road between two hedgerow-enclosed fields near Carillon, north of St. Lô. At lower left, a foxhole is dug into the berm, which is densely packed with roots. Carillon, a key objective of U.S. forces in Normandy, did not fall until July 18, 1944, after fierce fighting. For more than a month after the D-DAY beachheads were consolidated, the determined defense by an average of eight understrength German divisions—principally made up of infantry—skillfully held four U.S. corps at bay.

RIGHT: An American soldier rests the barrel of his Garand on a hedgerow berm near Mortain as he prepares to return fire. Although the munitions tube he carries is long enough for a 2.36-inch bazooka rocket, it may contain a much shorter rifle grenade. Along the way he has also picked up a German stick grenade, which is leaning against his right leg. The bandolier around his neck appears to be the twelve-clip variety with six two-clip pockets for carrying sixty .30-06–caliber rounds.

and more units were steadily consumed in the fighting around Caen, additional divisions were sent in to bolster the worsening situation, but the bulk of German power in the west, the Fifteenth Army, remained under lock and key. The German high command's firm conviction that the real invasion was yet to be launched against the Pas-de-Calais effectively prevented all but token reinforcements from being extracted from this formation.

Operations BODYGUARD and FORTITUDE succeeded beyond the wildest dreams of Allied planners. Designed to work at best for two weeks beyond D-DAY, the deception did not unravel until early August, despite some of the genuine U.S. divisions believed to be allotted to the coming invasion to the north appearing in the Normandy "feint." Even Rommel was deceived. Upon his arrival at Army Group B headquarters late in the evening of June 6, he ordered that several *Kampfgruppen* and divisions be sent from the Brittany Peninsula to the U.S. sector, but German Seventh Army requests to extract even more formations were rebuffed. Rommel feared that such a move

would leave the peninsula's valuable ports open to a strike by some of the six "uncommitted"—and mythical—U.S. airborne divisions created as part of the deception operation. Moreover, there was little understanding at this point of the Allies' ability to continuously pour men and matériel ashore without the use of established ports or even the use of the MULBERRY harbors, which did not become fully functional until the middle of June.

The number of American troops crossing the Channel to Normandy passed the one-million mark less than a month after D-DAY—ironically, on July 4th. Nevertheless, the Allies were extremely concerned about the flow of supplies. Although the landing of follow-on divisions was occurring more or less as planned, the personnel and equipment of the vast support structure needed to maintain the men in combat was far behind schedule. The expansion of "liberated France" was also proceeding much more slowly than expected: both British and U.S. commanders were growing increasingly nervous about being unable to establish bases in the prime real estate west and southwest of Caen, which was originally slated to support some thirty airfields. After a week of little movement on the ground, the word *stalemate* began to creep into the minutes of the daily Air Commander's Conference in England. Air Marshal Sir Arthur "Mary" Coningham's inability to move his Second Tactical Air Force headquarters to Normandy prompted severe criticism of Montgomery, not only by Coningham, but also by Eisenhower's deputy, Air Chief Marshal Arthur W. Tedder, and Air Chief Marshal Sir Tafford Leigh-Mallory as well.

🎙 *Taking care of the wounded, and rotating men in and out of France with others reporting to the replacement depot, became routine business for the Allies in the days, weeks, and months following D-Day. Sergeant Felix Branham required emergency medical attention after being wounded, but refused to allow a major injury to stand in the way of his returning to his men in the 29th Division.*

On the 11th of June, we were on the outskirts of Couvienes, on the way to St. Lô. Every time we got a foxhole dug in that hard clay of Normandy, they'd say we were moving on. We'd move out, go about two or three hours until we caught up with the enemy again. They'd move, fall back, and set up position when we approached them. We had done this about three times, when I said, "I'm so tired. Next time we stop, I'm not going to dig a foxhole." Three of us in the platoon made a pact that next time, we weren't going to do it.

I went to sleep in an apple orchard and woke up to mortars dropping all around like rice at a wedding. It didn't faze us. We moved up against the hedgerow and stayed there. We never dug in. We stayed there about three or four days until we could build up our forces. On the fourth day, two people would rest while the third watched the hedgerow. I saw a medical guy just about fifty yards (45.7m) down the hedgerow, and I assumed somebody was wounded. Suddenly a shell dropped right in the middle of the three of us.

LEFT: Dead Americans and a knocked-out M-10 tank destroyer mark the route that the 29th Infantry Division's Task Force C took during the assault that surprised St. Lô's defenders and seized the city. The M-10 was designed for use against German armor, but combat necessity invariably pulled it into infantry actions for which it was not well suited. In both the hedgerows and close-in street fighting, a tank destroyer crew in its open-top turret was vulnerable to mortar fire, grenades, or sniper fire from the upper stories of buildings. However, when operating behind effective infantry screens—and in settings where the threat from mortars was low—its big 3-inch gun provided devastating direct fire on enemy positions holding up an advance. Some two thousand men from the 35th Division and three thousand from the 29th became casualties during the prolonged fight for St. Lô.

ABOVE: Truckloads of 35th Infantry Division troops roll through the remains of St. Lô on a road swept clear of tons of debris by Army bulldozers. Approximately thirteen hundred French civilians were killed in a series of strikes by Allied aircraft, including B-17 heavy bombers, on the headquarters of the German LXXXIV Corps and other German targets, which began on D-DAY. The bulk of the survivors were sent to nearby Le Hurtrel, where they remained until late July. Then they were displaced yet again by the opening phase of the Allied breakout from Normandy.

When I came to, part of my leg was blown away. I looked over to one of the other fellows. His leg was pulled back over his shoulder, and he was unconscious. The other guy had lungs and other organs laying outside his chest. I crawled down the hedgerow. We had two morphine surrets. We were the first invasion troops to carry them, although paratroops always did. My ears, eyes, and nose were bleeding. The medic worked on me and gave me sulfa, then he crawled to the other guys. One was already dead. I was evacuated to about three field hospitals in three days. One was on OMAHA Beach. They told me we were being flown back to England. They loaded us on a C-47. They had racks in there for all of us on stretchers. Then they started tossing the parachutes out of the plane, and I asked why. The flight sergeant replied, "You can't use them anyway. You're on stretchers, so how could you use a parachute?"

We flew across the Channel and landed just outside of Swindon. There was a field hospital not far from where we had been stationed. When we landed, a doctor came on board and looked at our tags. He saw mine and said, "Son, this war's over for you. Can you stand about a twenty-minute ambulance ride?" I said after what I'd been through in the past eleven days, I could stand anything. He started walking away, stopped, then said, "You know you're going home." I said, "Major, you're nuts. I'm going back to France." He looked at me and winked. Ordinarily I wouldn't have said such a thing to a major, but I was pretty cocky.

They operated on me that night. I kept saying I was going back to France. I went to a rehabilitation center. One day a guy came in and hollered, "Anybody for the 1st Division? The 2d Division?" All the trucks and cars were lined up outside. I said I heard somebody calling for the 29th. I crawled into the back of a truck. I asked where they were going. He said to the coast and getting on a boat. I said, "Me too." We landed back at OMAHA Beach. By now the shore people had erected a huge sign on the hill: "UP THIS PATH MARCHED SOME OF AMERICA'S BEST FIGHTING MEN." About thirty of us ran up to this colonel. He said, "Full of vim and vigor, eh fellows?" I told him, "Colonel, we are back for seconds. We hit this beach on the first day, 6th of June." He just turned his head and walked away.

We checked in at the replacement depot and got something to eat. I met Ernie Pyle there. In the meantime I was watching trucks and jeeps, anything from the 116th [Infantry Regiment]. I saw a jeep coming down the road, and I crawled down an embankment and asked if he was in the 116th. He was. I asked where the third battalion was. He said they were about three miles (4.8km) away. I didn't tell anybody I was leaving. I just jumped into this jeep.

When we arrived, my company commander was hollering. I told them I was staying. They said I had to go back to the replacement depot to get cleared and return tomorrow. I couldn't believe we were still fighting near St. Lô. We had been about five miles (8km) away when I was wounded. Now twenty-four and half days later, we still hadn't taken the town. ▪

—Felix Branham

Private Frederick Glover of the British 9th Parachute Battalion had been wounded and captured June 6. He spent the following weeks under the care of the Germans in Paris.

After I was taken prisoner, the Germans brought us to a hospital for my wounds. The main building was a château in which they did the operations and the main treatment. All the rest were huts [filled] with Allied wounded. A German orderly came over and in a very pronounced American accent asked, "When do you think your buddies will be coming for you?" We had a short conversation. I learned that he'd been a waiter in New

ABOVE: A P-47 Thunderbolt bursts into flames after crash landing on the wire matting of a landing strip near Sainte Mère-Eglise, June 21, 1944. Chemical foam was used to suppress the fire near the cockpit, and a ground crewman attempts to control the spread of the flames with a spray of water. Note the clusters of undropped 20-pound fragmentation bombs dangling from the aircraft's starboard bomb rack.

York. He had been recalled to Germany when hostilities seemed imminent.

A short stay there and then I was taken on to a building that I discovered—for reasons I don't know—was called the American Hospital before the war. I stayed two or three weeks. We heard that wounded were being transported to Paris from there. That seemed to be the most likely opportunity if I was to be able to get away. At that particular time, the Allies were getting very close to Paris, and the Germans themselves were getting concerned that they weren't going to be taken prisoner. Security was particularly lax. I had made contact with some Resistance people who were working in the hospital. It was arranged on this particular night that I would get out, hopefully, and get into the grounds of the next building, which was an old people's home of some type.

I had actually adopted a situation that made it look as though I was having great difficulty in getting around, which, of course, I wasn't. But that's the picture that I'd painted. On this particular night I got down to the ground floor, out through a washroom window. The arrangement was, if I would get down this wall, Resistance people would be waiting for me to take me away.

It was dark and I misjudged the height of the wall. Hitting the ground didn't do my legs any good. The wounds opened up again, so they had to literally carry me away. I was taken to an FFI [French Forces of the Interior] headquarters and stayed there. They had a doctor examine me. This I delayed doing for fear of being sent to the hospital again and to Germany. I went back into the hospital after I knew that the Germans had gone. Eventually I was flown back to England. ▪

—Frederick Glover

Death from Above

A lack of airfields around Caen would hamper effective support of any British drive to the Seine and beyond, but British forces for now were well within range of even the notoriously "short-legged" Spitfires based in England. American P-51 Mustangs, P-47 Thunderbolts, and the tank-busting British Typhoons all made road movement during the light of day a deadly game of cat and mouse for the Germans. It became even more deadly when the June 27 capture of Cherbourg and the Cotentin Peninsula opened up valuable terrain for U.S. airfield development close to the front. German road and rail movements, previously measured in terms of hours, now were counted in days because of the combined actions of Allied pilots and the French Resistance. Hundreds, and ultimately thousands, of German troops were killed as they neared the Normandy battleground. The ones who did arrive often were sent off immediately to shore up a developing crisis along the line, instead of being gathered for a concerted effort against the Allied invaders.

The privileges of rank within the *Wehrmacht* and SS did not include safety from Allied attack:

June 8—During the tenth air attack of the day on Lieutenant General Fritz Bayerlein's Panzer-Lehr Division, his staff car was set ablaze by a string of 20-mm shells, killing the driver and peppering Bayerlein with shrapnel.

June 10—While preparing to launch the 1st SS Panzer Corps on a coordinated strike west of Caen, Panzer Group West commander General Geyr von Schweppenburg narrowly escaped death when rocket-firing Typhoons and B-25 Mitchell bombers wiped out his entire staff and nearly all of its forward echelon.

June 12—LXXXIV Corps commander General Erich Marcks was prevented from leaping quickly from his staff car by his wooden leg and was killed during a strafing attack, and Lieutenant General Fritz Witt of the 12th SS Panzer was killed by naval gunfire.

June 17—Lieutenant General Heinz Hellmich of the 243d Infantry Division was killed by a fighter-bomber.

June 18—Major General Rudolf Stegmann of the 77th Infantry Division suffered the same fate several miles from where Hellmich was attacked. Eventually, even Rommel's luck ran out: a pair of Typhoons caught up with his staff car in mid-July. He suffered severe injuries, including a fractured skull.

This steady attrition of German commanders in Normandy was only a foretaste of things to come. Remarkably, this dominance by Allied airpower was achieved even as the Pas-de-Calais remained the scene of an intense Allied bombing effort because of the ongoing deception operation. With FORTITUDE's target—the German Fifteenth Army—intact, out of the fight, and nearly impervious to pleas for reinforcements, OB West had to look elsewhere for help. The only major source of additional German armor was Army Group G in southern France, which saw most of its best formations moved one by one to railheads for their long, dangerous journey north to the Caen slugfest. Two costly British efforts to outflank the city from the west in June were beaten back, largely because of these reinforcements. Canadian and British forces finally broke into the northern half of the city in early July on the heels of a massive strike by Allied heavy bombers that killed some three thousand civilians as well as German combatants. The following operation, GOODWOOD, succeeded in pushing Montgomery's line more than two miles (3.2km) south of the city by July 20.

One of those appreciative of the Army Air Force was tank gunner Walter Stitt of the 3d Armored Regiment. Yet the very real possibility of being trapped in one's tank was on the mind of all who bravely served inside those metal coffins.

During my combat experience, I lost three tanks. One time I was in a tank and we'd been fighting, when suddenly a lieutenant came and ordered the tank commander out so he could take over. We found out later that the lieutenant had already lost two tanks that day. He got in, we sat still, then suddenly we heard the platoon sergeant yelling over the phone, "Lieutenant, they're shooting at you, back up, back up." When he did, I turned my periscope around and looked. I saw a fireball go by. Then the sergeant got on again, and said, "Lieutenant, back up, back up!" I looked out, and he was paralyzed. Then he grabbed his mike button, pushed it, and said, "Driver, back up."

Bang, just like that, we're hit, and the shell hit right in front of the gunner, and killed him and the tank commander both. The tank, of course, leaps up in the air. Everything got black for a minute, and it rattles your brains. You're just kind of stunned for a minute. And then I said to myself, We're hit. And I looked, and of course, for me to get out from where I am, I had to get underneath the cannon and out between these two people. When I looked, the gunner had fallen back, and the tank commander had fallen on top of him. I reached up, trying to pull them apart, but I couldn't get them. They were just wedged. So I dropped back down on the floor. Then I saw daylight, where the driver had gotten out. So I dove down out of the turret into the driver's seat and up over the side of the tank.

Just as I did, the tank got hit again, and then that time it exploded because they hit gas or ammunition or whatever. And I hit the ground. My shoulder kept coming out of joint, so I jumped up and pulled the shoulder back in place. It hurt. I started to run, snagging my foot on a piece of barbed wire fence, and went down again. This knocked my shoulder out again. I found a hot foxhole that wasn't very deep and got into that. Then I realized I was wounded; some shrapnel had gotten in my legs. They were not serious wounds, but a lot of scratches. And so I went

up to a light Stuart tank that was there, and said, "Hand me a bandage," and the guy said, "Come up and get it."

So I climbed up the side of the tank, and the guy handed the bandage out to me. As I'm climbing up and getting back down, all of a sudden there's a splatter of bullets go up the side of the tank, and I realize some German was shooting at me. I looked around, and here's this German underneath a bunch of bushes with his gun. And I yelled up to the light tank commander, "That guy with the gun is under those bushes." And he swung that little 37mm around like that, and *ka-boom,* they took care of that one.

The thing that I think I feared most was the tank catching on fire from a shell, because I'd seen that happen. Fellows come out of the tank on fire, or they'd been hit through the gas tank, and gas now was spewed all over.

With a Sherman tank, you couldn't come face to face with a German tank. The real strategy was to get around to the side of them. If you came [face to face] with a German tank, some of [our] crews would fire smoke shields right away, and see if they could fog it up for them, so they couldn't see you. Sometimes, if you were close enough, you could shoot a white phosphorous high-explosive shell. And if that got in, sometimes the German crews would abandon the tank.

But the best thing to do was to have somebody firing at the tank, and the German turrets couldn't traverse all the way, so they had to turn the tank to take another shot, over on the side. When they turned the tank, then somebody would come up on this side. The idea was to keep working on them, until somebody got a good shot that did him in. But if you shot right at them, oftentimes you could just see the shell just bounce right off. They could penetrate our armor with no trouble at all. Whereas most of our shots, head on, would bounce off. If our tank was hit on the side, that was bad, because that's where the gas tanks were. It had about a half an inch (1.3cm) of armor, which won't even slow down those German 88-mm shells. They just go right in there. So if they hit you from the side, it could go right on through. Our heaviest armor was in the front. The sides and the back were rather thin armor, and vulnerable.

Patton's philosophy was that tanks didn't fight tanks. He believed that tanks were to help out the infantry, but it didn't work that way. The infantry was essential for the tanks. We never wanted to get out and try to fight by ourselves, because the Germans were good fighters. The infantry and reconnaissance troops were good about spotting German tank positions. If they spotted one, then they'd call us, and we'd come up and start banging away to get rid of the German tanks or whatever they were having difficulty with. Once we got that air superiority, it was great, because you could call the Air Force. If the weather was good, they would come out and bomb it or strafe it. They were a big help to us that way. ▪

—Walter Stitt, E Company, 33d Armored Regiment, 3d Armored Division (US)

Members of the intelligence corps questioned the Germans the Allies had captured. Second Lieutenant Walter Bodlander of the 8th Infantry Regiment conducted his interrogations with usually good results. But occasionally a prisoner presented a challenge.

When a German soldier was captured or surrendered, he was immediately sent to me and my unit. We had him for about half an hour. We were the first people to talk to him. They usually came in groups of five or six. Often they were frightened, and it was very easy to get intelligence from them. They were willing to give name, rank, and serial number.

I then said, "Thank you. That was very nice and well done." Not sarcastically, but just

BELOW: German prisoners wait in temporary enclosures on Utah Beach for transportation back to England, and from there to a network of POW camps in the United States and Canada. More than ten thousand troops, many of them Russians and other non-Germans, were captured during the first week of the invasion. Daily transits across the English Channel remained frequent throughout the campaign and surged into the thousands after key events— the fall of Cherbourg, the opening of the breakout operation, the Falaise Pocket battles, and the pursuit to the Belgian border and eastern France.

in a friendly way, I pointed to a map on the ground and said, "Well, let's see. Do you know where you are?" They said they did. I asked them to show me because I didn't think they truly knew. They showed me. Then I asked if they knew where they had come from. They showed me that too. I then asked, "What is that?" And he said something like, "That's where our battalion is." Then he stopped. I told him I already knew they were commanded by so-and-so because another prisoner had told me. This way he realized he hadn't betrayed himself at all. I asked, "Is this where your artillery is?" He replied, "No, it's much farther behind the lines. I don't know where. All we have is machine guns here and here." That's exactly the kind of information I needed. It was easy enough to gain information. We were told not to torture anyone, and to my knowledge, no one ever did.

Occasionally an interrogation was difficult, and one was forced to do something more creative. After Falaise and on the way to Paris, we had just broken through but didn't know what was facing us. We had captured a lieutenant and two sergeants. I interrogated them, and they were really tough. They were convinced that they were fighting for their Fatherland and weren't giving anything.

I really needed information, since we had no idea about what unit we were facing—Reserve or frontline? Whose? Fresh unit? Older? When had they arrived? The more I asked, the more they clammed up. They felt relatively relaxed for some reason, and I remember being very frustrated because I needed information. And so I finally took one of the sergeants away from the group. I persuaded him to give me the name of the commanding officer of the regiment. I think it was in his little notebook he carried, but I couldn't read the name. I said, "It's signed by somebody—is this your commanding officer?" He said it was. I said I couldn't read the name, so he told me.

I took my pistol and shot in the air. I put a guard there and made sure that this guy was out of sight. Then I went back to the lieutenant, and told him, "You're next," and took him to another area. He asked, "What do you mean, 'I'm next'?" I told him that the sergeant didn't talk. All he gave me was the name of the regiment. I knew that. The regimental commander. I knew that too. And his company commander, I didn't care about. I wanted to know more. This guy really tensed up, because he had heard the shot, and he had found out that I knew something. Now he

was on the line. So he broke down, and I got information. Once I had his information, it was easy to get more from the other sergeant. This, though, was not common practice. ▪

—Walter Bodlander

Canadian Joseph Rivier was in the midst of the fighting. He came upon the ruins of what had been the city of Caen, whose William the Conqueror has succeeded in his own cross-channel invasion—of England— in 1066. Still, the reaction of the French people was warm.

When we went through Caen, it was just heaps of rubble. There was nothing left of Caen hardly anywhere. It was a big city, and I'm sure it was 99 percent destroyed from the bombing. One of our half-track operators adopted a little French boy who was orphaned. They called him Kao, and he traveled with us for months. They finally told him you can't do this; you've got to give him back. This little kid followed him everywhere just like a dog.

The French loved us. We would drive down the road in our tank and you could just hang over the side with one of our enameled teacups, and they'd fill it with apple whisky or whatever they had. If you were a drinker, you could really get quite a glow just driving down the road. They were giving us everything they had. They were so happy to see us. ▪

—Joseph "Al" Rivier, Gunner, 36th Battery, 3d Field Regiment, Artillery (CAN)

While infantry trudged their way across France, others were tasked with different duties. Second Lieutenant Walter Bodlander was now stationed in Cherbourg. There he stumbled upon a unique discovery.

My unit was ordered to guard a fortification in Cherbourg, which is a city where the mountains face the harbor. In those mountains the Germans built ground emplacements, and these ground emplacements went around the whole mountain edge facing the harbor. The 12th Infantry had captured this, which had been filled with guns,

ABOVE: Sprinting for the safety of a chapel wall in the Cotentin Peninsula, an American soldier holds his helmet to his head as his buddy watches for snipers. Although many German troops escaped, some twenty-five thousand were cut off in the Cherbourg area when the U.S. drive to the west was completed on June 18, 1944.

heavy artillery, and field artillery to be used against a possible sea invasion. Now, somebody had to be there to prevent roaming German units from recapturing those areas. I was assigned to guard these installations inside the mountain, including long endless corridors of tunnels.

There was no electricity, so the only way you could see anything was with a flashlight. All we really had to do was to guard the entrance to these tunnels. I went in a little bit further because I knew there was no danger.

I went in a little bit and realized this must be a command post. I figured this would be a great place to find documentation of plans of what they might be doing. I started to look into those dark little rooms and chambers with a flashlight. I found a sack, and inside was paper. I expected important documents but instead found French money. The room was filled with sacks and sacks of regular French currency. It was obviously a payroll for the whole region, so I opened a few of those sacks and there were 10,000 franc notes and 5,000 franc notes and 20,000 franc notes and 500 franc notes. I stuffed myself full of this thing, and I said, "Hey, that's a fun discovery." I figured it was play money we could use

Hell in the Hedgerows

ABOVE: Typical Norman countryside as seen from an artillery spotter aircraft. A platoon that succeeded in seizing a hedgerow—with the help of tanks and mortars, in a laborious, highly choreographed battle—might well find that the field beyond was actually two irregular fields separated and bordered by yet more hedgerows. The U.S. Army suffered forty thousand casualties in the five weeks of grinding combat it took to capture St. Lô and position itself for the breakthrough west of the town.

RIGHT: A soldier mans a heavy 50-caliber machine gun and watches for enemy activity from a break in the hedgerows.

when playing cribbage, which we did when there was nothing else to do. I took a lot of the money and eventually gave it to my friends and Major Todd. We began to play cribbage for 1,000 francs a point.

We were lighting cigarettes with French money until we decided it might be worthwhile to see if the French would use this money and honor it. So we went to the first farmhouse we came to on the way back from Normandy. The French were very willing to accept this money, so we got eggs and wine from the farmers.

About a month later we were being paid for the first time, and expected to be paid in invasion money. Instead we were paid in real French money. Had I held on to all that money I would've had an enormous amount of valuable American money, because we were paid in French money, but we had the right to send it home. Consequently, I could've sent thousands of dollars home, but it had all been burned up and given away. Later, I learned that there was forty million dollars' worth of French currency in that area, literally the payroll of the German Army for that whole region. Since there was so much currency available, the American Army decided to use it, and the French accepted it. ■

—Walter Bodlander

After the Allied landings, American soldiers immediately encountered the jumbled *bocage* country. German infantry skillfully turned the hedgerow-enclosed fields into deathtraps by combining well concealed automatic weapons and mortars with highly effective, portable *Panzerbuchse* and *Panzerfaust* antitank weapons. This determined defense by a handful of German grenadier and parachute divisions prevented significant U.S. advances to the south for weeks, and prompted concern at SHAEF that a military stalemate had been reached. Less than five miles (8km) from St. Lô on June 18, American troops would not enter the city for almost a month, and then only after some of the fiercest fighting of World War II as regiments and divisions independently developed tactics and techniques to isolate and reduce the Germans' mini fortresses in methodical, set-piece assaults.

By mid-July, bitter field-by-field fighting among the hedgerows had yielded the Americans a sufficient lodgment for the thousands of tons of supplies needed for Operation COBRA—the breakout and dash across France. While the British Second Army in the east around Caen continued to attract the bulk of the German armored forces to its sector, and strained for its own breakout, the U.S. First Army inexorably gained as much ground as possible to make room for the U.S. Third Army coming in behind it.

Aided by the recent development of a variety of field modifications to American tanks that allowed the machines to literally plow through the hedgerows' massive berms of roots and earth, the First Army planned to punch a hole through the German defenses, then hold the shoulders of the gap while its armor stampeded through into the German rear areas. Preceding the ground attack would be a massive bombardment by 1,500 American heavy bombers, which was designed to kill and shock the German defenders.

The carpet bombing of a "box" 7,000 yards (6,401m) wide by 2,500 yards (2,286m) deep essentially wiped out the one German armored division in the U.S. sector, Panzer-Lehr, on July 25. Tragically, 757 Americans were also killed and wounded in a series of bombing accidents as "shorts" fell into their jump-off positions. An initial wave of three armored divisions streamed through the broken German lines, and Avranches, where the Normandy and Brittany peninsulas meet, was seized on July 30. Patton rapidly exploited the breakthrough by launching his Third Army divisions at widely separated objectives far to the west, south, and east. The *Wehrmacht*, stretched to the limit by staggering troop losses in Normandy, had nothing that could stand in his way.

The Germans belatedly faced reality: Patton's "army" was not going to strike across the English Channel into the Pas-de-Calais and Flanders, but was running wild 250 miles (402.3km) to the southwest. The Fifteenth Army's infantry divisions, long held for the invasion that never came, took the place of Panzer divisions facing the British.

On August 6, the Panzer divisions were hurled through Mortain toward the narrow neck of the American breakout at Avranches. They never reached their goal. The "inexperienced" U.S. 30th Infantry Division refused to be intimidated by the curiously piecemeal attack of four Panzer divisions, and the German thrust was savaged from the land and air. The new German commander of Army Group B, Field Marshal Gunther von Kluge, found that the eastward-stretching arm of Patton's advance had not retracted to help counter the Panzers, but instead had turned abruptly north

BELOW: Infantry and armor of the Third Army's 5th Infantry Division fight their way into Montereau, southeast of Paris, on August 25, 1944. Although the Third Army did not officially become operational until August 1, Patton was immediately given control of the armored and mechanized divisions that surged through German lines during the July 25–27 breakthrough west of St. Lô.

30TH INFANTRY DIVISION

The U.S. 30th Infantry Division arrived in France on June 10, 1944, and defended along the Vire-Taute Canal line. The division forced a crossing on July 7 and repulsed a German counterattack as it advanced on St. Lô. On July 25, it and two other divisions punched a hole through the German lines for the U.S. Third Army's breakout from Normandy— Operation COBRA. On August 7, the day after taking over a new position along the front near Mortain, the 30th was subjected to a very strong German counterattack that temporarily ruptured its lines. The division resumed offensive operations on July 30 and quickly eliminated the German gains.

ABOVE: Shell casings litter the pavement of the Breton port of St. Malo, as soldiers from the 83d Infantry Division root out Germans trapped by the Third Army's rapid advance into the Brittany Peninsula on August 8, 1944.

The most important contribution that the Canadians made once they were ashore was south of Caen around the Verrières Ridge, conducting holding attacks. They didn't know they were holding attacks. On the afternoon of July 25th, the day the Americans broke out against a thin crust at their end of the bridge-head, the Canadians suffered 1,500 casualties in terms of wounded and dead—more than they suffered in wounded and dead at Dieppe. The Black Watch regiment alone, sustained 386 casualties. Only 10 men came back from the attack up the ridge. At the time we thought we were trying to break out. You can't very well tell troops they're going in for a bloodletting to let the Americans break out. So we really thought we were doing the job. They attacked courageously. But they did the job.

Having done that, with Patton's force zooming toward Paris with light opposition, the Canadians were now told, "Well, you have a chance to cut these Germans off. Hitler has sent his forces attacking, trying to cut the tail off the American advance." Eisenhower told them to cut through all the forces they'd been holding and cut the Germans off in a pocket. Later, he recognized that the most intensely held area of the whole bridgehead was the area that the Canadians were now expected to attack.

I think that it can be proven that one of the chief reasons for the Canadians' success was the strength of the artillery. Our guns fired more shells than ever had been dumped on gun positions before in British history. We were firing fifty rounds at some points on the Verrières Ridge when our units were smashed and overrun and nothing left between there and Caen of any consequence except the reserve battalions. The rounds overlapped.

toward Argentan, fifty miles (80.4km) behind the lead Panzers of the German counterattack. It was August 10 before von Kluge was finally able to persuade Hitler that he must break off the attack or face annihilation. Orders were issued for the Seventh and Fifth Panzer armies to quickly withdraw eastward before they were caught between the Americans and the new Canadian First Army.

As the Allies proceeded with the break-out, they encountered numerous pockets of resistance. George Blackburn of the Canadian 4th Field Regiment Artillery described the fierce fighting around the Verrières Ridge.

2D ARMORED DIVISION

Although the U.S. 2d Armored Division arrived in France within days of the invasion, it was held in reserve until Operation COBRA in late July. Surging through the hole punched in the German lines, the division completely unhinged the German defenses by striking far to the south, in the Percy area, taking St. Denis-le-Gast on July 28, 1944. It helped counter the Germans' August 7 attack toward Avranches, and overran Domfront on August 14. Five days later, west of Dreux, the division attacked north to cut off German forces retreating toward the Seine River, then struck northwest and reached Cambrai on September 1.

LEFT: An M-36 tank destroyer fires its 90mm gun at point-blank range into a German pillbox to clear a path through a side street in Brest in mid-September 1944. The conical-shaped structure, partially obscured by the dust kicked up by the M-36, is a portable air-raid shelter used by German sentries.

At one point, we were told, "Fire until you're told to stop." Our guns were red hot; the paint peeled off. They had to pour buckets of muddy water into the guns, creating great geysers of steam.

At one point, I came out of the command post, a little dugout, to fire some shells personally. As I'm walking over, this is what I saw. All six gunners at a gun, shoveling the shells in, cigarettes hanging out of their mouths, bare to the waist, their skin glistening with rain. Right in front of the gun, maybe fifty yards (45.7m) in front of the gun, a big black spout of mud and smoke went up from a German shell that landed. These guys never flinched. They didn't even look up, they were so tired. By this time, they had been going without sleep for a couple of days. They never whimpered. They never whined. They just did their business. It was just an outstanding job. They were wonderful. ▪

—George Blackburn,
4th Field Regiment, Artillery (CAN)

Aiding in the breakout effort were the troops manning the tanks and armored units. Many of these men had been sitting behind in England, awaiting orders to move. Canadian Joseph "Al" Rivier was one of those men.

The whole south coast of England was covered with camps. We were on "Buzz Bomb Alley." Day and night, buzz bombs went overhead toward London. When the V-1s flew over the Channel, the airplanes took them. If they missed them at the coast, the anti-aircraft took over. After they got inland maybe ten miles (16km), the airplanes took over again. I saw a Hurricane that came up and worked its way over. The pilot brought his wing under the wing of a buzz bomb. He rolled his airplane and just flipped it over. He dumped that buzz bomb right into the ground. Hardly any of them got through.

I landed in Normandy July 25th, on my birthday—got my draft notice the same day

in a mail call! D-DAY was a cheering time. We wanted to be there, too, but it was probably standing room only on the beaches. And they were also trying to play a game with Hitler thinking that the troops that were left in England would go to Calais. Make him think Normandy was only a diversionary thing.

Seeing the MULBERRY harbor coming up on you was an unbelievable feat. It was nice to land on it too. As we approached, you could see the sunken ships that they used for a breakwater. You might see the concrete caissons that they towed from England to sink to make the actual MULBERRY. And from there to shore I would estimate probably a half a mile (0.8km) of pontoon bridge going to shore. When we got our tank off and onto the MULBERRY itself, we had to sit and wait for a long time. We waited while a whole fleet of German prisoners came marching out to get on ships to be sent back to England. Then we finally headed for shore on the pontoon bridge. You don't put too many tanks on it too close together. You've got to space them out, 'cause they're pretty heavy. ▪

—Joseph "Al" Rivier

🎤 *Canadian war correspondent for Reuters Charles Lynch yearned to make his own breakout—and he did, with a most unexpected result.*

Eventually, we started to get beachhead fever, because the Canadian beachhead was only six miles deep, along with the Brits'. The American beachhead was similar until the American breakout. A couple of us got the idea of going to have a look at it. We had had enough of this same road, same place, same briefings, same bombings of Caen, same fierce opposition from the Germans. So we armed ourselves with a case of steak and kidney pie, which is the only thing in the Canadian and British rations that American troops wanted, and swapped for coffee and various things that the Americans had that were more to the Canadian taste than the British rations on which the Canadian Army fought.

We got behind Patton, and we were able to step on the gas. We had two jeeps, and we headed down the coast of Normandy toward Brittany. We discovered Mont St. Michel. I'd never heard of it. Suddenly this magic, Disney-esque sort of island appeared with this wonderful church and buildings.

We took a big causeway to get to it. It had been left undisturbed. It was one of the most famous antiquities of Europe. We got inside the walls and walked up a winding path and came to a restaurant, La Mère Poulard, famous for its omelettes. We went in, and here were the American correspondents who knew about this place. Here was Hemingway, Bob Capa, you name them, and they were there. Outside there was a huge staff car filled with guns. Patton had captured this German Mercedes and turned it over to Hemingway, who wanted to join the Free French Resistance. ▪

—Charles Lynch

Fighting in and among the hedgerows gave rise to some of the most haunting memories for survivors of those grim battlefields, including Private Bill True of the 101st Airborne Division.

Actually, our toughest fighting occurred a couple of days after taking Carentan, when the Germans were counterattacking. We were in a line just outside of town, on a hedgerow. I was with a machine gunner there, working as a second gunner. Ray, the first gunner, spotted some Germans in a little culvert and was really working it up and down. I said, "Ray, are you sure those are Germans? You know that that's not really far away." I can still remember the bodies stopped moving as he raked up and down. It turned out he was plenty right. They were Germans, because about that time a big tank showed up right where they had been and started firing at us. What in the world sense it made shooting either a 30-caliber machine gun or rifle at this tank, but we did. We saw the muzzle flash then duck down below the hedgerow. One of the shells hit in the tree, and the concussion killed two of our men. That was a tougher fight than taking the city of Carentan.

For the next month and a half that we were in Normandy, we had occasional fire-

fights like that, and lots of patrols. I got so sick of going out on patrols—Joe Flick and I vowed never to volunteer for another patrol. But one night our platoon commander, Lieutenant Tuck, got the assignment to send a patrol out to try to pick up a German prisoner. Joe and I had these handbooks to learn some basic French and German. We learned how to say "Hands up" and "Come with me" in German.

Lieutenant Tuck knew that we spoke a little bit of German. So he said, "Got a patrol goin' tonight, and I need one of you guys to volunteer to lead the patrol because I need somebody who can holler at those Germans to make 'em come with us." Joe and I looked at each other; we'd decided long ago we weren't going to volunteer anymore. [Tuck] says, "Come on, one of you has got to volunteer—ya gotta go!" Joe and I, at just about the same time, said, "Well, all right, I'll go." Tuck said, "Great! I can use both of you out there."

So we both got stuck on this night patrol. Going out way beyond your lines at night was frightening. You can't see your hand in front of your face. Joe and I led this patrol, walking and crawling, probably making a big circle of some kind. Fortunately, we didn't run into anything, and came back. But it taught us to shut up about our proficiency of the German language. ▪

—Bill True

Armored units were in no better shape to fight amid these monstrous growths of tangled tree roots and vines. Private Bertrand Close of the 3d Armored Division quickly learned the dangers of these nearly impenetrable obstacles.

I have letters that I wrote home when I was at Fort Knox, telling my folks that the Sherman tank was great. We were told it was the best in the world, perhaps a bit noisy, but still a wonderful tank. I believed that all the time I was in England before we went over into France.

I joined a tank crew in July. Our Sherman tank had a 76-mm gun, the only one in the company; the others were 75s. The difference was that the 76 had a much higher velocity

BERTRAND CLOSE

OPPOSITE, TOP: A German 75-mm round penetrated the port side of this Sherman tank just below the turret.

OPPOSITE, BOTTOM: Soldiers from the 3d Infantry Division walk slowly away from a still-burning Sherman after finding no survivors. Although these men are not wearing the coveralls still commonly worn by tankers at this stage of the war, their lack of gear and M-1 rifles other than a single carbine may indicate that they belong to the 3d's attached 756th Tank Battalion. The Sherman apparently took a hit to its starboard track before receiving a final, killing strike from a large 88-mm round directly through the add-on armor in front of the driver's position. Still-sealed hatches are another sign that none of the crew is likely to have survived, and the one open hatch on the hull may have been blown open by an internal explosion.

and was a much deadlier gun than the 75mms. It could pierce some of the smaller German tanks' armor. I felt pretty good about our tank, which was called *In the Mood*. It survived various battles right up until September 19th. I was with it about eighty days before it was destroyed.

After that, I was in three other Sherman tanks with 75-mm guns, and we really didn't have any ability to destroy German tanks with the 75mms. Those three tanks were

knocked out really without firing a telling shot. By January of 1945 I had pretty much a feeling of disgust. I had gone from thinking it was a great tank to seeing it as a piece of junk. I was angry, and felt we had been misled from the beginning when we were told what a wonderful tank it was. With the ability of American resources, we should have built the best tank in the world. Instead, German and Russian tanks were all superior, in my opinion, to American tanks.

USA 20383

4TH ARMORED DIVISION

Tanks of the U.S. 4th Armored Division rolled onto French soil less than two weeks before Operation COBRA. The division plunged through German lines west of the main breakthrough point on July 28, 1944, captured Avranches on July 30, and struck south to cut off the Brittany Peninsula. After capturing Vannes on August 5 and investing Lorient two days later, it was ordered to take part in the Third Army's drive toward the German border. The 4th seized Orléans on August 16 and established bridgeheads across the Meuse River on August 31.

I think the problem was that the Sherman tanks were designed to fight ground troops, not German emplacements or German tanks. My feeling was that there was no reason to use Sherman tanks in the hedgerows when they could be destroyed by bazookas at a range of twenty-five yards (23m). These hedgerows protected the Germans. They could pop up and you'd never see them. On the first day's battle, everyone thought that they could just go right through these hedgerows and destroy everything that was there. We soon learned that you had to machine-gun everything and blast the corners of the hedgerows with the 75- or 76-mm cannons, and hope you wouldn't be hit with anything.

In the Mood was credited with leading on twenty different occasions down the road as the point tank. Any time you got into a situation where you were the lead tank, it was risky, to say the very least. You moved down the road in northern France where there were clumps of trees, haystacks, farmhouses, sheds—anything that could hide a German tank or a German antitank gun. They would hit you, and you would never know where they were until they fired the first shot. If they missed, then we had a chance of eliminating them, or maybe the tanks behind us would see where that shot came from and join in the battle.

One reason we were usually the lead tank was due to the reputation of our tank commander—Lafayette Poole. During the breakout, we got onto the roadways and out of the hedgerows and orchards onto the roads. Poole was commander of the lead tank then. He was confident, and he created confidence in everyone else. He was smart and quick. He was a staff sergeant, but he never pulled rank. Everybody knew what they were supposed to do, and they did it, working well together. We used to kid him and say, "Lafayette, we are here!" He became known as a tank ace. Others had confidence in him as well; consequently, if we were not in the lead initially, we were often ordered to take that position.

In my first battle, about July 10th, we went through a hole in the hedgerow with the infantry following behind us, about three or four behind each tank. As the tanks passed through the hedge, they would spread out in a platoon of about four or five tanks. On this occasion, we probably got through a couple of fields before a tank gunner hit the attic in a house that was probably several hundred yards (about 300m) away, and just blew the attic to pieces. It could have been a place where a sharpshooter or a spotter was giving instructions to German artillery. Anyway, we went through these fields, and the tank maybe thirty yards (27.4m) in front of us was hit and started burning. All of its crew got out of that tank. We started backing up, and I think it was the bow gunner from the tank in front of us that was hit—stood right out there in front of our tank and gave directions with his arms, motioning the driver how to back up into the hole in the hedgerow that we'd come through. Then maybe a hundred to a hundred and fifty yards (91.4m–137m) in front of us, two or three P-47s came in and strafed and bombed that area and blew up whatever was in the way. We moved into the village. While infantry was running from door to door covering each other on each side of the street, we were firing at the end of the street with the 76-mm cannon. Meanwhile, I was firing machine guns. I didn't see anybody, but just in case there was anybody who wanted to pop out, we would keep them down. Bazooka men could've jumped out of a window above us and hit us. There would've been no way in the world that we could have stopped that.

When we were going through northern France, there were occasions when we would come upon Germans who were trying to escape back to Germany. One night, we saw a railroad car that was apparently filled with German ammunition, weapons, and troops. I think all of I Company fired on this train. It wasn't moving. That set the train on fire and had a tremendous blaze that night. Fighting went all through the night involving close combat with the German foot soldiers. ▪

—Bertrand Close, Private,
I Company, 32d Armored Regiment,
3d Armored Division (US)

OPPOSITE, INSET: A soldier from the welding section of an Army ordnance company assembles hedgerow cutters in Cerisy Forest, Normandy.

ABOVE: Third Army commander George S. Patton glances toward an Army photographer before taking off in his private plane to inspect his far-flung divisions running wild across France. In August 1944, Patton's formations often operated hundreds of miles apart. After the breakout, some divisions moved south then west into Brittany, while others plunged straight east toward Germany, and still more fought their way east, then north, then northwest to cut off retreating Germans.

The Hedge Cutter

First Lieutenant Belton Y. Cooper of the 3d Armored Division attended a meeting where the problem and solution of tanks fighting in the hedgerows was addressed during a presentation that included General George S. Patton, Jr. in the audience.

My combat command, CCB, did not land until D+20. Our mission was to get into the hedgerow country, build up our strength, and break out.

A smart young fellow named Culin came up with a simple idea for a hedgerow chopper. He took a piece of steel, about three feet long, and then he took some other steel and cut sharp spikes that extended out about two and a half feet in front. He rolled it up and put this thing on the tank's towing devices. Those spikes would dig into the hedge, keeping the tank from rearing back, the pressure of the tank would just pull out the whole earth and the tank could take out a hedge in about three seconds. It never stopped. The hedge choppers were so low to the ground that the Germans couldn't see which tanks had them and which ones didn't.

On about the 21st of July, I was told to report for a demonstration of this hedge chopper. Several officers reported as well, including General Patton. I looked across the field and I saw this tall and fine-looking man, a rugged-looking individual. He had a brass buckle, his pearl [ivory] -handled pistols, wearing riding breeches, boots and spurs, and, of course, his three stars. He was impressive looking.

Everyone watched the demonstration of the hedge chopper cutting through a hedge. They repeated it about three or four times. It just zipped through. I was amazed. The officers discussed how many would be needed. They decided on fifty-seven. General Patton ordered them to be ready to go for an attack that was planned the next day, so the tanks had to be equipped by 7:00 A.M.!

Some were ordered to take trucks and cutting torches and go to the beach to cut up all of the tetrahedron obstacles; otherwise, we wouldn't have had the steel to do it. We brought them into town and set up an assembly line. Douglas, the warrant officer, had run a welding shop back in civilian life and he was a good welder, so they put him in charge of the thing. He didn't have any drawings. He used scraps and backs of envelopes and sketched hedge choppers.

A different hedge chopper was required for each tank because the available parts were all different. We just cut up parts and tried to put them together any way we could. The individual men had to improvise and design their own hedge choppers. One guy got the steel, one guy was cutting up the steel, one guy was fitting the

BELTON COOPER

steel together, another crew would come and weld it down. We found out it took forty man-hours of labor to weld up a hedge chopper, forty man-hours to cut it and do all that. And we only had forty men, so we worked our butts off all night long. Instead of fifty-seven hedge choppers, we had seven the next morning; that's all we had.

Now, if the attack had gone off like that and General [Leroy] Watson had been counting on fifty-seven hedge choppers, we would have run fifty short. It would have been a damned disaster if they had planned it that way. Fortunately, the good Lord looked after us and storms came making the weather too bad for the Air Force to attack. It was delayed by three days. During that time, we got about half of them on there ready to go. We never had the fifty-seven, but we got about twenty-five or so. Those hedge choppers completely revolutionized the fighting in the hedgerows. Additionally, our tremendous air power and artillery support simply devastated the Germans. That's how we broke out. It was the single best innovation. We lost eighty-nine tanks in the first five hours of the hedgerows. That was a third of our force right there before we ever got going. ◼

—Belton Y. Cooper, First Lieutenant,
Combat Command B,
3d Armored Division (US)

OPPOSITE, TOP: Sergeant Curtis G. Culin of the 102d Cavalry Reconnaissance Squadron, an early proponent and developer of the cutter, climbs out of his M-5 Stuart light tank.

OPPOSITE, BOTTOM: The steel-toothed, berm-busting attachments, called hedge cutters, sometimes varied radically from one to the other because their designs were often determined by what kind of scrap metal or discarded German obstacles were available.

ABOVE: Three views of a hedge cutter, freshly welded to a Sherman tank, as it plows through a hedgerow with ease. Tanks fitted with some form of the device were called "rhinos."

BELOW: Medics clip a bottle of blood plasma to the collapsed screen of a DD-Sherman as they administer aid to a French woman wounded during invasion operations along the Riviera, August 15, 1944. The Sherman belongs to the 753d Tank Battalion, which supported the assault of the 36th Infantry Division seven miles (11km) southwest of Cannes. Launched in calm Mediterranean waters from only two thousand yards (1,829m) offshore, the 753d suffered none of the mishaps experienced by DD units at Normandy.

Attacking the torturous hedgerows with airpower also helped turn the tide for the Allies. The use of aircraft to see (and destroy) from above what tanks and infantry could not, made fighting on the ground easier. In his Hawker Typhoon, RAF pilot Ken Hanna flew some of those missions.

Most of the targets that the Army called us in on were ones where they would be looking down the road, and they'd know that the Germans would be at the crossroads or in that hedgerow, so rather than checking it out for themselves, which would be rather dangerous business, they'd call us in. Invariably they were correct that there was a bottleneck there, and we would go down to assist them. In Normandy the hedgerows had roads sunken to a point where a vehicle could be hidden there, and you'd never ever see it looking across the leveled ground. Being above, we could see a lot of the things they couldn't see.

By late June, we determined that the aircraft were suffering from dust inhalation because we were experiencing engine problems. Engineers [had gone] in with bulldozers and flattened fields. The quality of the dust that was generated was such that it gave us a lot of problems, and we had to go back to England to have filters attached.

We flew back to our base in England, re-equipped with filters, picked up some new aircraft, and then came back. I think it was June 26 that we started operating again from Normandy. From then on our trips were very limited, twenty-five or thirty minutes on an operation. After a week or two, they started pulling a pilot off the squadron and then sending him up with the Army. He would be on an advanced tank or half-track and call in. When we appeared on the scene, he would say, All right, the red smoke's going down on the target; it's at this particular corner. We knew approximately where it was, but they fine-tuned it, so he'd say the smoke will go down in one minute. The Germans, though, were also very smart because they would listen in, and on occasions they would put the smoke down on our own troops, so you'd be into your dive and suddenly the controller would call off, "Don't shoot! Don't shoot! They're our own boys!" so we'd pull off.

I feel that there were many instances where you had the feeling that what you were doing pleased the troops, whether you were successful in knocking the tank out or not. They just felt that you were in there helping. That was important for everybody's morale. ∎

—Ken Hanna

LEFT: Members of a 3d Infantry Division 81-mm mortar crew fire on German forces in the Rigney area of southern France, September 9, 1944. The 3d, along with the 36th and 45th Infantry Divisions, came ashore on D-Day in the Riviera three weeks earlier, and was then approaching the rugged Vosges Mountains, which barred their advance to the Rhine River and Germany. The U.S. 7th Army's three-division assault extended across a thirty-eight-mile (61km) front and included French commandos landing on both flanks. Unlike Normandy, the extreme distance from Allied air-fields necessitated that the invasion be supported by seven Royal Navy and two U.S. aircraft carriers of various sizes and types. There is also no significant tidal action in the Mediterranean, which meant that there would be no opportunity to employ Army and Navy demoli-tions teams against the underwater obstacles. Instead, remote-controlled boats laden with explo-sives and Underwater Demolitions Teams (UDTs) of frogmen blew gaps in the obstacle belts.

D-DAY—The Riviera

The Allies conducted two invasions of France during the summer of 1944. Although the British had pushed for expanding the Italian operations, U.S. planners argued that the OVERLORD landings in Normandy could best be supported by subsequent landings on the southern coast of France. An invasion along the Riviera coast would open up the huge ports of Marseilles and Toulon, bring the American-supplied French Army into play, and more effectively bring about victory by keeping the Allied armies massed for an unstoppable drive into Germany. With some of German Army Group G's best units already siphoned off to the fighting around Caen, there were excellent prospects for a quick victory in the south, fol-lowed by a dash up the Rhône Valley and then to the Rhine River itself.

Initially designated ANVIL, the August 1944 invasion of southern France was renamed DRAGOON because planners believed that the original name had been compromised to the enemy. The Allies again used an elaborate deception plan to disguise the operation's objectives. The Germans knew something was up but thought the strike would take place on the Italian peninsula. Allied efforts encouraged this belief. The cumulative effect of radar countermeasures, multiple diversions, decoys, airborne assaults with dummy parachutists, and a last-minute change in convoy direction was successful. While German troops were on alert in Genoa, Italy, along the French Riviera troops awoke to massive naval and aerial bom-bardments on August 15, 1944. Amphibious assault and airborne landings put more than 90,000 men of the U.S. Seventh Army ashore on the first day. By nightfall of August 16, almost 151,000 Free French and American fighting men were on the beachhead. For the first time in four years, a French army was battling the Germans on the soil of metropoli-tan France.

Is Paris Burning?

The French Resistance was active in Paris throughout the Nazi occupation, and many patriots or hostages were shot in retaliation for attacks on Germans. After Germany's invasion of the Soviet Union in June 1941, the French Communist Party, centered in Paris, rose up against Germany, with many leaders of the Resistance coming from the ranks of the Communist Party.

By 1944, the poorer districts of Paris were suffering, and only the well-off could afford black market prices for scarce goods. People yearned for liberation, particularly after the Normandy Invasion in June 1944. On August 19, as Allied forces neared Paris, the Communist wing of the Resistance called for a rising and a seizure of the city from the German occupiers in order to give themselves the upper hand in the future government of France.

Major General Dietrich von Choltitz, the German commander in Paris, was under orders from Hitler to defend the city at any cost—including its destruction. When the Resistance insurrection erupted, Choltitz at first attempted to negotiate. Through the Swedish consul general, Choltitz worked out a shaky truce with Free French Resistance supporters of General Charles de Gaulle. But the truce broke down, and Choltitz called out tanks.

Learning of the street fighting and the imminent Allied liberation, Hitler asked his military staff during a meeting in his Rastenburg headquarters, *"Brennt Paris?"* ("Is Paris burning?"). Even though Choltitz refused to carry out the order, serious confrontations loomed between Germans and patriots as Allied troops fought their way into Paris.

De Gaulle had convinced General Eisenhower, Supreme Allied Commander, that Allied forces would meet no opposition upon entering the city, which Eisehower had planned to bypass because of logistical problems. On August 25, U.S. forces entered against little opposition. Resistance fighters and jubilant citizens aided U.S. and French forces in silencing the few remaining strongpoints.

De Gaulle entered the city triumphantly on August 26, though collaborationist snipers opened fire during his arrival. When told to take cover, he said, "There are moments that go beyond each of our poor little lives. Paris! Paris outraged! Paris broken! Paris martyrized! But Paris liberated!"

—NP

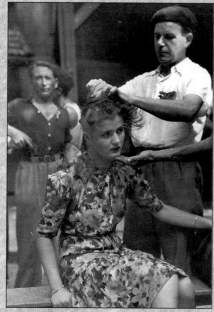

OPPOSITE: In a scene reminiscent of a Cecile B. DeMille movie, crowds of Parisians celebrating the entry of Allied troops into the city dive for cover as sniper fire erupts from a building on the *Place de la Concorde*.

TOP, LEFT: German prisoners of the French Resistance outside the *Académie Nationale de Musique*.

TOP, RIGHT: French civilians in Montélimar shave the head of a girl who had relations with a German soldier.

BOTTOM: Shouts, smiles, and preprinted signs bid welcome to General Charles de Gaulle.

Sergeant Norman Kirby recalls disturbing scenes of the rough justice inflicted on collaborators by the French Resistance.

The French Resistance were very uncompromising in their treatment of collaborators. One of the things that sickened me was the sight of French women with their heads shaved to the bone. Some of them were clutching their babies while they were dragged around the town in farm carts. They paraded these hairless girls and young women through the towns to the jeers and scorn of their neighbors because they'd had love affairs with German soldiers. These girls didn't really pose a security threat. It was none of my business, but we had never suffered as the French had suffered. So the fact that these girls were getting extra rations and lovely clothes while their neighbors were near starvation caused people to be full of hate and anger. Wanting revenge was understandable. It wasn't for me to judge these people. And it wasn't for me to judge the women either. ■

—Norman Kirby

ABOVE: *Wehrmacht* soldiers gather under the protective canopy of a small tree and look on as the trucks of their unlucky compatriots burn after a strafing by Allied fighters. One soldier, however, in the rear seat of the *Kübelwagen*, is more interested in scanning the skies for a repeat performance by the deadly "Jabos."

ABOVE: *Wehrmacht* soldiers gather under the protective canopy of a small tree and look on as the trucks of their unlucky compatriots burn after a strafing by Allied fighters. One soldier, however, in the rear seat of the *Kübelwagen*, is more interested in scanning the skies for a repeat performance by the deadly "Jabos."

OPPOSITE: A column of trucks, half-tracks, and horse-drawn 105mm howitzers lays smashed outside of Montelimer in southern France during the German retreat north. Although the savaging of German columns in Normandy is frequently recounted, the punishment dished out along the roads of southern France after Operation DRAGOON is less well known.

OPPOSITE, INSET: The ominous shadow of an artillery spotter aircraft traces a path over horse-drawn artillery—some of which appears intact and abandoned—during Army Group G's flight up the Rhône Valley to escape the U.S. and French forces pouring in from the Riviera.

Still the fighting continued. Some of the most horrific confrontations of the war occurred around Falaise. While with a reconnaissance group, British Sergeant Norman Kirby found himself stranded amid the grotesque scene.

After Caen fell, we moved deeper into Normandy, to Falaise. There, one of the worst things in the war happened to me. The Allies had hemmed in thousands of German troops in a valley called the pocket of Falaise. They sent in rocket-firing Typhoons, and there was no exit for these Germans because we were beginning to surround this pocket. Germans lay in heaps—ten thousand corpses, one on top of the other. Human beings, animals, chickens, there were cows and horses, dogs, cats, and people.

I was on my motorbike. I had already sustained an injury earlier, having been blown off the motorbike and having injured my ear. Damage to the motorbike was more hidden. One of my jobs was to go out with the reconnaissance party. We went through this dreadful valley, with all these dead people, looking for another site. We were still in Normandy. When the site was chosen, I had to come back through the same dreadful scene and then come back with the main body of the headquarters. It was while we were coming back that my motorbike broke down forever. It was

a workshop job. Normally I was responsible for the maintenance of the motorbike, but this was a workshop job, which could only be carried out by a motor transport section.

The whole convoy moved on because they didn't know about my motorbike. They thought I'd just stopped for a while by the roadside. Where I stopped there were heaps of dead Germans. One on top of the other, almost shoulder high where they'd been trapped by the bombing. The convoy moved on and went out of sight. I was left there alone. I couldn't get the motorbike to move. The heat was intense and the smell was absolutely nauseating. A war picture or a war film on television may show you some of the visual horrors of war, but one of the worst horrors is the smell, which you don't get on film.

I wanted to move away from this awful scene, and I thought I would move under the shadow of a tree, which I saw silhouetted in the distance. I pushed the motorbike toward this tree. But it wasn't a tree at all. It was a tank with the bodies of its crew trapped at the waist and their faces charred. With their burnt arms up, it appeared to be a tree from the distance. It was just a continuation of this awful horror.

Night started to fall, and I thought, When are they going to notice that I'm not there? Eventually headquarters must have realized something had happened. The motor transport section came back looking for me, and they found me. They picked me up and the motorbike and took me away.

It was then that I was sick with dysentery. It came from all of the terrible pollution that was around in the air. I suppose I suffered a kind of spiritual sickness. I'd been through D-DAY, which was quite disturbing but was exciting. At Falaise, seeing these heaps of Germans was bad enough, but what was even worse was that many of the dead were old men in their sixties and boys no older than fourteen. I was a teacher, and taught boys of that age. I'd taken them to scout camps, and they didn't look any different from some of the boys I'd taught, except they were dead, lying in heaps. ■

—Norman Kirby

Canadian gunner Joseph "Al" Rivier also witnessed this macabre scene on his way to Falaise.

At one gun position it seemed the Germans knew where we were all the time. They started firing air bursts at us, so we'd climb under the tank, and as soon as we got under, they started firing ground bursts. We'd run like hell from under the tank and jump into the tank itself to get protection from flying shrapnel. As soon as we got in, they fired air bursts again. We were in that tank for hours.

The first casualty I saw was when we were advancing through the wheat fields. Whole columns of our tanks. I guess this mortar dispatch rider went down with his motorbike in the wheat field, but nobody saw him. After being run over thousands of times, he and his motorbike were about two inches (5cm) thick.

Originally we started toward Falaise in daytime. Then they decided to do a twenty-four-hour deal because we needed to get

Spurts of fire flecked along the column and flashes of dust staccatoed along the road. Everyone was piling out of the vehicles and scuttling for the neighboring fields . . .
The march was now completely disrupted and every man was on his own, to pull out of this blazing column as best he could.
And it was none too soon, because an hour later the whole thing started again, only much worse this time.
—SS Division staff officer, in *The Second Front*

down to help trap the German Fifteenth Army. We didn't get them all, but we caught quite a bunch of them. After nightfall, they hurried us by making artificial moonlight with a bunch of searchlights. We had to stay between the searchlights and advance. We did once probably get a wrong reference point. We drove through the infantry. They were looking up at us from their trenches, figuring we were nuts. We went a mile (1.6km) or so before we finally realized that something was wrong. We stopped. Then the infantry finally moved up to cover us again.

As we moved closer to Falaise, we started to see all kinds of dead people. One cut we went through was where they must have dropped a bomb or a rocket in there. Germans had apparently been alive at the time but the blast just squished them into the clay bank. When we went by, they were black from the hot sun. There were maggots running in and out all over the place. They were kind of sickening.

Shortly after that we came to where the rockets came in and hit a whole monstrous, long column of German equipment and people. They blasted everything in the world, mixed there on the road. There were old wagons and horses. Trucks, tanks, and half-tracks were all destroyed. Off to the side, our people were digging monstrous long pits. Bulldozers came along and pushed everything into the pit. I'm sure that's where a lot of missing German soldiers were—soldiers who will never be found because they're just in that big pile of whatever.

We ate dinner that night in an apple orchard. Dead Germans were scattered all over the ground. One just had the upper part of his rib cage, arms, and head left—nothing else. Another one was split right up the middle, and pigs were pulling him apart, eating whatever they could. One of our guys couldn't eat for two or three days after that. We kept teasing him about it, but he kept refusing his food. ■

—Joseph "Al" Rivier

ABOVE: A burned-out half-track is the only piece of recognizable German equipment after bulldozers have pushed an obliterated convoy off to both sides of a road near Loriel in southern France. The vehicles speeding down the road belong to the U.S. Seventh Army.

Private First Class William Lee of the 1st Division survived the events of D-DAY and beyond. He watched as men replaced his comrades who had fallen or rotated out. Nearly another year of warfare loomed ahead. One only wanted to survive long enough to return home.

We were probably replaced three complete times. There's fifteen thousand people in a division. Fifty thousand men went through the 1st Infantry Division before they ended the war.

Replacements were these poor individuals who came into the division right out of the States and right out of the replacement depot. These people had not seen any action. They were raw recruits with just sixteen weeks of basic training, sent into a combat outfit whose missions always were the most deadly, the most treacherous missions you could ever be assigned. And how do you keep these people alive? I don't know. I don't think anybody's ever solved that. You just hoped they watched and learned.

They would come to us carrying two barracks bags with the latest equipment. We'd tell them to throw everything away except two blankets, a mess kit, the vital necessities to keep you warm, and your food. Your rifle was the only friend you had. The food you carried was the only food you were going to have to eat. That was the first thing they learned. Of course, to see a guy with pictures of his wife or family having to throw all of this stuff away was sad. But it's either that or be killed on the spot, because you can't survive and carry all that stuff. It was hard, but hopefully it saved somebody's life.

At the end I wouldn't even talk to the replacements when they came in. I didn't want anything to do with them. I didn't want to know who they were or their rank. I didn't want to know if they came from Texas or Carolina or Timbuktu. Stay away from me. They were only going to be trouble. I didn't want to know about them getting hurt. I never did know very many of those people who came to us toward the last. I couldn't tell you ten people when we were getting one to

TOP: French Forces of the Interior (FFI) guerrillas guard the wreckage of a German supply train destroyed by American tanks at Braine, September 8, 1944. Note the captured German machine gun and "potato masher" grenades near the wall. The late-model Tiger I tanks on the train's flatcars sport the special narrow tracks that it was necessary to mount on this type of vehicle when it was being transported by rail. These German cannons, the dreaded 88mms, will never see action against the Allies.

BOTTOM: Major General Hermann Ramke, German garrison commander at Brest, is escorted to the 8th Infantry Division headquarters after his surrender, September 19, 1944. Ramke had initially refused to surrender his force until the American general facing him showed his credentials. Without hesitation, Assistant Division Commander Charles D.W. Canham, at right, turned to the Garand-wielding soldiers accompanying him and replied, "These are my credentials." Another memorable quote of Canham's was made on D-DAY, when he commanded the 29th Infantry Division's 116th Regimental Combat Team on OMAHA Beach and refused to be evacuated after being shot through the wrist: "Get these men off their dead asses and over that wall."

ABOVE: The relationship between General George S. Patton, here with his famous ivory-handled pistol, General Omar Bradley, at center, and General Bernard Law Montgomery was often strained and contentious, but the headstrong Allies are all smiles in this photo, taken as their armies were routing German forces in France.

two hundred replacements a month. That's kind of a cold-hearted way of doing it. But it hurt so bad to get a good friend killed. It was easier to see that somebody we didn't know got killed.

The life of a young individual coming into the line companies wasn't exactly very long. Somebody once wrote that of the fifteen thousand people in the Big Red One that shipped out on the *Queen Mary* in 1942, only twenty-six were left at the end of the war. Not all were killed. Some were [became] prisoners; some rotated back to the States. Still, it was a phenomenal price to pay. I was one of the twenty-six. ■

—William Lee

A Postmortem

The establishment of a second front in the summer of 1944 marked the end of any chance that the Nazi regime had to survive the war. The blow to the German Army was nearly unimaginable. The captured and the dead in Normandy totaled at least 530,000 men. To this toll must be added the 103,000 German dead and prisoners lost to the U.S. and French

forces in southern France, plus 700,000 more men during the Soviet offensive timed to coincide with OVERLORD. Another 100,000 Germans were bottled up in a half-dozen French ports that, with the exception of Brest, the Allies did not believe were worth taking. Thus, excluding wounded, the *Wehrmacht* lost an average of a half-million men a month from June through August. Also worthwhile to note is that, thanks largely to an ongoing series of deception operations and Hitler's own proclivities, German troop strength in Norway and Denmark never dropped below 440,000. These soldiers sat out the war in relative comfort along with roughly 130,000 naval and *Luftwaffe* personnel.

There were 133,316 American plus 91,223 British and Canadian battle casualties from D-DAY through August 31, 1944.

Public controversy over the quality of Allied leadership began to bubble up—even as battles still raged around Caen and St. Lô—and frequently boiled over, as combatants and historians alike picked over the bones of opportunities unseen and challenges unmet on the killing fields of France. Eisenhower summed up the campaign from his unique vantage point in a May 23, 1946, letter to Montgomery.

I thoroughly agree with you that the line we had established as our dog (that is, D) +90 objective was not only attained at an earlier date, but the operations bringing us to that line generally followed the conceptions we had held before the invasion was launched.

On the other hand, the operations immediately following the landing diverged quite considerably, in a tactical sense, from what we had hoped to execute. Specifically, one of our earliest objectives was the open ground to the south and southeast of Caen and Falaise, which areas we wanted to seize quickly in order to establish airfields and to bring into play our superiority in armor . . . The fact that we were long delayed in obtaining this particular area, because of the intensive concentration of enemy forces in the Caen district, is some justification for those people that claim our early tactics had to adjust to enemy reaction. This I regard as normal in war and I would be the very last to subscribe to any plan or theory of operations that was compelled to depend for its

success on an exact sequence in the attainment of tactical objectives.

You will recall also that we felt before the invasion that the capture of open ground south of Caen would assist the Americans on the west to get through the difficult Bocage country following on the capture of Cherbourg. Thus we expected to have a dog [D] +17 line including Granville on the west, and including the line of the Orne on the east. From there we expected to break out largely according to the actual subsequent pattern of the operations, and depending upon developments to give such direction to troop masses as would most quickly accomplish the destruction of the enemy.

I repeat that while the intensive concentration and resistance of the enemy on the east compelled divergence from our anticipated tactical progress during the first 30 or 40 days, the instant adaptation of our own tactics to each day's requirements eventually enabled us to carry out a broad strategic program for the conquest of France that had been visualized long before dog [D] day.

Selected Bibliography

BOOKS:

Alanbrooke, Alan Brooke, Viscount. Alex Danchev and Daniel Todman, eds. *War Diaries 1939–1945: Field Marshal Lord Alanbrooke*. Berkeley, California: University of California Press, 2001.

Bando, Mark A. *The 191st Airborne at Normandy*. Osceola, Wisconsin: Motorbooks International (MBI), 1994.

———. *191st Airborne: The Screaming Eagles at Normandy*. Osceola, Wisconsin: MBI, 2001.

———. *Breakout at Normandy*. Osceola, Wisconsin: MBI, 1999.

Bland, Larry I., ed., *The Papers of George Catlett Marshall*, Vol. 4. *"Aggressive and Determined Leadership."* Baltimore: The Johns Hopkins University Press, 1996.

Blumenson, Martin. *Liberation*. Alexandria, Virginia: Time-Life Books, 1978.

———. *United States Army in World War II: Breakout and Pursuit*. Washington, D.C.: Center of Military History, United States Army, 1984.

Botting, Douglas. *The Second Front*. Alexandria, Virginia: Time-Life Books, 1978.

Brown, Anthony Cave. *Bodyguard of Lies*, Vol. 1. New York: Harper and Row, 1975.

———. *Bodyguard of Lies*, Vol. 2. New York: Harper and Row, 1975.

Buffetaut, Yves. *D-Day Ships: The Allied Invasion Fleet, June 1944*. Annapolis, M.D.: Naval Institute Press, 1994.

Churchill, Winston C. *Their Finest Hour*. Boston: Houghton Mifflin, 1949.

Clarke, Jeffrey J. and Robert Ross Smith. *United States Army in World War II: Riviera to the Rhine*. Washington, D.C.: Center of Military History, 1993.

Collins, Larry and Dominque Lapierre. *Is Paris Burning?* New York: Simon and Schuster, 1965.

Crookenoen, Napier. *Dropzone Normandy*. New York: Charles Scribner's Sons, 1976.

Crow, Duncan, ed. *American AFVs of World War II*. New York: Doubleday, 1972.

———. *British and Commonwealth AFVs 1940–46*. Garden City, N.Y.:Doubleday, 1971.

D'Este, Carlo. *Decision in Normandy*. New York: E.P. Dutton, 1983.

Dawne, Jonathan. *Spearheading D-Day: American Special Units in Normandy*. Paris: Histoire and Collections, 1999.

Doubler, Michael D. *Busting the Bocage: American Combined Arms Operations in France, 6 June–31 July 1944*. Fort Leavenworth, Kansas: Combat Studies Institute, 1988.

Eisenhower, Dwight D. *Crusade in Europe*. New York: Doubleday, 1948.

Eisenhower Foundation. *D-Day: The Normandy Invasion in Retrospect*. Lawrence, Kansas: University Press of Kansas, 1971.

Ellis, L.F. *Victory in the West*. Vol. 1, *The Battle of Normandy*. London: Her Majesty's Stationery Office, 1962.

English, John A. *The Canadian Army and the Normandy Campaign*. New York: Praeger, 1991.

Fleming, Peter. *Operation Sea Lion*. New York: Ace Books, 1957.

Gavin, James M. *On to Berlin*. New York: Bantam, 1978.

Giangreco, D.M. *Roosevelt, De Gaulle and the Posts*. Bonita, California: Joseph V. Bush, Inc., 1987.

Golley, John. *The Big Drop*. London: Jane's, 1982.

Hamilton, Nigel. *Monty's War Years, 1942–1944*. New York: McGraw-Hill, 1983.

Harrison, Gordon A. *United States Army in World War II: Cross-Channel Attack*. Washington, D.C.: Office of the Chief of Military History, 1951.

Hastings, Max. *Overlord: D-Day and the Battle for Normandy*. New York: Simon and Schuster, 1984.

Hogg, Ian V. *The American Arsenal*. London: Greenhill Books, 2001.

Horne, Alistair. *Monty: The Lonely Leader, 1944–1945*. New York: Harper Collins, 1994.

Insignia and Decorations of the U.S. Armed Forces. Washington, D.C.: National Geographic Society, revised edition, 1944.

Irving, David. *The Trail of the Fox*. New York: Avon, 1977.

Kaufmann, J.E. and H.W. *Fortress Third Reich: German Fortifications and Defense Systems in World War II*. Cambridge, Massachusetts: Da Capo Press, 2003.

Keegan, John. *Six Armies in Normandy*. New York: Viking Press, 1982.

Kershaw, Robert J. *D-Day: Piercing the Atlantic Wall*. Annapolis, Maryland: Naval Institute Press, 1994.

Mallory, Keith and Arvid Ottar. *The Architecture of War*. New York: Pantheon Books, 1973.

Matloff, Maurice. *United States Army in World War II: Strategic Planning for Coalition Warfare, 1943–1944*. Washington, D.C.: Office of the Chief of Military History, 1959.

Montgomery, Bernard Law. *The Memoirs of Field Marshal the Viscount Montgomery of Alamein*. Cleveland, Ohio: World Publishing, 1958.

Morison, Samuel Eliot. *History of United States Naval Operations in World War II*. Vol. 10, *The Atlantic Battle Won: May 1943–May 1945*. Boston: Little, Brown and Company, 1956.

———. *History of United States Naval Operations in World War II*. Vol. 11, *The Invasion of France and Germany: 1944–1945*. Boston: Little, Brown and Company, 1957.

Pogue, Forest C. *United States Army in World War II: The Supreme Command*. Washington, D.C.: Office of the Chief of Military History, 1954.

Polmar, Norman and Thomas B. Allen. *World War II: The Encyclopedia of the War Years 1941–1945*. New York: Random House, 1996.

Rommel, Erwin. Sir Basil Henry Liddell Hart, ed. *The Rommel Papers*. New York: Harcourt, Brace, 1953.

Ryan, Cornelius. *The Longest Day*. New York: Popular Library, 1959.

Shirer, William L. *The Rise and Fall of the Third Reich*. New York: Simon and Schuster, 1960.

Small Unit Actions: Pointe du Hoe–2d Ranger Battalion, 6 June 1944. Washington, D.C.: Center of Military History, 1991.

Speer, Albert. *Inside the Third Reich*. New York: Avon, 1970.

Stanton, Shelby L. *Order of Battle: U.S. Army in World War II*. Novato, California: Presidio, 1964.

von Senger und Etterlin, F.M. *German Tanks of World War II*. Harrisburg, Pennsylvania: Stackpole, 1969.

Weigley, Russell F. *Eisenhower's Lieutenants*. Bloomington, Indiana: Indiana University Press, 1981.

Wilson, Theodore A., ed. *D-Day 1944*. Lawrence, Kansas: University of Kansas Press, 1994.

Young, Desmond. *Rommel, The Desert Fox*. New York: Berkley Publishing, 1950.

ARTICLES:

Burrer, Douglas and Dennis Linton. "Juno Beach: The Canadians Avenge Dieppe." *Military Review* (June 1994).

Knight, James E. "The DD that Saved the Day." *Naval Institute Proceedings* (August 1989).

Koch, James R. "Operation Fortitude: The Backbone of Deception." *Military Review* (March 1992).

Weigley, Russell F. "From the Normandy Beaches to the Falaise-Argentan Pocket." *Military Review* (September 1990).

Index

Note: The names of the eyewitness veterans whose recollections appear in this book are indicated in boldface.

British, *62*, 99, 112
   U.S., 144–145, 148–150
   See also individual vessels
Devon, 45
Dieppe, 15, *21*, 24, 36, *118*
Dives River, 74, 82, 88, 210
Dollman, Gen. Friedrich, *31*, 202
Dorchester, 37
Dorset, 152
Douve River, 74, 95, 97, *114–115*, 210
Dover, 14
Doyle, 149
DuBroc, Nelson, 21, 112, *112*, 113–114
DUKWs, *49*, 75, *122*, *133*, *135*, *136*, *155*
Dunkirk, 13, 17, 22
"Dunkirked," 26
Duplay, Lt. Philippe, 245
Durban, 199

E
Eadie, Lt. Col. J.A., 205
Eastern Front, 24, 134
East Germany, 27
East Yorkshire Regiment (Britain), *172*
E-Boats, 45
Egypt, 32
Ehlers, Roland, 37
Ehlers, Walter, 37, 141–142, *142*
Eighth Air Force (U.S.), 67
Eisenhower, Gen. Dwight D., *12–13*, 14, *22–23*, 34, 36, 44–46, *53*, *63*, 65–66, 188–189, 247, 253
El Alamein, 32
Emmons, 149, *149*
Empire Rosebery, 121
Engineer troops, 59, *64*, 114, *146*. *See also specific units.*
English Channel, 18, 23, *74*
   D-Day conditions, 105–106
   German fortifications and, 28
   Operation Sea Lion and, 18
   ships on D-Day and, 72, 99
Erebus, 112, 124
Eureka transporters, 72, 84
Exercise Fabius, 45–46
Exercise Tiger, 45–46

F
Falaise, 162, 173, 228–229, 248, *253*
Falley, Maj. Gen. Wilhelm, 95
Fallschirmjägers. See Paratroopers (Germany)
Fécamp, *19*
Feuchtinger, Maj. Gen. Edgar, 160, 205
Fifteenth Army (Germany), 69, 72, 92, 227
Fire Support Area Four, 119
First Army (U.S.), 162
Flak guns, 77
Flak suits, 84
Flamethrowers, 78, 81
Flat-bottom barges. *See* Caissons
Flick, Joe, 195
"Flying Dustbin" demolition bomb, 163
"Fortress Europe," 14, 63
Foster, George, 166
France
   Communist Party, 246
   hospitality toward Allied soldiers, 212, 231, 245, *245*

liberation of, 72, 206, 222, 244–247
Riviera, 180, 243–244
soldiers, 35
southern invasion of, 243
See also names of cities
Frankford, 148
Franz, John, 213, 216
French Forces of the Interior (FFI), 226, *251*
French Resistance, 134, 225–226, 237, 244, 246–247
   treatment of collaborators, 247
Friendly fire, 185
Frigates, 72
Funnies, 28–29, 132, 163

G
Gara, William, 59, 63, 142–146, *146*
Gardner, Charlie, 89
Gas masks, *59*, *64*, 96, *201*
Gavin, Brig. Gen. James, 82, *86*
George Beach, 126
George VI, King, 16, 178, 188–189
German Armed Forces *(Wehrmacht). See* German Army, German Navy, *Luftwaffe*
German Army
   anti-aircraft artillery, 82, 84, 95
   booby-traps, 216
   combat formations, 27
   counterattacks, 191–219, 237
   in Denmark, 15, 252
   escape from Normandy, 207
   in Finland, 15
   Group B, 26–27, 31, 69, 192
   Group G, 26, 227, 248
   intelligence, 26
   in Norway, 15, 252
   Operation Bodyguard and, 23
   orders to withdraw and, 234
   post-war, 27
   recall of citizens before war, 225
   snipers, 216–217
   weapons, 211
German Navy, 18
   Group West, 27
Germany, Nazi
   declaration of war on the U.S., 14
   defeat of, 72
   defeat of Belgium and France, 18
   defenses against Great Britain, 14
   France and Low Countries Campaign, 32
   invasion of France, 26
   invasion of Great Britain, 19
   propagandists, 19
   Soviet Russia and, 23
   support for Japan, 14
   training for Operation Sea Lion, 19
Glasgow, 208
Gliders, 77, 81, 85, *88*, 89, 98, 200
   Hamilcar, 83
   Horsa, *79–80*, *83*, 85, 87, *94*, *200*
   Waco, *79–80*
Glennon, 122
Glocker, *27*
Glover, Frederick, 77, *78*, 81, 225–226
Gold Beach, 112, 162, 164–166, 173, 175, *179*, 191
Gooseberries, 199
Grandcamp Sector, 100
Great Britain

airfields, 42
blackout periods and, 42
civilian relations with U.S. soldiers, 36–39, 53
German sea invasion of, 13–14, 19
rail system, 35, *41*
U.S. Army Quartermaster Corps and, 36
See also names of cities
Greece, 24
Greenway, Lord, 201
Grenades, 71–72, 85, 89
   Gammon, 193
   launchers, *194*
   Panzerfaust, 197
   stick, *222*
   thermite, 109
Griswold bags, 75
Guderian, Gen. Heinz, 33
Guernsey Island, 98

H
Hagensen packs, 114
Hall, Adm. John L., 150
Hanna, Ken, 42, 242
Harding, 149
Harpagus, 121
Hausser, Paul, 208
Hedge cutter, *238*, 240–241, *240*, *241*. See also
   Rhino tanks
Hedgerows, *85*, 108, *194*, 220–222, 232, *232*, 233
Hellmich, Lt. Gen. Heinz, 226
Helmets, 36
Hemingway, Ernest, 113
Henrico, 146
Hermanville-sur-Mer, 172, 207
Higgins, Andrew, 120
Higgins boats, 120
Hill, O.B., 37, *39*, 96–97, 192–194
History of United States Naval Operations in World War II, 62
Hitler, Adolf, 27, 63
   conquest of Soviet Union and, 19
   "Führer directives" and, 14
   headquarters of, 214
   on invasion of Great Britain, 13, 18
   Operation Sea Lion and, 19
   Panzer-Lehr and, 31
   plot against, 27, 214–215
Hitlerjugend, 162, 207–208, 218
"Hitler's Hearse," *38*
Hope, Bob, *24*
Hospitals
   field, 224
   German, 225–226
   hospital ships, *72*, 126
Howard, Maj. John, 88–90, 92–93
"Human torpedos" (German), 120

I
Intelligence Corps (Britain), 27
Intrepid, 99
Irish Sea, 56
Irwin, Nathan, 117, 204
Isle of Wight, 39, 58, 72
Italy
   civilians, 92–93
   soldiers, 32

Photo Credits

Author's Collection: pp. 12–13, 14 left and right, 15, 16, 17 top and bottom, 20, 21, 22 bottom, 23, 24 right, 25 chart, 26 and 27 courtesy Geyr von Schweppenburg, 31, 32 bottom, 33 top and bottom, 38, 44, 47 left, 49 top, middle, and bottom left, 50–51, 52, 53, 54, 63, 66, 67 top and bottom, 70, 75, 77, 82, 86 top and bottom, 88 and 93 courtesy Marc Bando, 97 bottom, 100, 101, 107, 114–115, 118, 123 top, 124 bottom, 131 bottom, 132, 138, 140 top and bottom, 141, 143 top, 148 bottom, 151, 152, 153 bottom, 154 top, 158 top, 162 bottom, 164, 166, 170 bottom, 173 bottom, 196 top, 198, 199 top and bottom, 203 top, 204, 205, 208, 209 top, 210, Eva Braun Hitler Albums: p. 214 bottom; Heinrich Hoffman Albums: pp. 214 top, 215 bottom; Rommel Family Archive: p. 215 top; 217, 218 top and bottom, 220–221, 225, 232 top and bottom, 233 top and bottom, 234 top and bottom, 235 left, 238 top and bottom, 239, 241 left, 242, 243, 244, 246–47, 248, 249 top and bottom, 250, 251 top and bottom, 252 top and bottom, 253 right.

©Alexandra Boulat: pp. 5, 7, 101 inset

©Ed Calhoun: pp. 2–3, 10–11, endpapers

Corbis: pp. 34–35, 50–51; ©Michael St. Maur Sheil: p. 1

Imperial War Museum: pp. 83, 89, 91 top and bottom, 92, 94 top, 160–161, 170, 171, 172, 174–175, 179 top and bottom, 181, 183, 185, 186 top and bottom, 187, 188, 189

©Lou Reda Productions: pp. 139, 144, 165, 176, 184

National Archives: pp. 2 inset, 18, 19 top and bottom, 28, 29 top and bottom, 30 top and bottom, 32 top, 36, 37, 39, 40 top and bottom, 41 top and bottom, 42, 43, 45, 46, 48, 55 top and bottom, 56, 57, 58, 59, 60, 61, 62 top and bottom, 64 top and bottom, 68–69, 71, 73, 74, 76, 79, 80, 85 bottom, 87, 93, 94 bottom, 96, 97, 98 top right, 101, 102–103, 104, 108, 110–111, 113, 117 top and bottom, 123 bottom, 124 top, 125, 126, 127 top and bottom, 130, 131, 133, 134–135, 136, 137 top and bottom, 143 bottom, 144, 145 top and bottom, 146, 147, 148, 150, 154 bottom, 155 top and bottom, 156 and inset, 157, 158 bottom, 159, 163, 167, 168–169, 173, 177, 178, 180, 182, 190–191, 193, 194, 195, 196 bottom, 200, 201, 202–203, 207, 209 bottom, 211, 212, 222, 223, 224, 226, 227, 229, 230, 231, 232 left, 236 top and bottom, 238 inset, 239, 240 top, 241 all, 243 middle, 245, 249 and inset, 253 left and right; Army News Features: pp. 129, 140, 154 top, 222, 223, 224, 242, 252 inset; Canadian Overseas Photo: pp. 226, 228; 240 bottom; U.S. Army Photograph: pp. 9, 12–13, 21, 23, 49 bottom right, 53, 54, 65, 82, 159 bottom, 240 bottom

National Geographic Image Collection: pp. 120–122

U.S. Navy Art Collection: p. 149, The Battle for Fox Beach, D–Day Normandy, by Lt. Dwight C. Shepler; oil on canvas

A special thanks to the families who contributed portraits of the D–Day veterans whose firsthand accounts appear in this book.